"This is a wise and useful book that straddles the ¿ that does justice to both. Western science provides increasing support for the positive impact of the psychological processes of change engaged by meditation and contemplation, but Christians can feel left out of this conversation if the unique features of a Christian approach are not addressed and harmonized with what psychological science has found. Several other books link modern psychological intervention methods to the Christian faith, but this is the first book of which I am aware that dives deeply into the conceptual issues and practical psychological benefits of a Christian approach to meditation and contemplation, and then provides a step-by-step guide to implementing this understanding. The processes targeted by Dr. Knabb's approach to meditation, prayer, and contemplation—being better able to notice, to shift from a content (or 'earthly') perspective, to accept, and to act—are all empirically well supported. By laying them out so clearly and then providing practical methods to pursue them, the author empowers readers to judge for themselves how the practices in the book are landing in their life rather than being left to take the author's word for it. That is an honorable and empowering approach that is respectful of the reader. I highly recommend this book."

Steven C. Hayes, Foundation Professor of Psychology at the University of Nevada, Reno, and author of *A Liberated Mind: How to Pivot Toward What Matters*

"Research clearly shows that meditation is good for mental health and well-being. In this elegant book, Dr. Joshua Knabb explores the underlying processes of meditation and shows how to reap the benefits through Christian contemplative practices. It is a trustworthy guide for therapists and their clients who want to deepen their faith while managing psychological distress. Dr. Knabb offers truly beautiful practices that can be easily integrated into daily life. If you are Christian and want to learn meditation, you have come to the right place."

Christopher Germer, instructor in psychiatry at Harvard Medical School and coauthor of *The Mindful Self-Compassion Workbook*

"*Christian Meditation in Clinical Practice* by Joshua Knabb is a clearly written and substantial book on a distinctively Christian approach to mindful meditation based on Scripture and the writings of well-known Christian authors throughout church history. It contains very practical and helpful exercises in the practice of Christian meditation for repetitive negative thinking, impaired emotional clarity and distress intolerance, behavioral avoidance, perfectionism, and impaired mentalization, when associated with psychopathology, providing empirical support for the effectiveness of such Christian meditation interventions. A must-read for therapists, clients, researchers, and anyone interested in Christian meditation."

Siang-Yang Tan, senior professor of clinical psychology at Fuller Theological Seminary and author of *Counseling and Psychotherapy: A Christian Perspective*

"Not only does *Christian Meditation in Clinical Practice* ground the reader in excellent scriptural and psychological principles, providing well-researched treatment guidelines and practical exercises for mindful practice, but the reader also gains a level of understanding of Christian meditation that can't be found anywhere else. Knabb's book is comprehensive, thoroughly researched, and clearly written as a resource to therapists, spiritual directors, and anyone interested in growing in mindfulness as a Christian."

Jennifer Ripley, psychology professor and Hughes Chair of Integration at Regent University

"Mindfulness meditation is *the* current psychological bandwagon. But can it be Christian-compatible? Absolutely, argues Josh Knabb in *Christian Meditation in Clinical Practice*. It is a transdiagnostic treatment approach for people with one or several overlapping psychological struggles. Thoughtful. Practical. Hop on the bandwagon for an interesting and helpful ride."

Everett L. Worthington Jr., Commonwealth Professor Emeritus, Virginia Commonwealth University

"*Christian Meditation in Clinical Practice* is a helpful, practical guide through Christian meditation. Since the subject is often misunderstood by believers, Knabb delves into the history of Christian meditation as well as more secular types of meditation. It's a much-needed resource, because when we are hit by life's disasters, it can be tempting to view our suffering as something to avoid or defeat. Instead, Knabb encourages us to view suffering through the lens of faith and our eternity with God, so that we cannot fall prey to psychological traps that keep us fearful and anxious. By practicing the exercises in the book, readers can integrate meditation into their relationship with God and find better mental, emotional, and spiritual health. I highly recommend it to practicing therapists and their clients."

Jamie Aten, founder and codirector of the Humanitarian Disaster Institute at Wheaton College

"For Christian therapists working with Christian clients, it is hard to express strongly enough just how long overdue is a therapy workbook such as this one: an evidence-based treatment of Christian meditation that (1) explains its unique psychospiritual benefits, (2) differentiates itself from secular and Buddhist forms of mindfulness meditation, (3) documents its relevance for transdiagnostic problems affecting a broad range of psychological functions, and (4) offers numerous practical strategies for incorporating Christian meditation in the therapy process. I personally hope that more research in the future will be directed to forms of Christian meditation with greater biblical and theological content, but for those wanting to practice distinctly Christian therapy, this is the single best workbook on Christian meditation for therapy available in our day."

Eric L. Johnson, professor of Christian psychology at Houston Baptist University's Gideon Institute of Christian Psychology and Counseling

"Dr. Joshua Knabb provides needed clarity to an important issue in treating psychological symptoms today. He clarifies what Christian meditation is and how it can be used in practical ways to produce psychological and spiritual growth. Drawing on his years of experience as a practicing psychologist, researcher, and teacher, he addresses many complex issues with skill and practical advice. He bases his discussion of meditation on his wealth of knowledge of psychological research, Scripture, and the writings of early spiritual fathers and mothers. He is a practicing psychologist and researcher, and he communicates his synthetic understanding in easy-to-understand terms. After building a case for a transdiagnostic understanding of mental disorders and a four-step change model (noticing, shifting, accepting, and action), he provides useful exercises that will help clients deal with common symptoms impacting their cognition, affect, and action."

Clark Campbell, Rosemead School of Psychology, Biola University

CHRISTIAN MEDITATION

in CLINICAL PRACTICE

A Four-Step Model and Workbook for Therapists and Clients

JOSHUA J. KNABB

ĬVp
Academic
An imprint of InterVarsity Press
Downers Grove, Illinois

InterVarsity Press
P.O. Box 1400, Downers Grove, IL 60515-1426
ivpress.com
email@ivpress.com

InterVarsity Press® is the book-publishing division of InterVarsity Christian Fellowship/USA®, a movement of students and faculty active on campus at hundreds of universities, colleges, and schools of nursing in the United States of America, and a member movement of the International Fellowship of Evangelical Students. For information about local and regional activities, visit intervarsity.org.

All Scripture quotations, unless otherwise indicated, are taken from The Holy Bible, New International Version®, NIV®. Copyright © 1973, 1978, 1984, 2011 by Biblica, Inc.™ Used by permission of Zondervan. All rights reserved worldwide. www.zondervan.com. The "NIV" and "New International Version" are trademarks registered in the United States Patent and Trademark Office by Biblica, Inc.™

While any stories in this book are true, some names and identifying information may have been changed to protect the privacy of individuals.

The publisher cannot verify the accuracy or functionality of website URLs used in this book beyond the date of publication.

Cover design and image composite: Autumn Short
Interior design: Daniel van Loon
Image: brown background © Valentin Salja@valentinsalja / unsplash

ISBN 978-1-5140-0024-3 (print)
ISBN 978-1-5140-0025-0 (digital)

Printed in the United States of America ♾

Library of Congress Cataloging-in-Publication Data
A catalog record for this book is available from the Library of Congress.

P 29 28 27 26 25 24 23 22 21 20 19 18 17 16 15 14 13 12 11 10 9 8 7 6 5 4 3 2 1

Y 46 45 44 43 42 41 40 39 38 37 36 35 34 33 32 31 30 29 28 27 26 25 24 23 22 21

This workbook is dedicated to my wife,

ADRIENNE,

who gently reminds me, with just the right touch of grace,

to slow down and stay in the present moment

in order to savor all of God's blessings.

CONTENTS

ACKNOWLEDGMENTS

To begin, I would like to thank my wife, Adrienne, and children, Emory and Rowan, who inspire me to improve and grow as a husband, father, and fellow sojourner in this short and messy life. Also, I would like to recognize my editor, Jon Boyd, who has believed in this project ever since we had a brief, casual conversation upon meeting at a conference several years back. Moreover, I would like to express appreciation to the two anonymous reviewers, who took the time to provide helpful feedback so as to strengthen the project. Furthermore, I would like to acknowledge the many Christian authors who have traveled before me over the last two millennia, offering much-needed psychological and spiritual insights into the human condition from a distinctly biblical worldview. Finally, I would like to give thanks to God as my faithful, trustworthy tour guide, who gently and lovingly welcomes me back whenever I have wandered off the paths of life in a futile attempt to travel alone.

INTRODUCTION

*A man cannot look up to heaven and down to earth both at
the same time. There is an opposition between these
two, between the earthly-mindedness that has been
opened to you, and minding of heavenly things.*

JEREMIAH BURROUGHS, *A TREATISE
ON EARTHLY-MINDEDNESS*

Instead of seeing God man sees himself.

DIETRICH BONHOEFFER, *ETHICS*

REVERBERATIONS OF THE FALL

For a moment, try to imagine what it must have been like for Adam and Eve in those early days of human history. After God made Adam from dust and Eve from Adam's rib, both were naked and exposed yet seemingly experienced no sense of loneliness, inadequacy, or shame. Although we do not know the exact details, for a period of time they likely felt a sense of contentment in their daily communion with God, with no apparent awareness of the suffering that would emanate from a future estrangement. Yet, as this famous story unfolds, we quickly learn that Adam and Eve ate from the forbidden tree, then immediately realized they were naked, something they had previously failed to notice. Mindful of their exposed state, they automatically covered themselves with leaves, then lurked in the shadows, hoping God would not see them in their vulnerable condition. Along with the more obvious spiritual impact of this fateful decision, we can also envision a range of possible psychological consequences in those first few years of existence: rumination, worry, emotional distress and confusion, behavioral avoidance, guilt and shame, self-doubt and self-confusion, and a newfound, enduring uncertainty about living in an ambiguous, dangerous world.

Fast forward to the twenty-first century, and we continue to live in the midst of suffering. In fact, psychological pain seems to be a rather ubiquitous experience in contemporary Western society. In your own daily life, for example, you may be struggling with a range of difficult inner and outer experiences, losing hope that things will somehow get better in the near or distant future. Among other forms of psychological suffering, you may get stuck in unhelpful thinking processes, have a hard time identifying emotions or tolerating distress, use avoidance as an ineffective coping strategy, strive for unrealistic standards of perfection, and struggle to understand yourself and deepen your relationships with others.

Difficult thoughts, feelings, behaviors, self-judgments, and relationships may even prevent you from living the life God has called you to live as a Christian. If so, this workbook is for you, a Christian client in professional counseling or psychotherapy who is working with a mental health professional to experience positive psychological and spiritual change. In the pages that follow, I will be offering both a Christian and a psychological view of suffering in contemporary society, along with a wide variety of meditative exercises to help you (1) respond differently to difficult inner and outer experiences, and (2) improve your relationship with God and find a deeper contentment in him as you walk with him along the roads of life. Although the fall of humankind continues to impact us to this very day, as Christians we do have options for living a life of hope and endurance as we patiently wait for God's eventual restoration of a broken existence.

From this larger Christian perspective, the Bible has given us a "grand narrative" for making sense of human suffering.[1] Although God created us to be in communion with him and experience enduring contentment and psychological health, we turned away, leading to estrangement, discontentment, and psychological suffering. In other words, rather than walking with God, we frequently veer off the path he has called us to walk with him on. Still, God has offered us a redemptive plan, based on the incarnation and atoning work of Jesus Christ. Therefore, through our union with Christ, we have access to a restored communion with God, a deeper contentment in him, and psychological health, even in the midst of a fallen world. As we patiently wait for God to restore our fragmented existence, we can learn to steadily walk with him from moment to moment, cultivating a more lasting inner satisfaction, untethered to the adversities of life, which will never fully go away on this side of heaven.

In this introduction chapter, I discuss the importance of better understanding a Christian worldview, especially in the context of suffering, given Christianity

---

[1]Wolters (2005). Citations in this book will follow the typical social sciences style, but use footnotes to simplify the text. The full information for all sources can be found in the reference list at the end of the book.

will serve as the foundation for this workbook. Moreover, I explore some of the more recent trends in the psychology literature to help you understand the role that psychological science plays in ameliorating suffering. Then, I introduce you to some of the Christian concepts, writings, and interventions I draw from throughout the workbook, before concluding with a discussion on the workbook's intended audience, general outline, and format for each of the subsequent intervention chapters.

LAYING THE FOUNDATION OF THE PROVERBIAL PYRAMID: STARTING WITH A CHRISTIAN WORLDVIEW

A worldview is a powerful framework, laying a solid foundation for helping us to make sense of a fallen, confusing world.[2] Like the bottom layer of a pyramid, a Christian viewpoint can offer stability for an otherwise unstable, unpredictable existence. To be sure, as we move through life, we need a lens through which to view our unfolding reality, made up of an amalgam of beliefs and assumptions that we cannot necessarily test or prove.[3] For Christians, a comprehensive worldview comes from the Bible, which is considered God's revelation to humankind. Common assumptions that flow from a Christian view of the world include an understanding of God (theology), the universe (cosmology), reality (ontology), knowledge (epistemology), goals/purpose (teleology), human nature (biblical anthropology), and values (axiology).[4] To be more succinct, a distinctly Christian lens allows us to make sense of who we are (as human beings), where we are (in terms of our position in this world and the universe), what the problem is (within the world, individually and collectively), and what the remedy is (for daily suffering).[5]

Because a Christian framework extends to every aspect of life,[6] including psychological and spiritual functioning, beginning with a Christian worldview to make sense of health, dysfunction, and healing is key; still, because of recent advancements in the psychology literature, twenty-first-century science offers Christians a wide variety of insights into some of the causes of, and solutions to, psychological suffering. In other words, God offers his "common grace" in the form of secular advancements in psychological theory and research, in addition to his "special grace" to those who follow Jesus Christ.[7]

---

[2]Anderson et al. (2017).
[3]Koltko-Rivera (2004).
[4]Knabb, Johnson, Bates, and Sisemore (2019).
[5]Henriques (2019); Wright (1992).
[6]Anderson et al. (2017).
[7]Kuyper (2015).

ADDING LAYERS TO THE PROVERBIAL PYRAMID: DRAWING FROM THE PSYCHOLOGY LITERATURE

Although followers of Jesus Christ commonly turn to the Bible as a starting point for making sense of a fallen world, one way to expand our understanding of suffering is to examine the global prevalence of mental disorders, as revealed in the scientific literature. After reviewing 174 surveys in 63 countries from 1980 to 2013, researchers found that about one in five adults experienced a mental disorder (e.g., mood disorder, anxiety disorder) over a twelve-month period of time.[8] In the United States, more specifically, a survey from 2001 to 2003 revealed that about one in five adults experienced an anxiety disorder and one in three adults suffered from a mood disorder at some point in their lifetime.[9]

To better identify psychological pain around the globe, researchers have debated about whether or not to keep adding new diagnoses to the various psychiatric classification systems. A "splitting" strategy involves attempting to reduce broader diagnostic categories into narrower, more precise groupings, whereas "lumping" consists of the exact opposite approach.[10] With the former, specific diagnoses have more than doubled from the release of the first psychiatric diagnostic manual in the United States, the DSM-I, to the most recent version, the DSM-5.[11] Because of this, the latter involves attempting to identify common processes that link the various psychiatric disorders.[12]

One such movement of late in the psychology literature, the "transdiagnostic" approach to identifying psychological processes, involves researching key struggles (e.g., thoughts, feelings, behaviors) that contribute to multiple psychiatric diagnoses,[13] in line with a lumping strategy. Advantages to lumping rather than splitting include the recognition that many people struggle with more than one disorder at any given time, as well as improving our ability to understand common underlying processes across diagnoses.[14]

Also housed within this movement, treatment approaches have emerged that attempt to ameliorate a variety of symptoms across diagnostic categories.[15] In the cognitive behavioral tradition, mindfulness meditation has been converted into a "transdiagnostic" strategy for addressing a plethora of mental processes, such as repetitive negative thinking (e.g., rumination, worry) and experiential avoidance

---

[8]Steel et al. (2014).
[9]Kessler et al. (2012).
[10]Lilienfeld et al. (2017).
[11]Richter (2014).
[12]Siegel (2010).
[13]Harvey et al. (2004); Mansell et al. (2009).
[14]Harvey et al. (2004).
[15]Craske (2012).

(e.g., attempting to avoid unpleasant inner experiences).[16] Emanating from the Buddhist tradition, mindfulness meditation has quickly grown into a billion-dollar industry in the United States[17] and is commonly practiced in educational,[18] occupational,[19] and healthcare settings.[20] In publication format, references to mindfulness have steadily increased in the last several decades,[21] with both news and scientific publications growing from almost zero in the early 1970s to over 30,000 by 2015.[22] In addition, loving-kindness meditation, also derived from the Buddhist tradition, has received a considerable amount of attention in the psychology literature in recent years.[23]

Returning to a Christian perspective, a Christian worldview functions sort of like a lumping strategy, given there is a common thread that links psychiatric diagnoses. Psychological suffering, to be sure, can be traced back to the fall, and the Bible offers Christians a meta-understanding of God's story for humankind. Although we certainly live in a fallen world and can benefit from a scientific understanding of psychological suffering, prioritizing worldviews is paramount, as the secular psychology literature may have an accurate conceptualization of *some* of the individual ingredients that make up the remedy, but not the *full* recipe. In other words, the psychology literature can improve our understanding of contemporary suffering, functioning like added layers to the foundation (i.e., a Christian worldview) of a pyramid, but should not be automatically accepted in its entirety, given many of its untested secular assumptions (e.g., individualism, hedonism, determinism, materialism).[24]

See figure 0.1 for a visual depiction of the interaction between Christianity and secular psychological science, typically referred to as a "Christian psychology" perspective.[25] Notice how the Bible and historic Christian writings make up the base and bulk of the pyramid, offering a foundational understanding of life's most pressing questions, which leads to the ability to develop distinctly Christian theories and conduct uniquely Christian research, all filtered through a Christian worldview. The Bible, to be certain, is God's special revelation, helping us to better understand a meta-perspective on the human condition. As followers of Jesus Christ, God offers us his special grace, which allows us to commune with him based on our union with Christ.[26]

---

[16]Greeson et al. (2014).
[17]Wieczner (2016).
[18]Meiklejohn et al. (2012).
[19]Kachan et al. (2017).
[20]Mars and Abbey (2010).
[21]Valerio (2016).
[22]Van Dam et al. (2018).
[23]Hofmann et al. (2011).
[24]Slife and Whoolery (2006).
[25]Johnson (2007, 2010).
[26]Kuyper (2015).

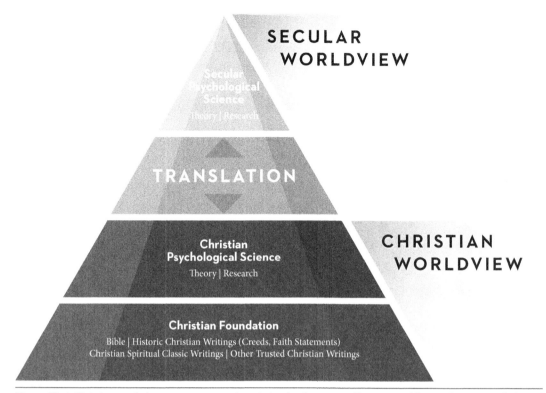

Figure 0.1. A Christian psychology perspective on the relationship between a Christian worldview, Christian psychological science, a secular worldview, and secular psychological science. Adapted from Johnson (2007, 2010); Knabb and Bates (2020b); and Knabb, Johnson, Bates, and Sisemore (2019).

Yet, we can also learn from secular psychological science, since God offers us common grace in the form of medical advancements, psychological insights, and so forth, just as long as a Christian worldview, emanating from Scripture, holds up the added layers of the proverbial pyramid.[27] In this interaction with the world, we need to ensure we are accurately translating secular theory and research in the psychology literature,[28] disentangling objective empirical data from arbitrarily constructed secular theories and conclusions that arise from the personal preferences and lived experiences of theorists and clearly conflict with a Christian worldview.[29] Although the secular psychology literature offers many helpful insights into psychological functioning in a fallen world, the lens through which secular and Christian researchers view health, dysfunction, and healing often differs. Because of this, in this workbook I attempt to offer a Christian approach to meditation in clinical and counseling practice, building upon a Christian worldview as a starting point, but also translating secular research in the psychology literature in a way that

---

[27]Kuyper (2015).
[28]Johnson (2007).
[29]Atwood and Stolorow (1993); Kuyper (1931).

is helpful for you as you learn to respond differently to psychological suffering. In this way, I hope to appeal to both those who advocate for an "integrationist" and "Christian psychology" perspective when considering the interaction between the Western secular psychology literature and Christian faith.[30]

PRIORITIZING DIFFERING WORLDVIEWS: CHRISTIANITY AND THE SECULAR PSYCHOLOGY LITERATURE

Although Christianity was the foundational worldview for many Western societies for almost two thousand years, offering answers to life's most fundamental questions—What is the world made of? Why is the world the way it is? What is the place of humans in the world?—the Enlightenment led to an alternative, secular understanding of the world, which psychologists adopted as the formal discipline of psychology emerged over a century ago.[31] As a result, although the psychological sciences, divorced from a Christian worldview, can certainly offer us different "streams" for better understanding human functioning, they do not point us to the proverbial "ocean."

For example, in the twenty-first century, secular psychologists have utilized the scientific method to develop a broad range of empirically supported treatments for a wide variety of mental disorders.[32] Still, when considering some of their unexamined worldview assumptions, a sharp contrast may begin to emerge when they are scrutinized alongside the Christian faith. As an example, naturalism pervades scientific research, which is the assumption that only the natural world, made up of natural laws, exists, in contrast with theism, consisting of the notion that God exists and influences the world.[33] In the psychology literature, "liberal individualism" tends to capture the contemporary zeitgeist, which suggests that (1) we are each isolated and independent, often developing and functioning outside the influence of relational systems; (2) as independent, we should be able to decide our own trajectory in the psychotherapy or counseling room; (3) our own self-fulfillment is central to life satisfaction and successful outcomes in psychotherapy and counseling; and (4) as independent, we can simply use others in an instrumental manner to achieve our own wishes and desires.[34]

With these secular assumptions in mind, my hope is that, as a Christian, you will consider turning to your own faith tradition to learn strategies to address your psychological suffering. Although psychological science, with recently popular

---

[30]Johnson (2010).
[31]Henriques (2019, p. 209).
[32]See www.div12.org/treatments.
[33]O'Grady and Slife (2017).
[34]Slife et al. (2017).

interventions like mindfulness and loving-kindness meditations in the psychology literature, can certainly offer some relief from the mental processes that exacerbate psychiatric disorders, it lacks the viewpoint necessary to "see the forest for the trees," as the saying goes. Thus, "Christian-derived" meditative practices can help us to begin and end from a biblical worldview, whereas "Christian-accommodative" meditative practices, which attempt to modify secular interventions by adding on Christianity, post hoc, may come up short,[35] commonly leading to a "square peg in a round hole" dynamic.

To offer a quick example, in his book *Christian Meditation: Experiencing the Presence of God*, the Christian psychologist and meditation teacher James Finley[36] reflected on his time spent with the late Trappist monk Thomas Merton, a widely popular twentieth-century spiritual writer on the contemplative life. As Finley revealed (and is commonly known), Thomas Merton devoted a significant amount of time furthering Buddhist-Christian relations in his later years, even traveling to Asia to better understand Buddhist culture and practices. Yet, on one such cross-cultural excursion, Merton apparently wrote a letter to his American monastery, concluding that "everything he was searching for was present in the monastery, was present in his own hermitage, was present in his own Christian tradition."[37] In other words, Christianity was, all along, offering Merton everything he needed for psychological and spiritual fulfillment.

In a similar vein, my hope with this workbook is that you can look to your own tradition, the Christian faith, to better understand a variety of ways to more effectively identify and respond to your suffering in contemporary society. Like Thomas Merton, you have the opportunity to draw from the rich Christian heritage that has been passed on to you, learning from the wisdom of writers from the last two millennia who have documented their psychological and spiritual insights as they faithfully walked with Jesus as a traveling companion on the roads of life. Instead of spending your time sifting through the vast secular psychology literature for help, my hope is that you will be able to pursue change in your own proverbial monastery, with Christianity serving as the familiar place you confidently return home to.

CHRISTIAN MEDITATION: A FOUR-STEP STRATEGY

Focusing on Christian meditative practices as the starting point, while also interacting with the psychology literature, I offer strategies to help you relate differently to an assortment of transdiagnostic processes that may be keeping you stuck in life.

---

[35]Johnson et al. (2013).
[36]Finley (2004).
[37]Finley (2004, p. 3).

Based on a range of Christian writings over the last two thousand years,[38] I define Christian meditation as follows:

> A broad collection of concentrative- and insight-oriented psychological and spiritual practices throughout historic Christianity, ranging from *apophatic* (emphasizing few to no words and no images) to *kataphatic* (emphasizing words and/or images), for shifting from earthly- to heavenly-mindedness and developing a deeper communion with God and enduring contentment in him in the midst of suffering.[39]

Or, simply put, the central aim of Christian spiritual practices is Christlikeness, given we are attempting to become more like Jesus Christ on a daily basis.[40] In our efforts to become more like Jesus, we are following a Suffering Servant (Is 53), who "empathize[s] with our weaknesses" (Heb 4:15). Therefore, because Jesus as our great high priest (Heb 4:14-16) fully understands our vulnerabilities, he offers his followers his mercy and grace from moment to moment, even in the midst of psychological suffering.

Worth mentioning, the Christian tradition tends to use words like *meditation, prayer,* and *contemplation* differently when describing ways to fellowship with the triune God. In fact, lectio divina brings these practices together in a four-step process (described in a subsequent chapter), moving from reading the Bible to meditating on a key passage to praying to God to resting in silence with God.[41] However, in this workbook I use the term *meditation* more generally to describe the vast array of psychological and spiritual practices in the Christian tradition for focusing the mind on God, cultivating a deeper awareness of his loving presence, and accepting his providential care in the midst of suffering, reconciling Christian exercises with the contemporary meditation literature and psychological science.[42]

As a result, throughout the workbook you will be practicing a four-step model of Christian meditation—housed within eight different bodies of Christian meditative writings throughout the ages and enhanced by contemporary research on the psychological benefits of meditation—to target a variety of transdiagnostic processes. Although I review each step in more detail in a subsequent chapter, below is a brief summary:

Step 1. In the first step, you will be learning to recognize a variety of "mind-brain-body-behavior" processes[43] that may be leading to psychological suffering and impaired functioning, focusing on changing unhelpful patterns with cognition, affect,

---

[38]For example, Ball (2016), Bangley (2006), Gallagher (2008), Hilhoit and Howard (2012), Lawrence (2015), and Ware (2000).

[39]Adapted from Knabb and Bates (2020b, p. 106).

[40]Whitney (2014).

[41]Finley (2004).

[42]Feldman et al. (2007); Walsh and Shapiro (2006).

[43]Greeson et al. (2014).

behavior, the self, and relationships. The following list offers a brief overview of the different types of transdiagnostic processes you will be working on within this workbook, all of which have been linked to mental disorders in the psychology literature:

Cognition

- Repetitive negative thinking: A perseverative type of thinking process that includes ruminating about the past and worrying about the future.[44]

Affect

- Impaired emotional clarity: The struggle to identify and understand emotional experiences.[45]

- Distress intolerance: The inability to endure unpleasant experiences, including uncertainty, frustration, emotions, and physical sensations.[46]

Behavior

- Behavioral avoidance: A type of experiential avoidance that involves avoiding behaviors that may lead to unpleasant thoughts, feelings, and sensations.[47]

The self

- Perfectionism: Frequently striving to meet a high set of personal standards and engaging in negative self-judgments when falling short of such standards.[48]

Relationships

- Impaired mentalization: The struggle to recognize and understand the thoughts and feelings of oneself and other people, especially in salient relational dynamics,[49] or having a hard time "seeing [one]self from the outside and others from the inside."[50]

Step 2. With the second step, you will be practicing turning from earthly-mindedness to heavenly-mindedness, consistent with the apostle Paul's letter to the Colossians (Col 3:1-2). The Puritans in the seventeenth century often distinguished between these two modes of awareness. Based on a review of several Puritan sources,[51] I define earthly-mindedness as follows:

> A past- to present-oriented, distracted mental state, preoccupied with the worries, uncertainties, and sufferings of the temporary physical world and struggling to maintain an awareness of a transcendent, spiritual reality, including heaven as an actual place and a real relationship with the triune God.[52]

---

[44]Ehring and Watkins (2008).
[45]Vine and Aldao (2014).
[46]Zvolensky et al. (2010).
[47]Gamez et al. (2011).
[48]Egan et al. (2011); Limburg et al. (2017).
[49]Allen (2008).
[50]Allen et al. (2008 p. 3).
[51]Burroughs (2010, 2014); Owen (2016); Rowe (1672).
[52]Knabb and Bates (2020b, p. 100).

On the other hand, in drawing from the same Puritan authors,[53] I define heavenly-mindedness as follows:

> A present- to future-oriented mental state of hope, prioritizing a moment-by-moment awareness of both a transcendent spiritual reality and heaven as an eternal, permanent place, wherein Christians will find their true home, free from suffering, and experience a perfect, face-to-face communion with the infinitely good, wise, and powerful triune God.[54]

Interestingly, the Puritans frequently advocated for meditating on heaven, given Jesus is there (although he is certainly omnipresent) and heaven is our future, permanent home.[55] In the midst of suffering, then, shifting from earthly- to heavenly-mindedness can help us maintain an awareness of this meta-view, or Christian worldview, enduring suffering with a deeper contentment as we patiently wait for Jesus Christ's return.

Step 3. As the third step, you will be practicing the following three mental skills,[56] which can help you accept God's active, loving presence from moment to moment, even in adverse life events and psychological suffering:

- *Attention*: Focusing on God with sustained attention.

- *Present-moment awareness*: Maintaining an awareness of God in the present moment.

- *Acceptance*: Accepting painful inner experiences because God is present.

Step 4. Finally, after moving through the first three steps, the fourth step involves deepening your communion with God and finding contentment in him, leading to the ability to make life decisions with an awareness of God's active, loving presence from moment to moment. Based on a review of a variety of Christian sources,[57] I define communion with God as follows:

> A mutual, intimate friendship with the Trinity, initiated by God and reciprocated by Christians through union with Christ, resulting in the psychological and spiritual benefits of being at peace with God, enjoying God's presence, feeling loved, accepted, and comforted by God, and communicating with God through prayer, meditation, and Bible study.[58]

In my own research with a Christian sample of community adults, I found that communion with God was positively linked to daily spiritual experiences and

---

[53]Burroughs (2010, 2014); Owen (2016); Rowe (1672).
[54]Knabb and Bates (2020b, pp. 100-101).
[55]Baxter (2015).
[56]Feldman et al. (2007); Knabb, Vazquez, and Pate (2019).
[57]Baxter (2017); Beeke and Jones (2012); Davis (2012); Henry (2011); Owen (2016); Packer (1990); Strong (2015).
[58]Knabb and Wang (2019, p. 4).

psychological well-being.[59] What is more, drawing from a range of Christian writings on contentment,[60] I define a distinctly Christian version of contentment in the following manner:

> An inner psychological state of enduring satisfaction, independent of outer circumstances, that is attributable to God's grace and involves freely and fully surrendering to God, finding pleasure in God, and thanking God in actively authoring every life event with perfect goodness and wisdom.[61]

In a recent study I conducted among a Christian sample of community adults, I found that Christian contentment was positively linked to a general state of contentment, life contentment, mindful qualities (attention, present focus, acceptance, awareness), equanimity, and daily spiritual experiences.[62]

See figure 0.2 for a visual depiction of this four-step Christian meditative strategy. As you can see, you will be starting off by learning to notice a variety of unhelpful transdiagnostic processes, then practicing shifting from earthly- to heavenly-mindedness, before accepting God's active, loving presence by cultivating focused, sustained attention on him, present-moment awareness of him, and acceptance of his providential care. As you get into the habit of taking these three steps with a range of Christian meditative practices, my hope is that you will be in a position to more deeply commune with God and rest in an enduring contentment found

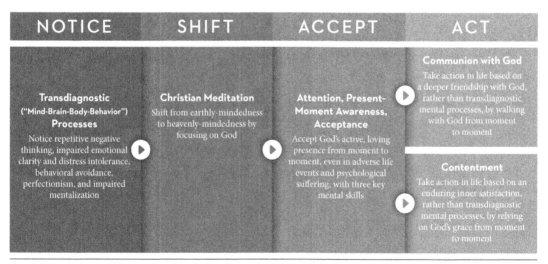

Figure 0.2. Theoretical four-step model of Christian meditation. Adapted from Ball (2016); Bangley (2006); Bishop et al. (2004); Feldman et al. (2007); Greeson et al. (2014); Hayes et al. (2012); Holzel et al. (2011); Knabb and Bates (2020b); Knabb, Vazquez, and Pate (2019); Kristeller and Johnson (2005); Saint-Jure and Colombiere (1980); Walsh and Shapiro (2006); and Ware (2000).

---

[59]Knabb and Wang (2019).
[60]Burroughs (2018); Colombiere (1983); Holman (1998); Kempis (1983); Watson (2017).
[61]Knabb, Vazquez, and Wang (2020, p. 8).
[62]Knabb, Vazquez, Garzon, Ford, Wang, Conner, Warren, and Weston (2020).

exclusively in him. By developing a more intimate relationship with God by *abiding* in him (Jn 15:5),[63] you will be working toward making life decisions that are rooted in becoming more like Jesus Christ,[64] rather than reacting to unhelpful transdiagnostic processes that point you away from living a life of meaning and purpose.

CHRISTIAN SOURCES AND USE OF CITATIONS

Consistent with *Streams of Living Water*,[65] I have organized historic Christian spiritual writings into eight overarching categories, or streams, taking into consideration factors such as their time period, denominational affiliation, characteristics, and themes. From my perspective, each body of writing (which, of course, has some overlap with the others) can help you in your struggle with unhelpful transdiagnostic processes, embedding the four-step meditative model along the way. To be sure, there is growing empirical evidence for the use of some of these historic Christian practices for psychological problems.[66] In subsequent pages, you will have the opportunity to practice these meditative exercises, with each body of writings offering strategies for cultivating sustained attention on God, present-moment awareness of God, and acceptance of unpleasant inner experiences because God is present.[67] Although many of these approaches will be explicated individually in subsequent chapters, I offer a brief introduction here:

Desert meditative practices. Beginning around the third and fourth centuries, Christians started moving to the deserts in Egypt and Syria to flee from society, attempting to be like Jesus in facing his temptations in the desert (Mt 4:1-11).[68] In this harsh terrain, they recited the Psalms to focus the mind, used Scripture to talk back to tempting, compulsive thoughts, and developed the skill of staying put in their "cell," a small room they lived in, mostly in solitude, to face their suffering.[69] In doing so, they worked toward developing patience in the midst of psychological pain (e.g., sadness, anxiety, boredom), a deeper awareness of God's presence, and sustained focus on him.

Orthodox meditative practices. The practice of reciting the Jesus Prayer ("Lord Jesus Christ, Son of God, have mercy on me") slowly evolved over time, possibly influenced by several passages in Scripture (e.g., 1 Thess 5:17; Lk 18:38). Eventually, writings on the Jesus Prayer (and other topics) from the fourth to the fifteenth

---

[63]Murray (1888).
[64]Whitney (2014).
[65]Foster (1998).
[66]For example, Knabb and Vazquez (2018); Knabb et al. (2017); Knabb, Vazquez, Garzon, Ford, Wang, Conner, Warren, and Weston (2020).
[67]Knabb, Vazquez, and Pate (2019).
[68]Burton-Christie (1993).
[69]Evagrius (2009); Farag (2012).

centuries were compiled into what is now known as the *Philokalia*,[70] a collection of spiritual teachings in the Eastern Orthodox Church. Among other benefits, reciting the Jesus Prayer can help us to remember Jesus, focus the mind, and rely on his mercy from moment to moment.[71]

Jesuit meditative practices. In the sixteenth-century work *Spiritual Exercises*, Ignatius of Loyola offered a variety of meditative practices, including the "Prayer of the Senses," which involves using each of the five senses to feel our way into a biblical story in the Gospels and interact more intimately with Jesus. He also described the examen, which consists of cultivating a deeper awareness of God's presence throughout the day.[72] With each of these practices, Christians are learning to "find God in all things," a popular saying among the Jesuits, even in experiences of suffering.

Medieval meditative practices. In the Christian tradition, there is a long list of medieval authors, such as the anonymous author of the *Cloud of Unknowing*,[73] Brother Lawrence,[74] Thomas à Kempis,[75] John of the Cross, Teresa of Àvila, and Julian of Norwich,[76] who all offered spiritual teachings on developing a deeper awareness of God's active, loving presence. In addition, lectio divina, or "divine reading," was a popular practice during this time.[77] Themes among these works, written in a time period of tremendous suffering and hardship, include staying connected to a spiritual reality, contemplating an awareness of God's active, loving presence and union with God, and trusting in God in the midst of psychological and spiritual struggles.[78]

Celtic meditative practices. Celtic spiritual writings emphasized the importance of recognizing God's omnipresence in all of creation, with love as a central theme, as well as the notion that we are embodied, with a physical form created by God.[79] "Breastplate prayers," for example, inspired by Paul's instruction to "put on the full armor of God" (Eph 6:11), are a powerful reminder of God's omnipresence and the need for God's protection.[80] Overall, themes among Celtic Christian works throughout the ages include an emphasis on the presence of the Trinity and Jesus' companionship as we walk through life, even during seemingly mundane tasks or activities.[81]

---

[70]Coniaris (1998).
[71]Johnson (2010).
[72]Hansen (2012).
[73]Bangley (2006).
[74]Lawrence (2015).
[75]Thomas (1983).
[76]McGinn (2006).
[77]Matter (2012).
[78]Jaoudi (2010).
[79]Earle (2011).
[80]Earle (2011).
[81]Earle and Maddox (2004).

French meditative practices. Several French writers offered meditative practices in the 1600s and 1700s, such as Francis de Sales,[82] Jeanne Guyon,[83] and François Fénelon.[84] Themes among these authors include specific directions on meditation and prayer to develop a deeper awareness of God's presence and surrender the self to God.

Protestant meditative practices. A variety of Protestant authors have outlined Christian meditative practices, such as the Puritans' focus on God's attributes and actions,[85] the Quakers' use of silence to experience God,[86] missionary Frank Laubach's "game of minutes,"[87] and A. W. Tozer's[88] *The Christian Book of Mystical Verse.* Among these writings, themes include an emphasis on thinking deeply throughout the day about God's qualities, both formally and informally, as well as the use of Scripture to guide meditative practices.

Contemporary meditative practices. Contemporary practices within the Christian tradition include the late Trappist monk Thomas Merton's instructions on meditation,[89] Thomas Keating's centering prayer (and, as a supplementary practice, the welcoming prayer),[90] John Main's mantra meditation,[91] and breath prayers,[92] often advocated for within writings on the spiritual disciplines. Among these writings and practices, a salient theme includes offering contemporary, updated instructions for Christians to practice historic Christian exercises, with a central aim of developing a deeper relationship with God.

To date, there is a considerable amount of research on the psychological benefits of secularized meditative practices,[93] with emerging research on the psychological benefits of Christian meditative practices.[94] Although some of the mental skills cultivated across these meditative traditions may be similar, such as developing focused, sustained attention,[95] the end goals (or *telos*) are highly different, given they are worldview-dependent. Therefore, this workbook is written for Christian clients receiving professional mental health services, taking into consideration that Christians need worldview-dependent strategies that overlap with what the contemporary

[82]Francis (2015).
[83]Guyon (2011).
[84]Fénelon (2010).
[85]Saxton (2015).
[86]Bill (2016).
[87]Laubach (2007).
[88]Tozer (1991).
[89]Merton (1960).
[90]Bourgeault (2004).
[91]Main (2001).
[92]Calhoun (2005).
[93]Khoury et al. (2013).
[94]Knabb et al. (2017); Knabb and Vazquez (2018); Knabb, Vazquez, Garzon, Ford, Wang, Conner, Warren, and Weston (2020).
[95]Walsh and Shapiro (2006).

psychology literature has shown to work in ameliorating psychological struggles. Within the pages that follow, psychotherapists and professional counselors can work directly with Christian clients to target transdiagnostic processes, using meditative practices that are firmly planted in historic Christianity and a biblical worldview. Quite often, the psychology literature possesses some of the building blocks to make sense of suffering and healing, but not the actual blueprint to fit the pieces together in a manner consistent with the Christian faith.[96]

Regarding the use of citations, I have chosen to employ footnotes at the bottom of each page, rather than in-text citations (which are common in academic writing), as a sort of compromise, so that clients can more easily follow along in a user-friendly manner, and academics and mental health professionals can more quickly track down references at the bottom of each page (if they choose to do so).

OUTLINE OF THE WORKBOOK

In the remainder of the workbook, I present the following chapters in an easy-to-follow format:

- Review of the transdiagnostic movement, including well-researched transdiagnostic processes that are linked to mental disorders (chap. 1)

- Review of meditative strategies throughout the ages, comparing and contrasting Buddhist, Christian, and secular psychological perspectives to better understand their similarities (e.g., mental skills developed) and differences (e.g., goal) (chap. 2)[97]

- Review of a theoretical four-step Christian meditative model for targeting transdiagnostic processes (see fig. 0.2) (chap. 3)

- Five intervention chapters, focusing on targeting transdiagnostic problems with thinking, feeling, behaving, the self, and relationships (chaps. 4 to 8)

FORMAT FOR THE INTERVENTION CHAPTERS

After laying the foundation for the workbook in the first three chapters, the five intervention chapters include the following format:

- Background on a specific transdiagnostic process and its link to mental disorders

- Background on specific meditative exercises used to target the transdiagnostic process

---

[96]Knabb, Johnson, Bates, and Sisemore (2019).
[97]Walsh and Shapiro (2006).

- Detailed, easy-to-follow instructions on the application of specific meditative exercises to the transdiagnostic process
- Journaling exercises to reflect on the meditative experiences
- Weekly logs to keep track of symptoms
- Transcripts and an audio recording to follow along with the meditative exercises

THE INTERCHANGEABILITY OF INTERVENTIONS

I link the long list of specific interventions throughout this workbook to a more general four-step process of Christian meditation because most of them are swappable across the five transdiagnostic process chapters. In other words, if you gravitate toward a certain intervention in one chapter (e.g., the Jesus Prayer), you can work with your psychotherapist or professional counselor to adapt it for use in another chapter. Ultimately, because the Christian practices threaded across this workbook are intended to help you notice the designated transdiagnostic process, then shift toward an awareness of God's active, loving presence, before accepting God's providential care and taking action in life by communing with God and finding a deeper contentment in him, the array of exercises offered from chapter to chapter are interchangeable, with only slight modifications necessary.

THE INTENDED AUDIENCE, THEOLOGICAL LENS, AND IMPORTANCE OF INFORMED CONSENT

This workbook is for graduate students in clinical and counseling (and related) programs and mental health professionals working with Christian clients to better understand Christian meditative practices in a clinical and counseling context. In fact, the workbook is written directly to motivated clients who identify with the Christian faith and wish to draw from their own meditative tradition to target transdiagnostic processes. More specifically, the "you" that I address throughout the workbook is a motivated client currently in psychotherapy or professional counseling, working with a psychotherapist or professional counselor who is guiding each step of the way. By writing directly to the Christian client, my hope is that mental health professionals—whether those currently pursuing a graduate degree, being supervised at a practicum or internship site, or independently practicing with a state license in the mental health field—will be able to use this workbook as an adjunct to the salient services they provide, attentively looking over their Christian clients' shoulders as they collaboratively dig deeper into the rich psychological wisdom of the Christian tradition.

During our time together, my goal is to serve as a miner, translator, and tour guide, given "there is nothing new under the sun" (Eccles 1:9). In other words, I will help you to mine the Christian tradition, translating the vast body of historic Christian writings over the last two millennia into accessible language and clear steps in order to point you in the direction of psychological and spiritual change. I will also function as a tour guide, walking with you as you dually attempt to better understand the problem and work toward a solution.

I do all of this from a Reformed, evangelical Protestant perspective, "embracing [the material] Evangelically."[98] Among other characteristics, evangelical Christians, who make up about 25 percent of adults in the United States,[99] identify as orthodox Protestants and believe in the authority of Bible as the Word of God, the need for a personal, sanctifying relationship with Jesus Christ, the importance of following the teachings of Jesus Christ to become more like him (i.e., "Christlikeness"), and the reality and impact of sin in a fallen world.[100] In the pages that follow, I write from this perspective, recognizing that "Scripture is the final authority over, but not the sole source of, Christian belief and practice"[101] and taking a "high view" of God's sovereignty, which means his providential care extends to *all* of creation.

In fact, Christians throughout history have advocated for the psychological and spiritual benefits of maintaining an awareness of God's providence in daily life, which includes God's redemptive work in suffering.[102] For instance, the Belgic Confession, a Reformed Protestant doctrine written in the 1500s, fittingly offers the following on God's providence:

> We believe that this good God, after creating all things, did not abandon them to chance or fortune but leads and governs them according to his holy will, in such a way that nothing happens in this world without God's orderly arrangement. . . . We do not wish to inquire with undue curiosity into what God does that surpasses human understanding and is beyond our ability to comprehend. But in all humility and reverence we adore the just judgments of God, which are hidden from us, being content to be Christ's disciplines, so as to learn only what God shows us in the Word, without going beyond those limits. This doctrine gives us unspeakable comfort since it teaches us that nothing can happen to us by chance but only by arrangement of our gracious heavenly father, who watches over us with fatherly care, sustaining all creatures under his lordship, so that not one of the hairs on our

---

[98]Goggin and Strobel (2013).

[99]Pew (2015).

[100]Goggin and Strobel (2013); Larsen (2007); Whitney (2014).

[101]Treier (2007, p. 35).

[102]Cosby (2012); Saint-Jure and Colombiere (1983).

heads (for they are all numbered) nor even a little bird can fall to the ground without the will of our Father. In this thought we rest.[103]

Undoubtedly, this psychological and spiritual understanding of God's providential care functions as the theological "glue" for this workbook, accepting life's challenges because God is the author of *every* event, which can bring Christians much-needed contentment on the dangerous roads of life, filled with potholes, cracks, ruts, and detours. Certainly, as a parallel process, the mindfulness literature also advocates for psychological acceptance, with the definition of acceptance over the years simply meaning "to consent to take what is offered"[104] or "receive willingly."[105]

Yet, for Christians, we relate differently to our most difficult inner and outer experiences because God's providential care extends to all of our thoughts, feelings, behaviors, self-preoccupations, and relationships, which can bring us "unspeakable comfort" and "rest" in our time of need. In other words, with the practices in this workbook, we are learning to "consent to take what is offered" or "receive willingly" from *God*, not accepting suffering from an impersonal universe solely because it is inevitable in this world, as may be the case with some secular mindfulness- and acceptance-based therapies in the twenty-first-century psychology literature. My hope, thus, is that you will benefit from these exercises as you work with your psychotherapist or counselor, deepening your relationship with God (which foundationally includes trusting in his providential care) along the way, given the Christian spiritual writings I utilize in this workbook offer "reflections on the lived experience of sanctification" among Christians throughout the ages.[106]

Finally, before choosing to use this workbook in clinical and counseling practice, it is important for you to talk to your psychotherapist or counselor about your options. In other words, "informed consent" is necessary, given the wide variety of interventions available in contemporary Western society to address psychological suffering.[107] In discussing this workbook with your psychotherapist or counselor, my hope is that you, as a Christian, will continue to identify ways to more intimately experience the love of God and find contentment in him throughout your day.

---

[103]Reformed Church in America (n.d.).
[104]American Dictionary and Cyclopedia (1900, p. 46).
[105]Merriam Webster's Desk Dictionary (1995, p. 4).
[106]Goggin and Strobel (2013, p. 24).
[107]Chappelle (2000).

TRANSDIAGNOSTIC PROCESSES

A New Approach to
Understanding Mental Disorders

God had one Son on earth without sin,
but never one without suffering.

AUGUSTINE OF HIPPO

IN THIS FIRST CHAPTER, I explore the burgeoning transdiagnostic literature,[1] including the difference between lumping and splitting strategies for psychiatric diagnosing,[2] and provide justification for a lumping approach (i.e., identifying and treating common psychological processes across diagnoses). I also present in more detail the different types of transdiagnostic processes in the psychology literature, which are organized around problems with cognition (repetitive negative thinking), affect (impaired emotional clarity and distress intolerance), behavior (behavioral avoidance), the self (perfectionism), and relationships (impaired mentalization).[3] Throughout the chapter, I offer explanations and an exercise for you to gain more insight into the nature of transdiagnostic processes.

THE PREVALENCE AND COMORBIDITY OF MENTAL DISORDERS IN CONTEMPORARY SOCIETY

In the United States, the lifetime prevalence among adults is about 20 percent for mood disorders and 35 percent for anxiety disorders,[4] which are two of the more

---

[1]Craske (2012); Harvey et al. (2004).
[2]Siegel (2010).
[3]Greeson et al. (2014); Harvey et al. (2004).
[4]Kessler et al. (2012).

common types of psychiatric disorders in contemporary Western society. In other words, about one in five adults will struggle with depression in their lifetime, to the point of meeting criteria for a formal psychiatric diagnosis, whereas about one in three will meet full criteria for an anxiety disorder. Beyond the United States, a recent worldwide survey revealed that about 30 percent of people will suffer from a common mental disorder (e.g., mood, anxiety) at some point in their adult years.[5] Even more troubling, the majority of people who suffer from a depressive disorder may also struggle with an anxiety disorder at the same time, referred to as "comorbidity."[6] These data suggest that depression and anxiety, which are often experienced together, may be quite common in both contemporary Western society and the non-Western world.

For depressive disorders (e.g., major depressive disorder), symptoms may include a low mood, a struggle to enjoy previously pleasurable activities, trouble sleeping, energy loss, impaired concentration, thoughts of worthlessness, and excessive guilt, among others.[7] With anxiety disorders (e.g., panic disorder, social anxiety disorder, generalized anxiety disorder), symptoms may include trouble breathing, shaking, dizziness, fear of judgment by others in social situations, and chronic worry, to name a few.[8] Combined, depressive and anxiety disorders are often referred to as emotional disorders in the psychology literature, since they frequently occur together among adult populations. Said differently, in recent years, psychologists have started to include these types of diagnoses in the same category in order to better understand their common ingredients and develop intervention strategies to treat an amalgam of psychiatric symptoms at the same time.

LUMPING VERSUS SPLITTING IN THE PSYCHOLOGY LITERATURE

In the psychology literature, psychologists often differentiate between lumping and splitting approaches to understanding and treating a variety of mental processes that impair functioning.[9] With lumping, researchers attempt to elucidate common psychological experiences that transcend any one particular diagnosis. In other words, an effort is made to make sense of patterns of thoughts, feelings, and behaviors that are observed across diagnostic categories. As an example, in the last decade, authors have identified "impaired emotional clarity" as a potential mental process that can help to explain the development and maintenance of a variety of psychiatric diagnoses.[10] More specifically, some people may struggle to identify

---

[5]Steel et al. (2014).
[6]Watson and Stasik (2014).
[7]American Psychiatric Association (APA) (2013).
[8]APA (2013).
[9]Siegel (2010); Taylor and Clark (2009).
[10]Vine and Aldao (2014).

and make sense of their emotional experiences, with this struggle linked to depression and anxiety.[11] As another example, openness to the future has been explored of late, with researchers identifying this positive emotional state as the ability to maintain a sense of confidence in, and acceptance of, future life experiences.[12] In a recent study, openness to the future was negatively linked to depression and anxiety, meaning people who have a more positive view of the future also report fewer symptoms of depression and anxiety.[13]

With splitting, researchers strive to cultivate an understanding of the unique psychological experiences for each mental disorder, then target the corresponding symptoms with disorder-specific interventions. For instance, psychologists may attempt to make better sense of the most salient symptoms of panic disorder, including panic-related thoughts, feelings, and behaviors and a preoccupation with subsequent panic attacks, then develop a manualized approach that teaches coping skills to ameliorate the disorder. As each new edition of the *Diagnostic and Statistical Manual of Mental Disorders* (DSM)[14] seems to add more diagnoses to its running list, a splitting approach requires additional manualized interventions to be researched in order to treat an ever-growing number of mental disorders.[15]

REASONS FOR A TRANSDIAGNOSTIC APPROACH IN THE PSYCHOLOGY LITERATURE

Yet, this splitting strategy may not be the most helpful approach for responding to psychological suffering in the twenty-first century, given some of the growing concerns about the DSM, now in its fifth edition.[16] First, although the DSM can be extremely helpful in identifying a cluster of symptoms and, thus, offering a common language for describing psychological struggles among both mental health professionals and consumers of mental health services, the vast number of diagnoses (currently over 300 in the latest DSM) leaves us vulnerable to pathologizing normal (albeit unfortunate) experiences of psychological suffering,[17] especially in a fallen, imperfect world. In other words, there is seldom a clear-cut dividing line between health and dysfunction when striving to understand the human continuum of thoughts, feelings, and behaviors.[18] What is more, many individuals struggle with

---

[11]Vine and Aldao (2014).
[12]Botella et al. (2018).
[13]Botella et al. (2018).
[14]APA (2013).
[15]Taylor and Clark (2009).
[16]APA (2013).
[17]Harvey et al. (2004).
[18]Harvey et al. (2004).

more than one diagnosis, which raises the question of whether dichotomous boundaries also exist from disorder to disorder in the real world.

Second, as we organize psychological suffering into more and more categories, we must, in turn, develop corresponding treatment approaches. However, someone with multiple diagnoses may not have the time, money, or energy to participate in multiple interventions to treat a list of psychiatric diagnoses.[19] This dilemma, too, goes for mental health professionals, who may not have the resources to deliver separate treatments, anchored to different diagnoses, to the same person seeking services. Rather, understanding and treating common mental processes that are experienced across diagnostic categories may be the most efficient option.

COMMON TRANSDIAGNOSTIC PROCESSES IN THE PSYCHOLOGY LITERATURE

As was briefly mentioned in the introduction chapter, we will be focusing on transdiagnostic processes within five domains: thinking, feeling, behaving, the self, and relationships. Although each of these areas is explored individually and in much more detail in subsequent chapters, below are some of their basic ingredients, including examples of how each mental process may impair daily functioning in the Christian life.

Cognition. With repetitive negative thinking, we may ruminate and worry, perseverating as a rigid thinking style on a daily basis.[20] This type of thinking, more specifically, involves ruminating about the past and worrying about the future. With ruminating, we may dwell on a past conversation or event, whereas worrying may consist of anticipating a dangerous situation in the near or distant future. In either case, we may end up getting lost in our thoughts, so much so that we have a hard time focusing on the life that is unfolding before us in the present moment. When this is the case, we may struggle to fulfill our daily obligations, since we are lost in a sea of cognitive distractions. Even more, we may struggle to recognize God's presence in the here-and-now. We may also get lost in the details of events, conversations, and so forth, and have a hard time seeing the bigger picture. In the psychology literature, perseverative thinking is linked to both depressive and anxiety-related symptoms.[21]

Affect. When it comes to impaired emotional clarity, we may struggle to identify and understand our emotional world,[22] especially when it comes to recognizing the role that our emotions play in daily life. In fact, we may end up having a hard

---

[19]Craske (2012).
[20]Ehring and Watkins (2008).
[21]Ehring et al. (2011).
[22]Vine and Aldao (2014).

time understanding even our most basic emotions (e.g., sadness, fear, anxiety, guilt), including their positive influence in helping us to make decisions, navigate relationships, and so on. With distress intolerance, we may struggle to accept the inevitable uncertainties, frustrations, emotions, and physical sensations of daily life.[23] When this happens, we may have a hard time fulfilling daily responsibilities and obligations, as well as recognizing what God is communicating to us in our emotional experiences. For example, if we struggle to accept the uncertainties of life, we may have a hard time making decisions about the future and recognizing God's will for the days, weeks, months, and years ahead, choosing instead to procrastinate in an attempt to delay committing to a course of action for fear of making a mistake. In the psychology literature, impaired emotional clarity is associated with both depressive and anxiety-related symptoms,[24] as is distress intolerance.[25]

Behavior. In the behavior domain, we may struggle to live the life God has called us to live, engaging in avoidance behaviors in an attempt to somehow rid ourselves of daily pain.[26] More specifically, we may withdraw or hide in an effort to eliminate unpleasant thoughts and feelings, which likely only makes matters worse given our psychological pain continues to persist, with the added struggle of falling behind on our daily obligations. Even more troubling, we may end up declining to follow Jesus because of the cost of letting go of the things we are dually distracted by and attached to (Mk 10:17-27). In the psychology literature, behavioral avoidance is linked to both depressive and anxiety-related symptoms.[27]

The self. Regarding the self, we may have perfectionistic tendencies, including standards that are unattainable.[28] In struggling to live up to our own expectations for ourselves, we may end up judging and criticizing ourselves, so much so that we withdraw in shame and waver in our ability to consent to God's will for our life. In other words, we may have a hard time extending the mercy and grace that God offers us to ourselves,[29] leading to impaired daily functioning. In the psychology literature, perfectionism is related to both depressive and anxiety-related symptoms.[30]

Relationships. In our relationships, we may struggle to understand ourselves and others, referred to as impaired mentalization, especially when it comes to making sense of the thoughts, feelings, and behaviors that drive key interpersonal exchanges.[31] When we have a hard time understanding these ingredients

---

[23]Zvolensky et al. (2010).
[24]Vine and Aldao (2014).
[25]Macatee et al. (2016).
[26]Gamez et al. (2011).
[27]Gamez et al. (2011).
[28]Egan et al. (2011); Limburg et al. (2017).
[29]Knabb (2018).
[30]Gnilka and Broda (2019); Maricutoiu et al. (2019).
[31]Allen (2008); Allen et al. (2008).

of relationships, many areas of our life can be impaired, such as family, work, church, and community. Even more, we may struggle to maintain an awareness of God's active, loving, compassionate presence in our daily encounters with others, leading to a disconnect between our relational world and experience of God. In the psychology literature, deficits in mentalizing are associated with anxiety in close relationships (i.e., attachment anxiety) and neuroticism (e.g., worry, anxiety),[32] as well as depressive symptoms.[33]

With each of these transdiagnostic domains, we may be unable to recognize when our mental processes get in the way of living the life God has called us to live. Therefore, simply recognizing when we are distracted by our imperfect mental processes in a fallen world can serve as a fitting first step. What follows, then, is a metaphor to better understand the dilemma of mental processes, followed by examples of the importance of identifying our mental habits from the psychology literature, the Eastern Orthodox Christian tradition, and Scripture, before concluding with an exercise to finish the first chapter.

IDENTIFYING TRANSDIAGNOSTIC PROCESSES: A STORY OF TWO FISH

There is an old story about two fish peacefully swimming along in the ocean. A third fish passes by and asks, "How's the water?" In response, one of the two fish turns to the other and asks with quite a bit of confusion, "What's water?" With this short story, we can easily draw a parallel with our mental processes. Because we are so close, so to speak, to these processes, swimming in a sea of thoughts and feelings throughout the day, we can struggle to attain the distance necessary to recognize them.

For example, someone may have the thought, *I'm worthless,* swimming in these seemingly powerful words for most of their adult years. Yet, just like fish in water, they may not have the necessary distance to simply observe the inner workings of the human mind. In fact, many of us struggle to develop the requisite psychological and spiritual practices to slow down and notice the mental processes that are unfolding from moment to moment. Without this inner awareness, we may end up making life decisions that are inconsistent with God's will.

Interestingly, both contemporary psychologists and Christians throughout history have advocated for practices to notice the inner world in a more open, curious, detached, and vigilant manner, recognizing the importance of doing so for psychological and spiritual health. Among the former, a wide variety of exercises

---

[32]Dimitrijevic et al. (2018).
[33]Fischer-Kern and Tmej (2019).

(e.g., mindfulness meditation) have been recently proposed for gaining a broader awareness of our inner experiences. With the latter, over the last two millennia, Christians have been slowing down to recognize the tempting, compulsive thoughts that can get in the way of a deeper, more restful experience of God's presence, employing both formal and informal spiritual practices to do so.

IDENTIFYING TRANSDIAGNOSTIC PROCESSES: "META-COGNITIVE SELF-REGULATION" IN THE PSYCHOLOGY LITERATURE

In the twenty-first-century psychology literature, researchers have identified several potential ingredients for understanding how meditation leads to positive psychological change. In particular, meditation may help to cultivate the "meta-cognitive self-regulatory capacity of the mind."[34] With self-regulation, we are developing the ability to simply notice our psychological experiences, including our thoughts, feelings, and behaviors.[35] Along the way, we are learning to observe these psychological processes, then shift toward another point of focus with sustained attention, doing so with an attitude of acceptance and nonjudgment.[36]

Ultimately, as we learn to engage in regular meditative practice, we begin to notice the inner world with greater awareness and distance, coupled with the ability to shift our attention in a more purposeful, nonjudgmental manner. In the context of the aforementioned transdiagnostic processes, meta-cognitive self-regulation[37] can help us to recognize when we are swimming in a sea of distractions, then gently shift toward an awareness of God's active, loving presence. In fact, some in the Christian tradition have been advocating for deepening our ability to notice and shift for centuries, referred to in the Eastern Orthodox tradition as *nepsis*.

IDENTIFYING TRANSDIAGNOSTIC PROCESSES: *NEPSIS* IN THE EASTERN ORTHODOX TRADITION

Housed within the Eastern Orthodox tradition, the *Philokalia* is an amalgam of Christian spiritual writings from the fourth to fifteenth centuries, which (among other themes) advocated for the use of the Jesus Prayer (i.e., "Lord Jesus Christ, Son of God, have mercy on me") as a way to cultivate an awareness of God's presence, attentiveness, and inner peace.[38] By repeatedly calling on Jesus' name and asking for his mercy, we are learning to notice the steady stream of tempting, compulsive

---

[34]Dorjee (2016).
[35]Dorjee (2016).
[36]Dorjee (2016).
[37]Dorjee (2016).
[38]Ware (2005).

thoughts (*logismoi*, Greek), then shift the mind toward Jesus.[39] Even more, Christians are developing an inner watchfulness and alertness (*nepsis*, Greek),[40] similar to the meta-cognitive self-regulation identified among contemporary mindfulness meditation researchers, which leads to a deeper awareness of a variety of transdiagnostic processes that may get in the way of following Jesus Christ.

As an example, in Hesychios's *On Watchfulness and Holiness* in the *Philokalia*, he states, "Watchfulness is a continual fixing and halting of thought at the entrance to the heart. In this way predatory and murderous thoughts are marked down as they approach and what they say and do is noted."[41] Or, as another example from Hesychios,

> When the mind, taking refuge in Christ and calling upon Him, stands firm and repels its unseen enemies, like a wild beast facing a pack of hounds from a good position of defence, then it inwardly anticipates their inner ambuscades well in advance. Through continually invoking Jesus the peacemaker against them, it remains invulnerable.[42]

Here we see that repeatedly calling on Jesus' name can lead to a deeper awareness of the "inner ambuscades" of the human mind, given we are noticing our mental processes, then pivoting toward Jesus by reaching for him as our source of mercy, comfort, and peace. In other words, we are cultivating a sort of vigilance, reminiscent of a guard on patrol to ensure no one scales the walls of a king's palace.

In a similar vein, in *Into the Silent Land: A Guide to the Christian Practice of Contemplation*, Martin Laird[43] discussed the use of a "prayer word" (e.g., "Jesus," "Abba") in the Christian tradition to maintain an awareness of God's loving presence from moment to moment. Given our attention will inevitably wander from God to other mental activities, a short word or phrase, anchored to Scripture, can help us to bring our focus back to God when it has drifted. Again, this simple process of noticing and shifting can help us to dually get to know the inner workings of the fallen human mind and maintain an awareness of God's merciful, compassionate presence in the here-and-now. As we learn to invite God into our inner experiences, we may begin to notice we can relate to our most difficult thoughts, feelings, and sensations with more compassion and acceptance, decreasing the tendency to judge and shame ourselves for inner experiences that may never fully go away. To deepen our understanding of this dynamic—noticing and inviting—the book of Hebrews can offer us a fitting example from Scripture.

---

[39]Ware (2005).
[40]Ware (2005).
[41]Nikodimos (1782).
[42]Nikodimos (1782).
[43]Laird (2006).

IDENTIFYING TRANSDIAGNOSTIC PROCESSES:
AN EXAMPLE IN SCRIPTURE

In Hebrews, the author explicates that, as a human being, Jesus suffered, which means he can assist us when we struggle: "Because he himself suffered when he was tempted, he is able to help those who are being tempted" (Heb 2:18). To help us in our suffering, the writer of Hebrews instructs us to "fix [our] thoughts on Jesus" (Heb 3:1), before going on to state the following:

> Therefore, since we have a great high priest who has ascended into heaven, Jesus the Son of God, let us hold firmly to the faith we profess. For we do not have a high priest who is unable to empathize with our weaknesses, but we have one who has been tempted in every way, just as we are—yet he did not sin. Let us then approach God's throne of grace with confidence, so that we may receive mercy and find grace to help us in our time of need. (Heb 4:14-16)

As the great high priest, Jesus understands our struggles because he has suffered just as we suffer. In fact, Jesus "learned obedience from what he suffered" (Heb 5:8), suggesting that suffering can teach us to yield to God's will and depend on his perfect love in our experience of daily psychological struggles.[44] In the midst of our suffering, then, we are called to persevere with a sense of hope, faithfully enduring with the recognition that God is with us (Heb 10:19-23). Ultimately, we are called to "throw off everything that hinders" in order to "run with perseverance the race marked out for us, fixing our eyes on Jesus, the pioneer and perfecter of faith" (Heb 12:1-2).

To reiterate, as Christians in a fallen world, we will inevitably suffer. Yet, from a Christian perspective, God is with us as we strive to press forward. To navigate our dimly lit paths on this side of heaven, the first step simply involves getting to know our suffering; then, as a second step, we are to shift our focus to God, reminiscent of Jesus' consent to the will of his Father in the midst of suffering.

As a reminder, throughout this workbook, you will be practicing a broader four-step process for responding to psychological suffering, with your struggles made up of a variety of psychiatric symptoms in our fast-paced, contemporary Western society. As the first step, you will be learning to notice the mental processes that are unfolding from moment to moment, before shifting to an awareness of God's active, loving presence in the here-and-now. Or, phrased differently, the first two steps involve recognizing and inviting—slowing down to identify a variety of trans-diagnostic processes, some of which may be getting in the way of living a fulfilling life, then asking God to be with you in the difficult experience by turning to a more

---

[44]Koessler (1999).

spiritual, transcendent perspective to make sense of your suffering. As you get into the habit of noticing and shifting, you will be, in turn, learning to rest in God's presence, recognizing that, although you cannot fully eliminate suffering on this side of heaven, you can relate differently to your psychological experiences as you patiently walk with God along the arduous roads of life. In other words, you can, like Jesus, learn to yield to God's providential care and trust in his plan, even when you suffer in this fallen world. As the fourth and final step, you are learning to patiently walk with God and find contentment in him, despite the psychological struggles—both internal and external—you may be experiencing on a daily basis.

But how, exactly, will you be learning to notice and shift as the first two (of four) steps? Christian meditation, prayer, and contemplation, anchored to Scripture, can help you to get into the daily habit of cultivating Christlikeness and a hopeful endurance in the midst of suffering. In the next chapter, you will get to know some of the spiritual practices that have been present within the Christian tradition for millennia, including the psychological role they can play in helping you to respond differently to the transdiagnostic processes that may be getting in the way of following Jesus on the roads of life. Before concluding the chapter, though, I would like to offer an exercise to help you begin to simply notice the patterns of your inner world.

IDENTIFYING TRANSDIAGNOSTIC PROCESSES: AN EXERCISE

For this exercise, please set aside ten minutes, finding a quiet location that is free from distractions. Sit in a comfortable chair, with your back straight and eyes closed. The purpose of this exercise is to simply watch whatever is unfolding within your inner world, recognizing that God is with you in the here-and-now.

First, slowly read the following passage in Scripture:

> That day when evening came, he said to his disciples, "Let us go over to the other side." Leaving the crowd behind, they took him along, just as he was, in the boat. There were also other boats with him. A furious squall came up, and the waves broke over the boat, so that it was nearly swamped. Jesus was in the stern, sleeping on a cushion. The disciples woke him and said to him, "Teacher, don't you care if we drown?"
>
> He got up, rebuked the wind and said to the waves, "Quiet! Be still!" Then the wind died down and it was completely calm.
>
> He said to his disciples, "Why are you so afraid? Do you still have no faith?"
>
> They were terrified and asked each other, "Who is this? Even the wind and the waves obey him!" (Mk 4:35-41)

Second, consider that Jesus was resting in the boat, despite the surrounding storm, before attempting to apply this passage to the subject matter from this chapter. In other words, in your own life you may feel like a "furious squall" is taking up all the space in your inner and outer world. For example, you may be ruminating about the past, worrying about the future, struggling to accept the uncertainties of life, isolating and withdrawing from the pains of life, and struggling to build and maintain healthy relationships with others. In the middle of the storm, you may easily lose sight of the fact that Jesus is with you on the boat, asking for you to faithfully trust in him as the wind and the waves surround. Stated differently, Jesus is in control and has the ability to simply say "be still" at any given moment, even as we question where he is in the midst of the winds and waves of life: "Teacher, don't you care if we drown?"

Third, begin to actually visualize yourself on the boat with Jesus. However, rather than noticing the winds and waves, you are observing your thoughts, feelings, and sensations, whether pleasant or unpleasant. Whatever inner experiences arise, simply notice them with a distant, curious attitude, given Jesus is with you on the boat. Because he is sovereign, there is nothing you need to do, other than get to know the patterns of your mental processes. Spend the next few minutes just observing, with no other goal in mind. Rather, your job is to just notice your patterns of thinking and feeling by attempting to answer the following questions:

- What am I thinking right now? Am I ruminating? Am I worrying? Am I getting stuck in a certain repetitive, perseverative type of thinking?
- What am I feeling right now? Am I feeling happy, sad, angry, afraid, anxious, or guilty? What other emotions might I be feeling right now? Where am I feeling these emotions in my body right now?

Fourth, once you have spent some time observing your thoughts and feelings, spend a few minutes journaling by answering the following questions:

What patterns of thinking did you notice in this exercise? Were you ruminating? Were you worrying? Were you getting stuck in a certain repetitive, perseverative type of thinking?

What emotions did you experience in this exercise? Did you feel happy, sad, angry, afraid, anxious, or guilty? Where did you feel these emotions in your body?

How well did you do in simply noticing your thoughts and feelings with an accepting, nonjudgmental curiosity? Did you struggle to allow these experiences to naturally unfold, without trying to change them in any way?

_____

_____

_____

_____

Where was Jesus during the exercise? Did you experience him as next to you in the boat? Did you experience him as in control, regardless of the thoughts and feelings that emerged? What other experiences did you have of Jesus during this exercise?

_____

_____

_____

_____

What are the strengths of this exercise? What about the limitations? How might this exercise help you to learn to notice your inner world, including the transdiagnostic processes that may be getting in the way of following Jesus on the roads of life? How can you extend this exercise to the rest of your day, recognizing that Jesus is with you, regardless of the thoughts and feelings that may arise?

_____

_____

_____

_____

CONCLUSION

In this chapter, we explored lumping and splitting strategies in the psychology literature,[45] including a rationale for focusing on a lumping approach in this workbook. We also reviewed the five different domains of mental processes we will be focusing on in subsequent chapters. To conclude, we completed an exercise to help you get to know your inner world. In the next chapter, we will review several common transdiagnostic treatment approaches for responding to the transdiagnostic processes that may be keeping you stuck in life.

---

[45]Craske (2012); Harvey et al. (2004); Siegel (2010).

TRANSDIAGNOSTIC INTERVENTIONS

Buddhist, Christian, and Secularized Meditation

Meditation is to be the motion of the heavenly spirit heavenward;
to carry it up to heaven and keep it a time there; a looking of
the eye of the mind, and a lifting up of the heart, a making a
stay, and taking a spiritual solace in heaven with God.

Nathanael Ranew

In this chapter, I review different types of meditation in the psychology literature, including "focused attention" and "open monitoring,"[1] which typically emanate from the Buddhist tradition. In addition, I explore the main ingredients of meditation, such as the type of attention utilized, the relationship to cognitive processes, and the goal of the various types of practices.[2]

With Buddhist-influenced meditation, I cover its religious roots, along with examples of secularized versions that are popular in the psychology literature, such as mindfulness and loving-kindness meditations. In this review, I also briefly discuss the theoretical and empirical support for these meditative practices that originate from Buddhism.

Alongside Buddhist-informed meditative strategies, I provide a Christian perspective, including *apophatic* and *kataphatic* forms of meditation in the Christian

---

[1]Kok et al. (2013); Kristeller and Johnson (2005); Lippelt et al. (2014); Lutz et al. (2008); Perez-De-Albeniz and Holmes (2000); Walsh and Shapiro (2006).
[2]Walsh and Shapiro (2006).

tradition. In particular, I discuss the various terms used to describe meditation in Christianity, such as *contemplation, prayer,* and *meditation.*[3] I also explore the religious roots of Christian meditation, including references to meditation in the Bible and historical Christian writings across several classic sources, as well as contemporary delivery systems for Christian meditation, such as popular organizations,[4] the Eastern Orthodox Church, and burgeoning movements in Protestant Christianity. Then, I briefly touch on Christian meditation and related research in the peer-reviewed psychology literature.[5]

In the remainder of the chapter, I cover the similarities and differences between Buddhist, Christian, and secularized forms of meditation. Despite the fact that two of the three main ingredients for these practices can often be similar (i.e., the type of attention and relationship to cognitive processes), the third ingredient, the goal (or *telos*), tends to be very different.[6] In other words, although it can certainly be healthy for Christians to "realize [their] attachment to things," then "let those attachments go and see things from a new, more flexible and open perspective,"[7] Buddhist-influenced (and sometimes secularized) meditation is about achieving oneness and equanimity versus communion with God and contentment as the ultimate aim across many of the Christian meditative traditions.[8]

I conclude the chapter with a brief exercise for you to "try on" Christian meditation within historic Christianity. Overall, as one of the lengthier chapters in this workbook, I pose a fundamental question for you to consider: should meditative practices be used in an instrumental manner (e.g., for symptom reduction) or to deepen your relationship with God,[9] with symptom reduction as a possible by-product? From my perspective, as you focus on deepening your relationship with God and finding contentment in him, you will be moving in the direction of either (1) getting *some* relief from psychological suffering, or (2) relating differently to psychological suffering because of a newfound ability to persevere with God by your side. In either case, Christian meditation is really a relational strategy to draw you closer to God, recognizing that Jesus empathizes with your weaknesses and wants you to approach him with confidence (Heb 4:14-16) as you learn to "run with perseverance the race marked out before [you]" (Heb 12:1).

---

[3]Finley (2004); Walsh and Shapiro (2006).

[4]See www.contemplativeoutreach.org.

[5]Knabb et al. (2017); Knabb and Vazquez (2018); Knabb and Wang (2019); Knabb, Vazquez, and Wang (2020); Knabb, Pate, Sullivan, Salley, Miller, and Boyer (2020); Knabb, Vazquez, Garzon, Ford, Wang, Conner, Warren, and Weston (2020).

[6]Walsh and Shapiro (2006).

[7]Greeson et al. (2014).

[8]Knabb and Wang (2019); Knabb, Vazquez, and Wang (2020).

[9]Slife and Reber (2012).

TYPES OF MEDITATION

In twenty-first-century Western society, the use of meditative practices appears to be rapidly increasing from year to year. In just a five-year period, for example, the percentage of United States adults who say they practice meditation jumped from 4 percent to 14 percent.[10] At some point in their lifetime, according to recent survey data, about 3 percent of adults in the United States will engage in either mantra or mindfulness meditation, whereas roughly 4 percent will utilize some sort of spiritual meditation.[11] With this latter category, about half of Christians indicate they meditate every week.[12]

Different types of meditation in contemporary Western society include concentrative- and insight-related practices. With concentrative, or focused attention, meditation, practitioners are typically directing their attention to one aspect of their awareness, including a mantra (e.g., a sound, a word, a short phrase), one of the five senses, or the breath, in a voluntary, purposeful manner.[13] Over time, practitioners are cultivating focused, sustained attention, as they repeatedly concentrate on the designated object of awareness, then deliberately return their attention to the object if their focus drifts.[14] In this process, practitioners commonly appraise whatever they were distracted by (e.g., labeling a thought as "worrying"), before gently returning to their original object of focus,[15] doing so over and over again during a formal period of time (e.g., 20 to 30 minutes). Examples of Buddhist practices that use concentration are meditating on the breath and repeating a predetermined mantra.[16]

With insight, or open monitoring, meditation practitioners are cultivating a meta-awareness of whatever experiences arise in the inner or outer world, exercising a nonjudgmental curiosity in the process.[17] In other words, there is no one object of focus, as is the case with concentrative meditation; rather, participants are developing a broader, more expansive perspective as they observe whatever emerges in the present moment.[18] Along the way, each and every experience is attended to, with no one experience being preferred or prioritized over another.[19] Said another way, practitioners are utilizing a detached, open stance toward whatever emerges, rather than holding on to or pushing away thoughts, feelings,

---

[10]Clark et al. (2018).
[11]Cramer et al. (2016).
[12]Pew (2018).
[13]Kok et al. (2013); Kristeller and Johnson (2005); Lutz et al. (2008).
[14]Kok et al. (2013).
[15]Lutz et al. (2008).
[16]Rubin (2003).
[17]Kok et al. (2013).
[18]Lutz et al. (2008).
[19]Kok et al. (2013).

sensations, or any of the five senses.[20] An example of this type of meditation in Buddhism is mindfulness, which focuses on gaining an awareness of the "three marks of existence" (described below).[21]

As a third category, some meditative practices may oscillate between the field and object, meaning practitioners begin with a specific object to focus on, then pivot toward a broader awareness of the background of the object.[22] Ultimately, many meditative traditions combine concentrative and insight elements.[23] Therefore, a clear dividing line between the two may not be fully possible when attempting to organize the different types of meditation that emanate from the world religions (e.g., Buddhism, Hinduism, Judaism, Islam, Christianity).

INGREDIENTS IN MEDITATION

To better understand the various meditative traditions, it may be helpful to review the individual ingredients that are combined to form each practice. First, the type of attention is an important consideration.[24] Some practices, such as concentrative forms of meditation, focus on one object within the mind, including one of the five senses (e.g., sound, touch), a word or phrase (e.g., a mantra, a prayer, a passage from a sacred text), or the breath. On the other hand, insight meditations tend to advocate for a more open, fluid type of awareness, observing whatever object enters into the practitioner's experience with an attitude of curiosity and flexibility.[25] With attention, ultimately, practitioners may zoom in or zoom out (to use a camera metaphor), depending on what they wish to focus on.

Second, the relationship to cognitive processes is worth considering.[26] With some practices, the meditation involves noticing whatever cognitive experiences emerge, including the thoughts that enter into awareness, without attempting to modify them in any way.[27] In other words, practitioners are exercising a nonjudgmental, open, curious attitude toward cognition, whether the thought or image is pleasant or unpleasant. This type of an open attitude toward thinking is common among insight forms of meditation, such as mindfulness. Conversely, some meditations may attempt to actually alter thinking in some way during formal practice.[28]

---

[20]Kok et al. (2013).
[21]Walsh and Shapiro (2006).
[22]Perez-De-Albeniz and Holmes (2000).
[23]Walsh and Shapiro (2006).
[24]Walsh and Shapiro (2006).
[25]Walsh and Shapiro (2006).
[26]Walsh and Shapiro (2006).
[27]Walsh and Shapiro (2006).
[28]Walsh and Shapiro (2006).

Finally, the goal (or *telos*) is a salient part of each practice,[29] especially when considering meditation in a cultural context.[30] Put differently, when attempting to understand the purpose, motive, or aim for each practice, it is important to make sense of the actual heritage that has given rise to the various types of meditation from around the world. For instance, is the goal of a particular practice to better understand the nature of reality, mitigate suffering, cultivate well-being and psychological health, generate a sense of compassion for the self and others, or develop a deeper relationship with God, to name a few possibilities? If so, where do these goals originate? Does the *telos* flow from a religious or secular worldview? A sacred text? A doctrine within a community? Relatedly, is meditation used as an instrument in the service of some other aim or as an end in and of itself?

When used as an instrument, some authors have been critical of the recent emphasis on mindfulness and loving-kindness meditations in Western psychology, since such practices are often divorced from their Buddhist roots and may create unrealistic expectations for practitioners who are looking to fully eliminate psychological pain.[31] In other words, when meditation is removed from its religious heritage, its ultimate purpose may be obscured, given it is converted from a way of life, embedded within a comprehensive worldview, to merely a coping skill.[32]

When employed as an end in and of itself, on the other hand, meditation may indirectly lead to certain psychological benefits (e.g., symptom reduction), but is primarily practiced as a way to deepen relationships (with God and others), cultivate compassion (for the self and others), better understand the nature of existence (e.g., suffering), and so on. Stated differently, meditation is practiced because of its inherent value, rather than what it seemingly offers on a more superficial level. What follows, then, is a review of meditation in Buddhist, Christian, and secular contexts so as to gain a deeper understanding of the types, ingredients, and *telos* of each, before exploring the similarities and differences between some of the more common meditative practices circulating in contemporary Western society.

MEDITATION IN THE BUDDHIST TRADITION

Types of Buddhist meditation: Concentrative and insight. In the Buddhist tradition, there are typically two overarching types of meditation. The first type of Buddhist meditation is concentrative (*samatha*), or "focused attention,"[33] and emphasizes the importance of attending to one particular object for a prolonged

---

[29]Walsh and Shapiro (2006).
[30]Kok et al. (2013).
[31]Farb (2014).
[32]Farb (2014).
[33]Kok et al. (2013).

period of time in order to cultivate stillness, tranquility, loving-kindness, and so forth.[34] In general, practitioners are learning to settle the mind by focusing on one thing in the present moment, letting go of the tendency to dwell on the past or future.[35] Whenever a distracting thought or feeling emerges, practitioners notice it, then gently return to their point of focus, doing so over and over again during the formal, designated period of time.[36] Ultimately, the *telos* of concentrative meditations in the Buddhist tradition may be tranquility and related emotional experiences (e.g., compassion, joy).

The second type of Buddhist meditation is insight (*vipassana*), or "open monitoring,"[37] and is practiced in order to cultivate wisdom, gain a deeper awareness of reality, and better understand the "three marks of existence" (i.e., impermanence, unsatisfactoriness/suffering, no-self/non-self).[38] With mindfulness meditation, the aim is to recognize that everything in life is temporary and will pass away, life is suffering and filled with unsatisfying experiences, and there is no such thing as an individual, separate self.[39] Ultimately, the *telos* of insight meditations in the Buddhist tradition may be a deeper awareness of a Buddhist interpretation of reality (i.e., everything is impermanent, life is suffering, there is no individual self).[40]

Sometimes, however, focused attention may be combined with open awareness meditative practices, with concentration preceding insight. In other words, among the vast array of Buddhist meditations, practitioners may first focus on one object of awareness, before letting go of the designated object in an effort to monitor awareness in general, prioritizing the foreground (by zooming in) or background (by zooming out) at various points in the formal practice.[41]

Examples of Buddhist meditations that employ focused attention (concentration) include simply attending to the breath or repeating a mantra for a designated period of time,[42] whereas mindfulness meditation is used as an open awareness (insight) exercise.[43] Of course, some Buddhist practices may utilize a combination of concentration and insight, as is the case with loving kindness (*metta*) meditation.[44]

---

[34]Eifring (2016); Kyabgon (2014); McCown et al. (2010); Raffone and Srinivasan (2010).
[35]McCown et al. (2010).
[36]McCown et al. (2010).
[37]Kok et al. (2013).
[38]Eifring (2016); McCown et al. (2010).
[39]Kyabgon (2014); McCown et al. (2010).
[40]Morgan (2010).
[41]Shankman (2015).
[42]Shankman (2015).
[43]Kok et al. (2013); Lippelt et al. (2014).
[44]Gunaratana (2017); Lippelt et al. (2014).

With mindfulness meditation, practitioners may observe sensations in the body, emotions, or the mind during formal practice, sitting up straight with their eyes closed.[45] In this practice, the goal is to begin to notice how experiences seemingly change from moment to moment and there is no apparent separate self—everything is interconnected and one.[46] For example, being mindful of breathing means practitioners spend a designated amount of time focusing their attention on the breath cycle in the present moment, then bring their concentration back to an awareness of each in-breath and out-breath when their attention has drifted to something else.[47] To be sure, the breath is often a starting point for mindfulness meditation, since breathing occurs naturally and the in-breath and out-breath are an anchor to the present moment.[48] In sum, concentrating on the breath is commonly used as a stepping stone toward insight into the oneness of everything.[49] Thus, concentration and insight approaches to Buddhist meditation may be combined.

With loving kindness meditation, practitioners repeat predetermined mantras—typically directed toward the self (e.g., "May I be happy"), then extended to others (e.g., "May others be free from suffering")—in order to cultivate compassion, equanimity, and so forth.[50] The goal (or *telos*) of loving kindness meditation is to develop positive thoughts and feelings (e.g., loving kindness, equanimity, joy),[51] as well as a perception of oneness with every living being.[52] Whereas mindfulness meditation tends to be neutral toward inner and outer experiences, exercising an attitude of nonjudgment toward whatever arises in the here-and-now, loving kindness meditation is about purposefully developing a positive emotional experience.[53]

Contemporary delivery systems for Buddhist meditation. In contemporary Western society, Buddhist meditation has often been secularized, disentangled from its religious roots in order to serve as a vehicle through which psychological change is pursued in a variety of integrated healthcare settings. For example, mindfulness-based stress reduction (MBSR) is a popular eight-week group intervention for lowering stress and improving daily living,[54] and Buddhist-influenced mindfulness meditation appears to be integral to dialectical behavior therapy (DBT) and mindfulness-based cognitive therapy (MBCT),[55] whereas loving

---

[45]Kyabgon (2014).
[46]Kyabgon (2014).
[47]Nhat Hanh (1976).
[48]Nhat Hanh (1976).
[49]Nhat Hanh (1976).
[50]Gunaratana (2017); Neff and Germer (2018).
[51]Thondup (2008).
[52]Salzberg (1995).
[53]Germer (2009).
[54]Lehrhaupt and Meibert (2017).
[55]See Robins et al. (2004); Segal et al. (2004).

kindness meditations are foundational to the mindful self-compassion program (MSC).[56] In the last decade, a review of 209 studies elucidated that mindfulness meditation is effective in decreasing symptoms of depression, anxiety, and stress,[57] a review of 47 studies highlighted that mindfulness meditation is effective in decreasing symptoms of depression, anxiety, and pain,[58] and a review of 24 studies revealed that loving kindness meditation is effective in increasing positive emotions (e.g., happiness).[59]

More specifically, Buddhist-influenced mindfulness meditation may be helpful for a variety of transdiagnostic processes, such as perseverative thinking, distress intolerance, a preoccupation with the self, and perfectionistic thinking,[60] given its main ingredients in the psychology literature (i.e., attending to/concentrating on one thing at a time, staying focused on the present moment, maintaining an awareness of thoughts and feelings with openness and nonjudgment, accepting unpleasant emotions).[61] For instance, concentrative practices may help practitioners focus on one object in awareness, anchoring themselves to the present, rather than ruminating about the past or worrying about the future. What is more, insight practices may allow practitioners to let go of the expectation that the present moment should somehow be different by accepting that inner experience is impermanent. Insight practices, in addition, may assist practitioners in relinquishing their grip on perfectionistic tendencies, given their emphasis on oneness and the amelioration of the notion of a separate, individual self. Finally, concentrative practices may help practitioners to improve negative interpretations of life events, as they focus on cultivating compassion, joy, equanimity, and loving kindness in the present moment, as well as gaining a deeper insight into the nature of reality. Although the research literature on Buddhist-influenced meditative practices for transdiagnostic processes is further reviewed in subsequent chapters of this workbook, for now, there seems to be some theoretical support for engaging in concentrative- and insight-oriented practices in response to unhelpful psychological processes that get in the way of daily living.

Buddhist meditation in the psychology literature: A summary. Overall, the current psychology literature reveals that (1) Buddhist-influenced meditative practices are integrated into a wide variety of intervention approaches, and (2) such practices (whether secularized or anchored to Buddhism) may help Western individuals who are suffering from psychiatric symptoms. Yet, because the *telos* of these

---

[56]Germer and Neff (2019).
[57]Khoury et al. (2013).
[58]Goyal et al. (2014).
[59]Zeng et al. (2015).
[60]Greeson et al. (2014).
[61]Feldman et al. (2007).

Buddhist-informed practices may not be fully consistent with a Christian worldview, this workbook offers you, as a Christian client in professional counseling or psychotherapy, a worldview-sensitive alternative, helping you turn to your own religious heritage for meditative approaches to improve psychological suffering. What follows, then, is a review of the various forms of meditation in Christianity so that you can begin to "try on" a plethora of practices that are housed within your own religious tradition.

MEDITATION IN THE CHRISTIAN TRADITION

In the Christian tradition, there are a variety of practices to respond to psychological suffering in a fallen world. Although the previously mentioned types of meditation (i.e., concentrative, insight) tend to be labeled as such in both Buddhism and Western psychology, I also employ these labels to compare and contrast the varying practices across Buddhist, psychology, and Christian literatures. Worth noting, however, Christianity often categorizes historic spiritual practices with the more familiar language of meditation, prayer, and contemplation (based on the four-step medieval practice of lectio divina, or "divine reading"), as well as *kataphatic* (using words and images) and *apophatic* (using few to no words and no images).

Meditation, prayer, and contemplation: Basic definitions from lectio divina. To better understand the different types of spiritual practices that Christians have been using throughout the last two millennia to draw closer to God and find a deeper contentment in him, lectio divina may be a useful starting point. Lectio divina typically includes four steps—reading, meditating, praying, and contemplating—and has roots in the monastic Christian tradition.[62] With lectio divina, we are opening ourselves to God's active, loving presence through ruminating on the words of the Bible, reminiscent of a cow slowly chewing cud in a field.[63] In the twelfth century, Guigo II[64] captured lectio divina in his famous work *The Ladder of Monks*, describing its four steps using the metaphor of eating a meal.

With the first step, reading, we are settling into the practice by slowly reading the Bible in a relaxed, deliberate manner, word by word and phrase by phrase, consistent with taking the first bite of a savory dish of food as we fully enter into the experience.[65] In this first step, we are striving to read Scripture relationally and reverentially, as if God is actually speaking and a reciprocal, interpersonal exchange is unfolding with God in the here-and-now, one that Christians cherish as the most

---

[62]Benner (2010); Wilhoit and Howard (2012).
[63]Paintner (2011).
[64]Guigo II (2012).
[65]Guigo II (2012); Paintner (2011); Wilhoit and Howard (2012).

important thing in life.[66] In other words, we are listening to God, who communicates throughout the pages of the Bible.[67] Ultimately, reading is an "outer exercise" as we begin the process.[68]

With the second step, meditating, we are deeply and carefully thinking about (i.e., pondering) the text by using our God-given cognitive, discursive capacities, similar to beginning to chew a bite of food.[69] In this step, we are absorbing the words of the Bible by examining them from multiple perspectives,[70] then allowing them to linger for a period of time.[71] Here we are employing the intellect to understand, on a deeper level, the chosen passage in Scripture. Ultimately, meditating is "an inner act of the mind" as we continue to move through the practice.[72]

With the third step, praying, we are communicating with God, responding to him based on whatever spontaneously arises during the first two steps of lectio divina, consistent with tasting the bite of food that we are slowly chewing.[73] In this response to God, we may petition him with a request, convey that we trust him, or simply thank him and praise him.[74] Along the way, we are engaging in a reciprocal exchange to commune with God, both speaking and listening in our prayer time with him.[75] Ultimately, praying is "the action of the soul," in that we convey a deeper longing for communion with God.[76]

With the fourth step, contemplating, we are learning to rest in God, which typically means letting go of the tendency to overly rely on words in our fellowship with him.[77] Here, we are savoring the bite of food, having interacted with God's Word through reading, meditating, and praying, and focusing on simply being with God.[78] Ultimately, contemplating is "beyond all feeling and knowledge" and described as a "stage of the blessed."[79]

Meditation, prayer, and contemplation: Similarities and differences. Of course, beyond the basic four steps of lectio divina, writers from the various Christian traditions have defined these terms somewhat differently over the years. For instance, several centuries ago, in *Treatise on the Love of God*, Francis de Sales defined meditation as "dwelling on a single thought with great attention" and contemplation

---

[66]Paintner (2011).
[67]Paintner (2011).
[68]Guigo II (2012).
[69]Benner (2010); Guigo II (2012); Wilhoit and Howard (2012).
[70]Benner (2010).
[71]Paintner (2011).
[72]Guigo II (2012).
[73]Benner (2010); Guigo II (2012); Paintner (2011).
[74]Benner (2010).
[75]Wilhoit and Howard (2012).
[76]Guigo II (2012).
[77]Wilhoit and Howard (2012).
[78]Guigo II (2012); Paintner (2011).
[79]Guigo II (2012).

as "an adoring, uncomplicated, and enduring attention of the soul to divine things," then went on to explain that "meditation examines the details," whereas "contemplation considers the larger picture."[80] Also several centuries ago, in *A Treatise of Divine Meditation*, the Puritan author John Ball defined meditation as

> the steadfast and earnest bending of the mind on some spiritual and heavenly matter, discoursing on it with ourselves, until we bring it to some profitable point, both for the settling of our judgments, and the bettering of our hearts and lives.[81]

More recently, in the *Westminster Dictionary of Christian Spirituality*, meditation is defined as "the mind [reflecting] on some Christian truth or passage of scripture or personal experience, using words and ideas in more or less logical progression, with the aim of reaching fuller understanding and personal appropriation of the truth considered."[82] What is more, prayer involves conversing with God by adoring God, interceding to God on behalf of others, petitioning God with a request, and giving thanks to God, to name a few themes.[83] Finally, contemplation is defined as "the kind of prayer in which the mind does not function discursively but is arrested in a simple attention and one-pointedness," with the practitioner desiring "the opportunity simply to express to God one's loving, hoping, trusting, thanking, in as few words as possible."[84] Or, simply put, contemplation is about cultivating an "awareness of the divine presence."[85] In many Christian writings, including the four steps of lectio divina,[86] meditating with words and images prepares the practitioner to contemplate with few to no words and no images, reaching out to God in faith and love, rather than overly focusing on knowledge.[87]

In consideration of these practices, the twentieth-century Trappist monk Thomas Merton argued that meditation and contemplation should be grouped together: "[Meditation] is part of a continuous whole. . . . To separate meditation from prayer, reading, and contemplation is to falsify our picture of the monastic way of prayer."[88] In agreement, the English Methodist J. Neville Ward noted that "contemplation and meditation, main sources of nourishment in the life of faith as they are, need each other," as meditation without contemplation can lead to "self-preoccupation" and prevent Christians from engaging in "wordless loving," whereas

---

[80]Francis (2011, pp. 44, 46, 49).
[81]Ball (2016, p. 25).
[82]Ward (1983, p. 95).
[83]Ballester (1983).
[84]Ward (1983, p. 95).
[85]Egan (2005, p. 211).
[86]Guigo II (2012).
[87]Bangley (2006).
[88]Merton (1969, p. 4).

contemplation without meditation can lead to Christians forgeting about "earth and the word made flesh."[89]

In sum, then, I believe it is helpful for us to continue to discuss and learn these practices—meditation, prayer, and contemplation—within the framework of lectio divina, rather than separating them out and attempting to understand and practice these Christian approaches in isolation. As a common theme across these practices, the aforementioned definitions seem to convey that focusing on God is central, as is anchoring (on at least some level) attempts to commune with God to Scripture. Yet, worth mentioning, with reading, meditating, and praying, we are typically relying on the intellect, words, and images (*via positiva*), whereas contemplation often downplays the use of these faculties in an attempt to lovingly gaze upon, and rest in, God (*via negativa*).[90]

Apophatic versus kataphatic. In returning to lectio divina, the first three steps—reading, meditating, and praying—are typically conceptualized as *kataphatic* practices, which means they employ words, images, and so forth to relate to God.[91] Conversely, the fourth step of lectio divina, contemplation, is often considered an *apophatic* practice, which means contemplation downplays the use of words and images to commune with God.[92]

More specifically, with *kataphatic* (i.e., "positive," *via positiva*) approaches, we typically use words and images to know God, as well as relate to him, consistent with the fact that God has revealed himself to us through the Bible.[93] So, for example, we can view God as our Father because Scripture reveals him as such.[94] Or, we can know about who God is, since his attributes are revealed throughout the pages of the Bible. In the *kataphatic* Christian tradition, we are "praying with our eyes open," with rich descriptions and images of who God is.[95]

However, with *apophatic* (i.e., "negative," *via negativa*) approaches, we are recognizing the limitations of human language in fully capturing God.[96] In other words, as soon as we assign a label to God, we may be attempting to confine God to such a label.[97] In the *apophatic* Christian tradition, we are "praying with our eyes shut" by accepting the mystery of God, including his ineffability.[98]

---

[89]Ward (1983, p. 96).
[90]Francis (2011).
[91]Paintner (2011).
[92]Paintner (2011).
[93]McGrath (2011).
[94]McGrath (2011).
[95]Hoare (2016).
[96]McGrath (2011).
[97]McGrath (2011).
[98]Hoare (2016).

Religious roots: The Bible. *Kataphatic* spiritual practices have deep roots in the Bible. Throughout Scripture, there are several Hebrew words for meditation, including *hagah* and *siyach*. The former is captured in the following passage: "Keep this Book of the Law always on your lips; meditate on it day and night, so that you may be careful to do everything written in it. Then you will be prosperous and successful" (Josh 1:8).[99] The latter, on the other hand, is used in the following verse: "I will consider all your works and meditate on all your mighty deeds" (Ps 77:12).[100] Here we see that meditation in the Old Testament involves pondering God, including his Book of the Law, attributes, and actions.

Since Christians believe God has revealed himself through Scripture, meditating on God's word means we are able to gain a deeper knowledge of God through pondering his attributes and actions in the Bible. Examples of a *kataphatic* approach to knowing and relating to God include Jesus' incarnation (Col 1:15-19) and scriptural support for the notion that Christians can experience God through Jesus Christ (Jn 14:9; 1 Jn 1:1-3).[101] In these passages we see that God the Father has clearly revealed himself to humankind through the incarnation of Jesus Christ, God the Son. Therefore, God is knowable through Jesus Christ.

Conversely, *apophatic* spiritual practices are often influenced by a handful of passages in Scripture. For instance, Moses encountered God in "the thick darkness" (Ex 20:21), God told Moses, "I AM WHO I AM" (Ex 3:14), and God revealed himself to Elijah in a "gentle whisper" (1 Kings 19:11-13).[102] In these passages, we see that God has certainly revealed himself to humankind through Scripture, but is also beyond words. Therefore, although we, as humans, can speak of God through the use of language, God is also beyond language. [103]

Religious roots: Key historic Christian writings. Over the last two millennia, Christian authors have developed spiritual practices to help Christians commune with God, find a deeper contentment in him, and become more like Jesus Christ. In fact, in the vast array of Eastern Orthodox, Catholic, and Protestant writings, instructions on meditation, prayer, and contemplation are widely available, though many present-day Christians are often unaware of these psychological and spiritual resources. My hope here is to convey the reality that the Christian tradition has a deep appreciation for the need to develop daily habits to improve psychological and spiritual functioning, and for practices that can help Christians both deepen their relationship with God and respond differently to many psychiatric symptoms that will not fully go away in a fallen world.

---

[99]Strong (2001a).
[100]Strong (2001a).
[101]Ruffing (2005).
[102]Howells (2005).
[103]Augustine (2011).

Beginning around the third century, some Christians started to move to the deserts of Egypt and Syria to emulate Jesus' temptations in the desert (Mt 4:1-11).[104] In moving to these desert terrains, Christians sought to reject the materialism of the societies from which they came, face their temptations, and rely exclusively on God.[105] In fact, the desert can represent our inner world as Christians, regardless of our actual geographic location or the time period we live in, since it is "ultimately a metaphor for inner attentiveness, vulnerability, and transformation."[106] In the process of relocating to the desert, Christians developed strategies for responding to the tempting, compulsive thoughts they inevitably faced on a daily basis. These desert strategies included reciting the Psalms, as well as talking back to their thoughts with Scripture.[107] Over time, Christians organized monastic communities in the desert, with elders offering instruction on this type of Christian living.[108] Eventually, these teachings were documented in the *Sayings of the Desert Fathers*, with topics rich in psychological and spiritual content, such as cultivating peace and inner stillness, self-control, endurance and patience, watchfulness, humility, and living out Christian virtues.[109]

With possible roots in the use of "monologic" or "arrow" prayers (i.e., repeating a short word or phrase) among early desert communities in Egypt,[110] the Jesus Prayer ("Lord Jesus Christ, Son of God, have mercy on me") gradually emerged as a way for Christians to cry out to God for his mercy (i.e., God's loving responsiveness and healing), focus the mind through repetition of the words of the prayer, cultivate inner peace and stillness, and maintain an awareness of Jesus' name throughout the day.[111] To this day, Eastern Orthodox Christians rely on the Jesus Prayer, presented in the *Philokalia*, for psychological and spiritual health.[112] Although reciting short passages in Scripture is typically understood as a *kataphatic* practice, the Jesus Prayer is commonly viewed as an *apophatic* approach, since (other than the actual words of the prayer) practitioners do not rely on words and images.[113] Fast-forward to the twenty-first century, and Christians are still struggling to gain a deeper awareness of the inner workings of the mind, slowing down to notice our thoughts and feelings, before shifting toward an awareness of God's active, loving presence for psychological and spiritual growth.

---

[104]Burton-Christie (1993).
[105]Paintner (2012).
[106]Paintner (2012, p. xiv).
[107]Evagrius (2009); Farag (2012).
[108]Wortley (2012).
[109]Wortley (2012).
[110]Ware (2013).
[111]Ware (2014).
[112]Coniaris (2004).
[113]Johnson (2010).

From a transdiagnostic perspective, these historic practices may help Christians to notice unhelpful psychological processes, before pivoting toward a more spiritual perspective, with God at the center of Christians' functioning, not on the periphery.

As another example of a Christian approach, the Jesuit tradition offers the foundational work *Spiritual Exercises* for psychological and spiritual health, teaching Christians to "find God in all things," as the famous Jesuit saying goes. Originally written by Ignatius of Loyola in the sixteenth century, *Spiritual Exercises* includes four weeks of activities.[114] The various themes include learning to trust in God's enduring love despite human brokenness and fallenness, following Jesus by communing with him as a trustworthy traveling companion, and sharing Jesus' suffering and resurrection,[115] with corresponding meditative, prayer, and contemplative exercises to help Christians "develop their attentiveness, their openness, and their responsiveness to God."[116] In other words, as Ignatius mentioned, the exercises are about allowing "the soul to rid itself of all inordinate attachments, and, after their removal, disposition of our life for the salvation of our soul," meaning Christians are dually identifying the various obstacles to fellowshiping with God and living a life devoted to him.[117] Here we are attempting to develop a sort of spiritual-mindedness, finding God in each and every experience in both the inner and outer world. Whether engaging in meditation, prayer, or contemplation, the practices within *Spiritual Exercises* are commonly viewed as *kataphatic*, given the use of both words and images. From a transdiagnostic perspective, these historic exercises may help us to notice our unhelpful attachments to the psychological processes that can get in the way of loving and following Jesus, then shift toward a deeper awareness that God is active and present in all things, before enduring painful experiences in a fallen world with a newfound sense of hope by communing with God and finding contentment in him.

To offer an additional example, medieval writers on contemplation include Julian of Norwich, Walter Hilton, and the anonymous author of the *Cloud of Unknowing*. For them, contemplation captures a state and a way of engaging with the world, filled with "attentiveness and receptiveness" to God's activity, an attitude of humility, a willingness to surrender to God, and self-denial in the service of following God's will.[118] More specifically, the author of the *Cloud of Unknowing* advocated for the use of a short, simple word (e.g., *God*) to symbolize Christians' willingness to reach out to God in love in a "cloud of unknowing," rather than

---

[114]Society of Jesus (n.d.).
[115]Barry (1991).
[116]Society of Jesus (n.d.).
[117]Barry (1991, p. 14).
[118]Fanous and Gillespie (2011).

overly relying on knowledge.[119] In this contemplative effort, Christians are to place everything else (e.g., thoughts, feelings, memories) beneath a "cloud of forgetting," given these mental processes can be barriers to a deeper experience of God.[120] What is more, in *The Stairway of Perfection*, Walter Hilton advocated for the first three steps of lectio divina—reading, meditating, and praying—as a path toward contemplation, at one point powerfully declaring,

> if you want to speed your travels and make a good journey each day, you should hold these two things often in your mind—humility and love. That is: I am nothing, I have nothing, I desire only one thing [Jesus]. You shall have the meaning of these words continually in your intention, and in the habit of your soul.[121]

Consistent with the *Cloud* author's advice, Hilton was arguing for a shift from earthly preoccupations (including the self) to God, exercised with humility and love. Many of these writings from the Middle Ages are *apophatic*; that is, they downplay an overreliance on words and images when contemplating God. From a transdiagnostic perspective, these practices may help Christians to recognize the limitations of the human mind, shifting from distracting inner experiences to God through the vehicle of love. Along the way, Christians are deepening their trust in God in the midst of the chronic inner and outer trials that may never go away.

As one final example, Protestant sources over the last several centuries have advocated for the use of meditative practices. The Puritans, in particular, wrote widely on Christian meditation, highlighting the role that pondering both the Trinity and God's attributes and actions can have in different areas of life.[122] One Puritan author, Edmund Calamy, defined meditation as

> a dwelling and abiding upon things that are holy; it is not only a knowing of God, and a knowing of Christ, but it is a dwelling upon the things we know; as the bee that dwells and abides upon the flower, to suck out all the sweetness that is in the flower.[123]

Puritan meditation, then, is about filling the mind with God, prioritizing him above our own fallen thoughts that may, at times, lead us away from God, who resides at the center of our existence. In this meditative process, the Puritans advocated for both formal practice during designated periods of time and informal practice throughout the day, balancing the head and the heart, or the intellect and affections.[124] Interestingly, the Puritans often argued that meditating on heaven should be the central aim in the Christian life, given heaven is our

---

[119]Bangley (2006).
[120]Bangley (2006).
[121]Hilton (1991, p. 228).
[122]Beeke and Jones (2012).
[123]Calamy (1680, p. 23).
[124]Beeke and Jones (2012).

destination and source of hope and Jesus Christ is in heaven.[125] Of course, since the Puritans frequently utilized words in their spiritual practices, Puritan meditation is typically considered *kataphatic*.[126] From a transdiagnostic perspective, these historic practices may help Christians to focus the wandering mind on God, balancing the head and heart in the process. In other words, as we get distracted by earthly preoccupations, we can learn to gently shift toward savoring our knowledge of, and relationship with, God.

To summarize, Christians throughout the ages have practiced meditation, prayer, and contemplation, whether *kataphatic* or *apophatic*. In spite of the popularity of Buddhist-influenced meditative practices in contemporary society, Christians do have other options, especially when considering the *telos* of these approaches to psychological and spiritual health can be wildly different. From a transdiagnostic perspective, these historic practices may help Christians to develop several mental skills, such as concentration, insight, and present-moment awareness[127] in order to relate differently to a wide variety of distracting mental processes via recognizing that God is sovereign over both the inner and outer world. Beyond a theoretical understanding of the potential benefits of these historic practices for transdiagnostic processes, several Christian researchers have empirically investigated historic Christian practices for psychological problems.

Religious roots: Contemporary delivery systems. Today there are a wide variety of church and parachurch delivery systems for Christian meditation and contemplation. For example, Contemplative Outreach[128] offers instruction and training in centering prayer,[129] which draws upon the teachings of the *Cloud of Unknowing*. In centering prayer, practitioners are engaging in a multi-step approach, which involves selecting a prayer word to represent a willingness to yield to God's active, loving presence within the inner world, then reciting the chosen word whenever a distracting thought or feeling emerges, followed by resting in a few minutes of silence to conclude the practice.[130]

In addition, the World Community for Christian Meditation[131] offers resources and education in Christian meditation, drawing on the teachings of John Main.[132] With this approach, Christians recite a mantra—*Maranatha*, or "Come, Lord" (see 1 Cor 16:22)—for a formal period of time to cultivate a deeper relationship with God.[133]

---

[125]Beeke and Jones (2012).
[126]For an exception, see Schwanda (2012).
[127]Feldman et al. (2007).
[128]See www.contemplativeoutreach.org.
[129]Keating (2019).
[130]Keating (2019).
[131]See www.wccm.org.
[132]Main (2006).
[133]Main (2006).

Moreover, the Eastern Orthodox Church continues to advocate for the use of the Jesus Prayer in contemporary society as a way to cultivate psychological and spiritual health, drawing on the *Philokalia*.[134]

Finally, the Society of Jesus, linked to the Catholic Church, advocates for the use of the *Spiritual Exercises* in daily life,[135] anchored to Jesuit spirituality. Among other practices, the examen is prioritized as a foundational daily meditative exercise to help practitioners recognize God's presence throughout the day, especially in our senses, thoughts, feelings, and behaviors, as well as seemingly unimportant, trivial tasks (e.g., washing the dishes, getting the mail).[136]

Worth mentioning, there seems to be a lack of contemporary, well-organized, parallel Protestant movements (whether church or parachurch) that advocate for the regular use of these spiritual practices for psychological and spiritual health.

Nevertheless, beyond church and parachurch organizations, a variety of writings that focus on the spiritual disciplines advocate for the use of Christian meditation, prayer, and contemplation as a way to draw closer to God, cultivate spiritual health, and become more like Jesus Christ.[137] Yet, many of these writings have rarely, if ever, been converted into step-by-step processes so they can be investigated as interventions in the psychology literature, paralleling the Buddhist-influenced mindfulness movement in Western psychology.[138] To be sure, while Buddhist-influenced mindfulness has been researched as both an intervention[139] and construct for measurement,[140] there seem to be very few Christian efforts to engage in similar scientific explorations, drawing from the Christian tradition to better understand the impact that classic Christian spiritual practices have on psychological health. In fact, many of the current writings on Christian practices appear to be housed within theological, church, or parachurch circles, along with spiritual direction sources.

However, Christian spiritual writers from the past can offer deep psychological insights into health, dysfunction, and change processes. Certainly, from a Christian perspective, one mistake is to assume spirituality merely consists of psychological processes, as is the case with many secular psychologists studying the psychology of religion and spirituality.[141] As another mistake, we may artificially separate psychology and spirituality in an overly reductionistic manner, assuming psychological and spiritual functioning somehow occur independently.[142]

---

[134]Coniaris (1998).
[135]See www.jesuits.org.
[136]See www.jesuits.org.
[137]Calhoun (2015); Classic Christian eBooks (2019); Whitney (2014); Willard (1999).
[138]Singh et al. (2008).
[139]Khoury et al. (2013).
[140]Sauer et al. (2013).
[141]Benner (1989); Sisemore and Knabb (2020).
[142]Benner (1989).

Ultimately, given that Jesus lived a fully human life—with human thoughts, feelings, behaviors, and relationships—communing with God, finding contentment in him, and cultivating Christlikeness all involve the pursuit of both psychological and spiritual health, "[situating] our spiritual life in the heart of our psychological being."[143] In other words, psychology and spirituality are integrated and work in unison because we are embodied as human beings living in a fallen world. Certainly, "we are psychospiritual beings," and "no step of psychological development is devoid of spiritual significance nor is spiritual development ever devoid of psychological significance."[144] Therefore, when we engage in the historic spiritual disciplines, we are aiming for "transformation of the total state of the soul," including "differences in thought, feeling, and character."[145] A biopsychosocial-spiritual model of functioning, then, offers a holistic understanding of the human condition, which includes a central role for the transcendent, made up of spiritual practices, spiritual well-being, and spiritual needs.[146] Stated differently, human biological, psychological, social, and spiritual dimensions interact in an integrated, dynamic manner, and "no one aspect can be disaggregated from the whole."[147] Overall, with the import of Buddhist practices into contemporary psychology, distinctly Christian practices need equal attention in the psychology literature so Christian clients have worldview-consistent choices in the psychotherapy room.

With this need for uniquely Christian perspectives in mind, in recent years I have worked with several colleagues to draw from, define, map out with clear steps, and empirically investigate a range of meditative, prayer, and contemplative concepts and practices from the Bible and historic Christian sources, aiming to offer a parallel to the mindfulness movement that seems to be sweeping through Western society in general, as well as the psychology literature in particular.[148] Although several Christian psychologists have pointed out the potential for utilizing historic Christian practices in professional counseling and psychotherapy,[149] only recently have empirical studies been conducted in the psychology literature. Again, if the *telos* of the spiritual disciplines is Christlikeness,[150] and Jesus lived a *fully* human life, becoming more like Jesus as the Suffering Servant (Is 53) means both psychological and spiritual change—or psychospiritual change, given the two often work in an integrated manner—is necessary.

---

[143]Benner (1989, p. 19).

[144]Benner (1989, p. 24).

[145]Willard (1998, p. 107).

[146]Sulmasy (2002).

[147]Sulmasy (2002, p. 27).

[148]Knabb et al. (2017); Knabb and Vazquez (2018); Knabb et al. (2018); Knabb and Wang (2019); Knabb, Vazquez, and Pate (2019); Knabb, Pate, Sullivan, Salley, Miller, and Boyer (2020); Knabb, Vazquez, Garzon, Ford, Wang, Conner, Warren, and Weston (2020).

[149]Eck (2002); McMinn and McRay (1997).

[150]Whitney (2014).

To offer a few quick examples on the role that distinctly Christian spiritual exercises can play in influencing both psychiatric symptoms and transdiagnostic processes, in an eight-week pilot study, I found that a combination of several Christian practices (e.g., the Jesus Prayer, practices from *Spiritual Exercises*, centering prayer) can be helpful in reducing worry, symptoms of depression, anxiety, and stress, and intolerance of uncertainty among Christian adults.[151] In addition, among a sample of Christian college students, I found that practicing the Jesus Prayer over a fourteen-day period of time was helpful in reducing daily stress.[152] Moreover, among a sample of Christian college students at two different universities, I found that the use of a combination of *kataphatic* (Puritan meditation) and *apophatic* (instructions from the *Cloud of Unknowing*) practices over a four-week period of time was helpful in reducing repetitive negative thinking.[153] Finally, in a recent pilot study, I found that combining daily walking with Brother Lawrence's instructions from *The Practice of the Presence of God* and Puritan meditation over a four-week time period was helpful in reducing stress among a sample of eight community Christian adults.[154]

Although this burgeoning literature is certainly lagging behind the abundance of empirical research on Buddhist-influenced constructs and practices in the psychology literature, the above studies elucidate that Christian practices hold promise as a psychological response to psychiatric symptoms and unhelpful transdiagnostic processes. Still, employing meditation, prayer, and contemplation in pursuit of psychological change prompts a fundamental question: should these practices be used as an instrument or an end in and of itself?

A Christian instrument toward another end, an end in and of itself, or both?
In the psychological study of religion and spirituality, many researchers examine practices within religious communities as predictors that are hypothesized to lead to certain psychological outcomes. For example, prayer is often expected to positively affect stress, anxiety, and mental well-being.[155] More specifically, the particular type of prayer may play a certain role based on the (1) intended use, and (2) expectation of a psychological benefit. Christians, for instance, who engage in petitionary prayer (e.g., requesting "material things" from God, asking God for forgiveness, requesting that God eliminate suffering) may be doing so to achieve some other end, whereas ritualistic (e.g., reciting the Psalms) and meditative (e.g., experiencing God's presence, sitting in silence with God) prayer may be utilized as a

---

[151]Knabb et al. (2017).
[152]Knabb and Vazquez (2018).
[153]Knabb, Vazquez, Garzon, Ford, Wang, Conner, Warren, and Weston (2020).
[154]Knabb, Pate, Sullivan, Salley, Miller, and Boyer (2020).
[155]Ferguson et al. (2010).

way to commune with God and find a deeper contentment in him.[156] In this line of research, results have revealed that both petitionary and meditative types of prayer are positively related to well-being.[157]

However, as Christians, are these types of practices (e.g., meditation, prayer, contemplation) merely an instrument in the service of our own aims (e.g., happiness, the improvement of psychiatric symptoms)?[158] Or, should our ultimate goal—or *telos*—in this life be worshipfulness and a deeper relationship with God, regardless of the perceived psychological benefit?[159]

Throughout this workbook, I argue for both, with the latter often influencing the former. Stated differently, the classic Christian practices in this workbook function as an indirect method,[160] helping you to notice unhelpful psychological processes, then shift toward God. In this process, psychiatric symptoms may or may not go away. In either case, prioritizing God as the center of life allows you to relate differently to your symptoms in a fallen world, persevering in the midst of suffering with a sense of hope and confidence as you walk home with God to your final destination.[161]

Christian concentration, insight, or both? Although some historic Christian practices—whether meditation, prayer, or contemplation—tend to primarily emphasize *either* concentration *or* insight, I believe most offer a helpful balance, given their purpose is to dually focus our attention on God and gain deeper insight into a spiritual reality while living in a fallen world, filled with unhelpful, distracting psychological processes that may keep us stuck from time to time. Consistent with Peter's difficulty in keeping his eyes on Jesus as he walked toward Jesus on the water (Mt 14:22-33), we, too, may become preoccupied with the proverbial winds of the mind, struggling to maintain an awareness that God is loving us from moment to moment and offering his infinite wisdom as we navigate the stormy seas of this world, all while holding our experiences in the palm of his hand.

Ultimately, I believe most of these Christian practices, whether labeled as meditation, prayer, or contemplation, are designed to cultivate a deeper awareness of God's active, loving presence by shifting from earthly, time-limited distractions to a more transcendent, spiritual perspective in order to commune with God and find contentment in him. To be more succinct, many of these exercises aim to develop a present-moment loving awareness of God, which requires both "focused attention" and "open monitoring."[162] To be sure, in our efforts, we are focusing all of

---

[156]Poloma and Pendleton (1991).
[157]Poloma and Pendleton (1991).
[158]Slife and Reber (2012).
[159]Knabb and Bates (2020b); Peterson (1992).
[160]Ware (2000).
[161]Knabb and Bates (2020b).
[162]Kok et al. (2013).

our attention on God, letting go of our self-preoccupation in the process, as well as maintaining an open posture toward God, monitoring his active, loving presence with an attitude of trust and acceptance.

From a Christian mystical viewpoint, union with God is entirely about "presence,"[163] meaning the purpose of the various practices within classic Christian spiritual writings is commonly about recognizing God's presence and becoming more like Jesus Christ from moment to moment. With all of the distractions in life, it is easy to get lost in an earthly perspective, wherein we are distracted by a long list of unhelpful thoughts, feelings, behaviors, and relationships that are inevitable in a fallen world.

To offer a fitting example, C. S. Lewis captured this ubiquitous human dilemma in *The Screwtape Letters*, which he wrote as a fictional exchange between a demon uncle and nephew, designed to elucidate how demons might go about tempting humans in a fallen world and drawing humans away from God.[164] In their initial exchange, the uncle instructs his nephew to "fix [the human's] attention on the stream [of human experience]," rather than "universal issues," recognizing that humans are "enslaved" "to the pressure of the ordinary."[165] In other words, distracted by the material world (e.g., a bus driving down the street), we often struggle to embrace "realities [we] can't touch and see,"[166] which is what the Puritans referred to as "heavenly-mindedness," in contrast with our default mode, "earthly-mindedness," in a fallen world.[167]

Christian meditation: A summary. With the above definitions in mind, for the purpose of this workbook, I have decided to use the term *meditation* to capture all of the aforementioned classic Christian spiritual practices from the last two millennia in order to avoid any added confusion. In other words, because (1) the psychology literature tends to use the term *meditation* to capture a variety of the previously discussed practices, and (2) Buddhism, as the most popular practice in the psychology literature, uses the term *meditation* to represent two of its most common forms (i.e., concentrative, insight), I have elected to use this term throughout the current workbook, which I define[168] (consistent with the introduction chapter) as follows:

A broad collection of concentrative- and insight-oriented psychological and spiritual practices throughout historic Christianity, ranging from *apophatic* (emphasizing few to no words and no images) to *kataphatic* (emphasizing words

---

[163]McGinn (2006).
[164]Lewis (2001).
[165]Lewis (2001, p. 2).
[166]Lewis (2001, p. 4).
[167]Burroughs (2014).
[168]Ball (2016); Bangley (2006); Gallagher (2008); Lawrence (2015); Ware (2000); Wilhoit and Howard (2012).

and/or images), for shifting from earthly- to heavenly-mindedness and developing a deeper communion with God and enduring contentment in him in the midst of suffering.[169]

At this point in the chapter, I would like to compare and contrast the different types of practices in the present day, making the case that a distinctly Christian approach to meditation should be considered as a more fitting alternative to the Buddhist or secular variety for Christian clients in professional counseling and psychotherapy.

BUDDHIST, CHRISTIAN, AND SECULAR MEDITATION: SIMILARITIES AND DIFFERENCES

Because "the philosophical, spiritual and cultural roots of a meditative practice . . . are integral to understanding the mechanisms of that practice,"[170] it is important to compare and contrast the Buddhist, Christian, and secular forms of meditation that are circulating in contemporary Western society. As you can see in table 2.1, Buddhist mindfulness and loving kindness meditation, secularized meditation, and Christian meditation all employ various combinations of concentration and insight.

However, the object of awareness is different across these traditions, given Buddhist-influenced and secularized practices tend to be individualized, unilaterally focusing on the breath, the senses, or a mantra. Even with loving kindness meditation, which often employs mantras that are directed toward others (e.g., "May my coworker be happy and free from suffering"), the individual practitioner is alone in the exercise. Yet, with Christian meditative practices, a relational understanding is embraced, with God at the center of the approach. To be certain, whether Christians are meditating on God's presence, attributes (e.g., love, wisdom, power), actions, or providence, an interpersonal strategy is utilized, wherein reading Scripture leads to thinking more deeply about God (who is revealed in the pages of the Bible), followed by praying to God and resting in him, all with the goal of improving this divine-human relationship.

With Buddhist, secularized, and Christian approaches, moreover, the skills that are developed during formal practice can certainly overlap, although there are some differences. For example, although attention, an awareness of the present moment, acceptance, and an attitude of openness, curiosity, and nonjudgment may be cultivated, Christians are aware of God's presence in the midst of their inner and outer experiences, rather than the experiences in and of themselves. Also, for

---

[169]Adapted from Knabb and Bates (2020b, p. 106).
[170]Kok et al. (2013, p. 28).

	Type of Meditation	Typical Object of Awareness	Skills Developed	Goal/Purpose/Design (*Telos*)
Buddhist Mindfulness	Concentrative/ "focused attention" and/or insight/ "open monitoring"	The breath or senses	Attention; present-moment awareness; nonjudgment; acceptance; nonattachment	Three "marks of existence" (insight into the nature of suffering, no-self, impermanence); amelioration of suffering
Buddhist Loving Kindness Meditation	Concentrative/ "focused attention" and/or insight/ "open monitoring"	A mantra	Attention; present-moment awareness; nonjudgment; acceptance; nonattachment	Loving kindness, compassion, joy, equanimity; oneness
Secularized Meditation	Concentrative/ "focused attention" and/or insight/ "open monitoring"	The breath, the senses, a mantra	Attention; present-moment awareness; nonjudgment; acceptance; nonattachment	Coping skill for psychiatric symptom reduction; eliminating or relating differently to psychiatric symptoms
Christian Meditation	Concentrative/ "focused attention" and/or insight/ "open monitoring"	God's presence, attributes (e.g., love, wisdom, power), actions, and providence	Attention; present-moment awareness; nonjudgment (e.g., grace, mercy); acceptance; detachment	Communion with God through union with Christ; Christian contentment; amelioration of suffering is a potential byproduct

Table 2.1. Adapted from Feldman et al. (2007); Greeson et al. (2014); Gunaratana (2017); Hayes et al. (2004); Knabb (2018); Kok et al. (2013); Kyabgon (2010); McCown et al. (2010); Neff and Germer (2018); Nhat Hanh (1976); Salzberg (1995); and Walsh and Shapiro (2006).

Christians, nonjudgment is about extending God's mercy and grace to ourselves, regardless of the inner and outer experiences that emerge in a fallen world, as we can commune with God through our union with Christ. On the other hand, nonjudgment, openness, and acceptance are commonly embraced in Buddhist and secular practices for pragmatic reasons (e.g., to decrease suffering). Furthermore, for Christians, shifting from earthly preoccupations to a more transcendent, spiritual reality involves detachment, which is about "correcting one's own anxious grasping in order to free oneself for committed relationship to God,"[171] whereas Buddhist nonattachment is about "not being stuck or fixated on ideas, images, or sensory objects and not feeling an internal pressure to acquire, hold, avoid, or change."[172] In essence, Christians accept inner and outer experiences because God is present, generously extending his providential care each step of the way, not to achieve oneness or eradicate suffering on this side of heaven.

---

[171]Miles (1983, p. 111).
[172]Sahdra et al. (2010, p. 118).

Finally, in consideration of the *telos* of each practice, Buddhist loving kindness meditation is employed to enhance a variety of emotions, such as compassion, joy, and equanimity, cultivating oneness and a deeper connection to others, whereas Buddhist mindfulness meditation is utilized to gain a broader understanding of the "three marks of existence" and decrease suffering, consistent with the intention of secularized meditative practices. Secularized versions, to be sure, are employed as an instrument (e.g., coping skill) in the service of psychological change, whether to reduce or eliminate symptoms or relate differently to them. Conversely, Christian meditation, prayer, and contemplation are about communion with God through union with Christ, with the elimination of suffering as a possible byproduct. In other words, at the end of the day, the spiritual disciplines in Christianity are about Christlikeness and aligning our will with God's will (Lk 22:42), which may or may not include relief from psychological pain. Certainly, because God is active and present in the here-and-now, we can trust that his providential care extends to each unfolding experience, including our inner world.

With these differences in mind, we now turn to an example of Christian meditation in Scripture, before concluding the second chapter with an exercise. In this process, my hope is that you will begin to try on your rich Christian heritage, recognizing that a long list of Christian writings throughout historic Christianity offer astute psychological insights into the role that God plays in the human response to suffering in a fallen, broken, fragmented world.

CHRISTIAN MEDITATION: AN EXERCISE

In Psalm 62:5-8, David offers the following:

> Yes, my soul, find rest in God;
>> my hope comes from him.
> Truly he is my rock and my salvation;
>> he is my fortress, I will not be shaken.
> My salvation and my honor depend on God. . . .
> Trust in him at all times, you people;
>> pour out your hearts to him,
>> for God is our refuge.

For David, God is the spiritual source of peace and hope, with the "meaning of life [found] in God, and in God alone."[173] Therefore, in the midst of suffering, as Christians, we can learn to trust in God, even when we are uncertain about the near or distant future.

---

[173]Bullock (2015).

In this exercise, try to set aside ten minutes to sit with God, taking the following four steps of lectio divina (bite, chew, taste, savor)[174] in a deliberate, intentional manner:

Bite. Slowly read Psalm 62, approaching the text with the understanding that God is speaking to you in this very moment. Notice some of the key phrases (e.g., "my soul finds rest," "my hope comes from him," "trust in him at all times," "with you, LORD, is unfailing love") by taking a small bite out of each of them.

Chew. Once you have read through Psalm 62, deeply ponder its theme—God is your spiritual source of peace, hope, and love, and you can patiently wait on him in silence, trusting that he will respond to your needs as your refuge and source of salvation. Begin to chew on these words as you think about their meaning.

Taste. Pray to God, asking him to reveal himself to you during this time, as well as thanking and praising him for offering his infinite goodness, wisdom, and power in this very moment. Taste God's goodness, recognizing that he is all you need in this unfolding experience.

Savor. Rest in God, gently repeating the short phrase "my soul finds rest in you," then returning to these words whenever your mind has shifted toward another thought or feeling. Savor this biblical language, relishing the notion that God is your rock and refuge in the here-and-now.

Once you have concluded this exercise, spend a few minutes journaling by answering the following questions:

How well did you do in biting, chewing, tasting, and savoring Psalm 62?

_____

_____

_____

What thoughts and feelings emerged as you attempted to spend this time with God?

_____

_____

_____

Where was God during the exercise? Did you experience him as with you? Did you experience him as your source of peace and hope? What other experiences did you have of God during this time?

_____

_____

_____

[174]Guigo II (2012).

_____

_____

_____

What are the strengths of this exercise? What about the limitations? How might this exercise help you to respond differently to unhelpful transdiagnostic processes? How can you continue with this exercise throughout your day?

_____

_____

_____

_____

_____

CONCLUSION

In this chapter, we have covered a lot of territory with the goal of recognizing and differentiating the different meditative practices (including their ingredients and *telos*) in contemporary Western society. For Christians struggling with psychiatric symptoms and unhelpful transdiagnostic processes, the Christian tradition offers meditative alternatives to Buddhist-influenced or secularized practices. Because the ultimate aim of Christian meditation, prayer, and contemplation is typically communion with God, Christians have a more relational opportunity to find contentment in him, relating differently to inner experiences that may not fully go away on this side of heaven. Certainly, because we have hope in God's eventual restoration of all things, we can press forward on the roads of life with confidence, maintaining an awareness of a more transcendent reality, wherein God is at the center. Rather than practicing concentrative- and insight-oriented exercises for mere pragmatic reasons (e.g., reducing symptoms), as Christians, we are learning to focus on God and recognize his active, loving presence from moment to moment. In the next chapter we explore the four-step model in this workbook, focusing primarily on learning to shift from earthly preoccupations to a more heavenly, spiritual perspective, in which we see God as the author of each and every one of life's occurrences in both the inner and outer world.

CHRISTIAN MEDITATION *for* TARGETING TRANSDIAGNOSTIC PROCESSES

The mind of man is not quieted (neither indeed can it be) until it meets with something that will be happiness to it; and it never meets with happiness, until it finds all the good it would have, and also knows it shall have that good always, without diminution, intermission or cessation. God alone is an infinite and an eternal good. Nothing can be happiness to the reasonable creature, but to enjoy him as the chief good, and to acquiesce in him as its last end; and then is the mind quieted, when it comes to fix and rest in him. The scope of the whole Discourse is, to gather in our souls from sensible things unto God, and to fix them in the contemplation of that which must be our happiness at last.

JOHN ROWE

So we fix our eyes not on what is seen, but on what is unseen, since what is seen is temporary, but what is unseen is eternal.

2 CORINTHIANS 4:18

IN THIS THIRD CHAPTER, I draw from a variety of Christian and non-Christian sources to define and review a four-step, distinctly Christian type of meditation, practiced in various forms throughout the ages. In addition, I focus on the second step—pivoting from earthly-mindedness to heavenly-mindedness (2 Cor 4:18)—as a more condensed, one-step version. Along the way, I offer a breakdown of the four steps, as well as the ingredients of both earthly and heavenly perspectives. Then, I relate these perspectives to several transdiagnostic processes, before concluding with a biblical example of a more transcendent, spiritual perspective and exercise to try on this viewpoint. In essence, my hope is that this chapter prepares you for the remaining five chapters of the workbook, which focus on the application of Christian meditation to a variety of domains of psychological functioning— thinking, feeling, behaving, the self, and relationships.

CHRISTIAN MEDITATION IN FOUR STEPS: AN EXPANDED VERSION

Throughout this workbook, you will be practicing a four-step model of Christian meditation, with the ultimate aim of deepening your relationship with God. I use an indirect method in this approach,[1] since you are learning to notice unhelpful inner experiences, then shift toward a more transcendent understanding, with God at the center. With a newfound awareness that God is active and present, even in the midst of suffering, you are working to trust in him, relating differently to some of the more enduring mental processes that may never fully go away in a fallen, broken world. Along the way, you are developing the ability to approach the throne of grace (Heb 4:16), minute by minute, as you walk with God on the sometimes-dangerous roads of life.

In discussing the four steps, as well as focusing on the second step in particular, my hope is that you will begin to internalize this four-step process as we move forward with each remaining chapter. Thus, we begin with the first step, which simply involves noticing the proverbial sea of mental processes we are swimming in.

Step 1: Notice. In a variety of transdiagnostic domains, we may struggle to notice the "mind-brain-body-behavior" patterns we get stuck in.[2] First, with our thoughts, we may ruminate about the past or worry about the future, perseverating with repetitive thinking from moment to moment.[3] In doing so, our thinking patterns may distract us from the road ahead, reminiscent of a parent driving a minivan with two arguing children in the backseat. Over time, we may find ourselves regularly turning around to intervene, only to find out that we are unaware (sometimes tragically) of the obstacles in the road ahead. In the Christian tradition, though, our thinking may not always be fully reliable,[4] leading us in directions that are inconsistent with the path God has prepared for us. As a result, learning to simply notice our thought patterns can be a crucial first step.

Second, we may do whatever we can to avoid distressing emotional experiences, believing that somehow eradicating emotional pain will mean we can live the life

---

[1]Ware (2000).
[2]Greeson et al. (2014).
[3]Ehring and Watkins (2008).
[4]Goodwin (2015).

we want to live. In this process, we may struggle to identify even our most basic emotions (e.g., sadness, fear, anxiety, guilt, shame), as well as understand their role in helping us to make sense of daily life.[5] As a quick example, sadness tells us we have lost something important, whereas fear alerts us to a present danger and anxiety helps us to anticipate a future catastrophe. However, gradually, we may discover that our avoidance of distress, whether coming from unpleasant physical sensations, painful emotions, frustration and unmet expectations, or the uncertainties of life,[6] causes more problems than the distress in and of itself.[7] Therefore, we can begin to notice and relate differently to the different types of distress we experience in life. From a Christian perspective, this change means we can learn to recognize that God has given us our emotions as signals,[8] which help us to make sense of both our relationships (including our relationship with God) and life events so we can choose the best path forward.

Third, we may avoid people, places, and events in order to seemingly reduce or eliminate unpleasant thoughts, feelings, and sensations.[9] For example, we may delay starting a task if we believe it will lead to discomfort, avoid pursuing a goal if there is any chance it will result in psychological pain, or stay away from relational encounters that make us uncomfortable.[10] When behavioral avoidance is the primary strategy we rely on to manage psychological pain, though, we may stay stuck on the sidelines of life, watching other people live a life of meaning and purpose.[11] For Christians, we may delay following Jesus because of the anticipation of psychological suffering; yet, minute by minute, Jesus asks us to practice self-denial as we bear our cross and follow him (Mt 16:24-26). As a result, learning to stay fully engaged in life is paramount, since we only have a limited time on this planet to fulfill God's will. As a useful first step, we can begin to notice when we are struggling to accept the inevitable distress that arises in daily living, including the impact this intolerance has on the different areas of life (e.g., work, family, church).

Fourth, we might engage in chronic self-criticism and self-judgment, based on perfectionistic tendencies, which can lead to psychopathology and other types of psychological suffering.[12] With this legalistic approach to life, we may constantly fall short of our unilaterally constructed standards, as well as struggle to fully rest in God's forgiveness, mercy, and grace.[13] From a Christian vantage point, though,

---

[5]Vine and Aldao (2014).
[6]Zvolensky et al. (2010).
[7]Hayes et al. (2012).
[8]Knabb, Johnson, Bates, and Sisemore (2019).
[9]Gamez et al. (2011).
[10]Gamez et al. (2011).
[11]Hayes et al. (2012).
[12]Egan et al. (2011); Limburg et al. (2017).
[13]Knabb (2018).

"because [Jesus] suffered when he was tempted, he is able to help those who are being tempted" (Heb 2:18). Thus, we can "approach God's throne of grace with confidence, so that we may receive mercy and find grace to help us in our time of need" (Heb 4:16). When it comes to perfectionism, as Christians, we can first notice when we are being overly critical toward ourselves, before learning to draw on God's grace (i.e., God's undeserved kindness) and mercy (i.e., God's leniency and compassion).[14] In this process, we are coming to recognize that Jesus has already reconciled us to God, who is a loving father with outstretched arms, running to us when we turn back home because we have lost our way (Lk 15:11-32).

Fifth, we may struggle to understand our relationships, including the thoughts and feelings we have in our most salient interpersonal exchanges, as well as the thoughts, feelings, and intentions of others.[15] Because of this, we may have an especially hard time deepening our relationships. Yet, because relationships are central in the Christian life and should be grounded in love (Jn 13:34-36), a useful first step involves beginning to develop a "balcony view" of our exchanges with others, seeing ourselves from the outside and striving to understand others from the inside.[16] Certainly, in Christian living, we are called to "be kind and compassionate to one another, forgiving each other just as in Christ God forgave [us]" (Eph 4:32). Overall, by noticing our relational habits, including gaining a deeper insight into these self-in-relationship dynamics, we are in a better position to love others and navigate difficult interpersonal exchanges with grace and mercy.

Ultimately, when problems emerge in life, we may view them as somehow threatening and doubt our own ability to respond in an effective manner.[17] Along the way, as Christians, we may even struggle to understand God's will for our life, possibly viewing God as distant or absent amid the perceived chaos. If this is the case, a helpful first step may be to notice our negative interpretation of life's challenges, then work toward reinterpreting them with God at the center. In other words, because God is active and present, governing and preserving his creation with his providential care,[18] we can trust that he is guiding daily events, whether large or small (Acts 17:25-28). As outlined in the Heidelberg Catechism, a famous summary of Christian teachings on Scripture from the 1500s, God's providence involves

> the Almighty and everywhere present power of God; whereby, as it were by his hand, he upholds and governs heaven, earth, and all creatures; so that herbs and grass,

---

[14]Douglas and Tenney (2011).
[15]Allen (2008); Allen et al. (2008).
[16]Allen et al. (2008, p. 3).
[17]Robichaud and Dugas (2005).
[18]Ursinus (1852).

rain and drought, fruitful and barren years, meat and drink, health and sickness, riches and poverty, yes all things come not by chance, but by his fatherly hand.[19]

If this is the case, as Christians we can learn to "find God in all things," as the Jesuit saying goes, even life's challenges, with God as a trustworthy traveling companion on the sometimes-treacherous roads of life.

To summarize this first step, we are beginning the meditative process by slowing down to recognize the unhelpful "mind-brain-body-behavior" processes[20] that can get in the way of living a fulfilling life, becoming more like Jesus Christ from moment to moment.[21] As we gain a bit of distance from these processes, we are able to notice them with more clarity, which leads to the second step.

Step 2: Shift. In this second step, we are learning to shift from earthly preoccupations to a more heavenly, spiritual perspective, with God at the center (described in more detail in the next section of this chapter). To return to a camera metaphor, we are zooming out, attempting to see the transdiagnostic process from a wider perspective. In this effort, we are learning to endure suffering (because we recognize it is time-limited), let go of our preoccupation with earthly possessions (since they are temporary), prioritize godliness, and become more and more like Jesus Christ, recognizing this world is not our home and we will eventually be face-to-face with God, our source of perfect joy.[22] When we repeatedly shift from looking at the ground to fixing our eyes on the horizon, we gain a deeper awareness of (1) Jesus as our traveling companion, and (2) our final destination of heaven. In doing so, we are strengthening our ability to persevere with inner and outer trials, reminiscent of the hope of a marathon runner who has a friend running side-by-side and sees the finish line in sight. This crucial shift can help us relate differently to unhelpful "mind-brain-body-behavior" processes,[23] accepting them because of our newfound awareness that God is with us in the here-and-now.

Step 3: Accept. In this third step, we are working toward focusing our attention on God, recognizing God's active, loving presence in the present, and accepting God's influence as the author of all events, even our most difficult experiences. In other words, these three mental skills—attention, present-moment awareness, and acceptance[24]—are key in shifting from unhelpful transdiagnostic processes (e.g., rumination) to focusing on God.[25] To be sure, as we pivot from a worldly, earthly perspective to a more transcendent, spiritual recognition of God at the center of

---

[19]Ursinus (1852, pp. 146-47).
[20]Greeson et al. (2014).
[21]Whitney (2014).
[22]Yuille (2013).
[23]Greeson et al. (2014).
[24]Feldman et al. (2007).
[25]Knabb, Vazquez, and Pate (2019).

daily life, cultivating these mental skills can help us to relate differently to the difficult "mind-brain-body-behavior" processes[26] that may be keeping us stuck in life.

For instance, attention helps us to keep our focus on God, rather than getting "hindered" by difficult thoughts, feelings, behaviors, perfectionistic tendencies, and relationships, "[running] with perseverance the race marked out for us, fixing our eyes on Jesus, the pioneer and perfecter of faith" (Heb 12:1-2).[27] Stated differently, Jesus is our motivation for pressing forward, running toward him as we maintain a sense of hope in our efforts to one day see him face-to-face in heaven.[28] As the medieval monk Brother Lawrence stated,

> Thoughts spoil everything; that's how trouble starts! We must be careful to reject them as soon as we notice that they have nothing to do with our present occupation or our salvation, and begin again our conversation with God, which is where our good is found.[29]

Moreover, maintaining a present-moment awareness of God allows us to settle into the here-and-now, wherein God is revealing his will to us as each second passes by. To be sure, so much of our suffering stems from being preoccupied with a past that is behind us or catastrophizing about a yet-to-be-determined future. Yet, as we come to focus our attention on God, we find that he is moving in each particular moment of life. In fact, to grow roots in the present moment is a source of peace, given God's will is being revealed to us right now. As the Jesuit author Jean-Pierre de Caussade stated some three centuries ago, "To be satisfied with the present moment is to delight in and to adore God's will in all that comes to us to do or suffer through the succession of events each passing moment brings."[30] Even more, according to Jean-Pierre, "A soul can be nourished, strengthened, purified, and made holy only by the fullness of the present moment. What more could you have? Since you can find all that is good here, why search for it anywhere else?"[31] So, anchoring ourselves to the present moment—rather than being on automatic pilot,[32] lost in our heads because we are ruminating about the past, worrying about the future, avoiding the inevitable distress of daily living, or being preoccupied with troubled relationships—is an antidote to suffering.

Finally, acceptance allows us to make peace with the psychological pain that may never fully go away. In other words, our avoidance of psychiatric symptoms may

---

[26]Greeson et al. (2014).
[27]Pink (2012).
[28]Pink (2012).
[29]Lawrence (2015, pp. 101-2).
[30]Jean-Pierre (2008, chap. 11, para. 4).
[31]Jean-Pierre (2008, chap. 7, para. 1).
[32]Segal et al. (2012).

cause us more pain than the psychiatric symptoms in and of themselves.[33] Paradoxically, by learning to make room for (i.e., compassionately accept) the "mind-brain-body-behavior" processes[34] that keep us distracted in life, we can continue to follow Jesus on the road ahead.[35] In fact, if God is the author of all of life's events, even the inner and outer experiences we perceive to be painful may have a purpose. As an example, the Jesuit tradition advocates for the importance of surrendering to God's providence as the remedy to suffering in a fallen world, suggesting that the "secret to peace and happiness" involves recognizing God's presence in every one of our experiences. Jean-Pierre explained this understanding of God's role in life with the following:

> There is not a moment in which God is not present with us under the cover of some pain to be endured, some obligation or some duty to be performed, or some consolation to be enjoyed. All that takes place within us, around us, or through us involves and conceals his divine hand.[36]

Consistent with this perspective, writing about a century before Jean-Pierre, the Jesuit author Claude de la Colombiere offered the following teaching on the remedy for living in a fallen world, filled with hardship and suffering:

> Let us suppose that you turn to God with blind trust and surrender yourself unconditionally and unreservedly to Him, entirely resolved to put aside your own hopes and fears; in short, determined to wish nothing except what He wishes and to wish all that He wishes. From this moment you will acquire perfect liberty and will never again be able to feel troubled or uneasy, and there is no power on earth capable of doing you violence or giving you a moment's unrest.[37]

In these two famous Jesuit works, we see that (1) God is active and present in each and every life occurrence, and (2) surrendering to God's will is key to communing with him and maintaining a deeper contentment, regardless of the inner and outer suffering that life brings.

Ultimately, in the secular psychology literature, acceptance-based coping skills (sometimes drawing upon the ingredients of mindfulness meditation) are commonly advocated for in a pragmatic fashion, since the alternative (avoidance) simply does not work in the long run and may end up impairing daily functioning. However, for Christians, we can learn to accept the experiences we cannot change by trusting that God has a purpose and plan, even in the middle of pain and suffering. Responding to suffering, then, is about learning to walk with God and find a more stable contentment in him, which is our fourth and final meditative step.

---

[33]Hayes et al. (2012).
[34]Greeson et al. (2014).
[35]Knabb (2016).
[36]Jean-Pierre (2008, chap. 10, para. 2).
[37]Claude, d. l. C. (1983, chap. 4, sect. 4, para. 2).

Step 4: Act. Once we have noticed, shifted, and accepted because God is at the center of even our most difficult and enduring transdiagnostic processes, we are better prepared to fellowship with him and find a deeper contentment in his perfect love, which are founational to the Christian life. In fact, God created us to "glorify" and "enjoy him forever," consistent with the Westminster Shorter Catechism,[38] a popular Protestant doctrine from the 1600s.

According to the Puritan theologian John Owen, communion with God is defined as "that mutual communication in giving and receiving, after a most holy and spiritual manner, which is between God and the saints while they walk together in a covenant of peace, ratified in the blood of Jesus."[39] In our communion with God, then, we have an ongoing, reciprocal exchange, based on our union with Christ, which is built upon peace and a more transcendent, spiritual reality. As we walk together with God, in turn, we are able to cultivate a deeper, more contented peace, regardless of the inner or outer struggles we may face, because God is with us and we are delighting in him.

Another Puritan, Jeremiah Burroughs, defined contentment as "that sweet, inward, quiet, grace-filled condition of spirit which freely submits to and delights in God's wise and fatherly management in every condition."[40] In agreement, the Puritan author Thomas Watson likened contentment to a wrist watch: "though you carry it up and down with you, yet its spring is not shaken nor the gears out of order; but the watch keeps its perfect motion."[41] Or, as another metaphor,

> the ship that lies at anchor may sometimes be a little shaken, but it never sinks; flesh and blood may have its fears and disquiets, but grace checks them. A Christian, having cast anchor in heaven, never has his heart sink. A gracious spirit is a contented spirit.[42]

Finding a deeper, more enduring contentment in God's perfect love means we are not easily swayed by the inner or outer experiences in a fallen world that change from moment to moment, whether emanating from our thoughts, feelings, behaviors, sense of self, or relationships. Rather, we are "anchored in heaven," a perspective that requires regular practice to maintain. Therefore, next I offer a more condensed version of this four-step process, emphasizing the shift from an earthly, worldly perspective to a more transcendent, spiritual viewpoint, something that is definitely difficult to maintain on this side of heaven.

---

[38]Westminster Shorter Catechism (n.d.).

[39]Owen (2007, p. 94).

[40]Burroughs (2018, chap. 1, para. 8).

[41]Watson (2017, chap. 2, sect. 3, para. 8).

[42]Watson (2017, chap. 2, sect. 3, para. 9).

CHRISTIAN MEDITATION IN ONE STEP: A CONDENSED VERSION

Several centuries ago, the Puritans wrote on the distinction between earthly-mindedness and heavenly-mindedness, arguing that an awareness of heaven as our destination is especially important in navigating the dangerous terrain of a fallen world.[43] On the other hand, when we are overly preoccupied with this temporary world, we may end up experiencing added suffering as we lose sight of the destination ahead and a broader, more transcendent understanding of the reality before us.[44] In this section, then, I focus on the second step of the four-step meditative model in this workbook, especially since this pivot is crucial for maintaining a spiritual perspective on difficult situations. With this salient shift, we are learning to trust in God as we walk with him on the sometimes-dangerous roads of life.[45]

Earthly-mindedness: Basic ingredients. With earthly-mindedness, we are talking about the things and experiences that take place on this earth, such as "the beauty, the glory, the pageantry of the earth; the profits that are earthly, the pleasures and honors of the world; who mind any things inordinately that are sublunary [i.e., on the earth] accommodations."[46] In the third chapter of the apostle Paul's letter to the Philippians, he explicates that we are to "put no confidence in the flesh," given we "serve God by his Spirit" (Phil 3:3-4) and need to "press on toward the goal to win the prize for which God has called [us] heavenward in Christ Jesus" (Phil 3:14). Rather than focusing our mind on "earthly things," we are to place our attention on "our citizenship in heaven" (Phil 3:19).

With earthly-mindedness, we may prioritize worldly possessions and happiness, believing that the people, places, possessions, and circumstances of this life are the ultimate source of human fulfillment and worthy of our highest esteem.[47] In other words, we place our hope in temporary things, seeking our comfort in them as a remedy for the lows of life.[48] In this state of preoccupation, we may end up perseverating on "distracting cares about the earth, what [we] shall eat and drink, what [we] shall put on, how we shall provide for [ourselves] and [our] family, and what shall become of [us]."[49] In this distracted mental state, we may attempt to avoid some sort of perceived pain or negative situation (whether current or future), expecting that we will be unable to cope with the future we have in store, as well as struggle to trust that God will provide for our needs in this fallen world.[50] Stated

---

[43]Burroughs (2010, 2014); Jollie (2015); Owen (2016); Rowe (1672).
[44]Burroughs (2010, 2014); Jollie (2015); Owen (2016); Rowe (1672).
[45]Knabb and Bates (2020b).
[46]Burroughs (2014, chap. 1, para. 2).
[47]Burroughs (2014); Rowe (1672).
[48]Rowe (1672).
[49]Burroughs (2014, chap. 2, para. 10).
[50]Burroughs (2014).

more succinctly, we (1) worry about the future, and (2) struggle to trust that God will provide for our needs.

Heavenly-mindedness: Basic ingredients. In contrast to earthly-mindedness, heavenly-mindedness is about keeping things in perspective in a fallen, broken world, prioritizing an eternal, spiritual perspective above a more limited, temporary understanding of our current state.[51] Stated differently, we are recognizing that we will never be fully satisfied in the things of this earth, our adversities and hardships are time-limited, we have a more trustworthy hope in God (through our union with Christ), and our final destination is in heaven, not within this world.[52] Ultimately, when we are heavenly-minded, we have confidence that we will be able to persevere with God by our side, holding on to a spiritual understanding (i.e., looking beyond what we can currently see around us) of our present, earthly state.[53] In this shift, to be sure, we are focusing our mind on the triune God, with a hopeful confidence and more transcendent understanding of our current struggles, as well as looking ahead to heaven as our eventual source of perfect happiness.[54]

Earthly- versus heavenly-mindedness: A summary. As a quick reference to some of the main differences between earthly- and heavenly-minded perspectives, consider the following:

- Past versus future
- Self versus other
- Permanent versus temporary
- Hopeless versus hopeful
- Meaningless versus meaningful
- Material versus transcendent
- Far versus near
- Passive versus active

With earthly-mindedness, we tend to dwell on the past, look to the self, view pain and suffering as permanent, quickly lose hope and meaning, only see the material world, and believe God is far away and passive, whereas heavenly-mindedness is about focusing on the future, looking to God, viewing pain as temporary, holding on to hope and meaning, seeing a transcendent reality, and believing that God is near and active, even in the midst of suffering. These very different perspectives can also be applied to transdiagnostic processes, explored further below.

---

[51] Burroughs (2014); Rowe (1672).
[52] Burroughs (2014); Rowe (1672).
[53] Rowe (1672).
[54] Rowe (1672).

Earthly-mindedness, heavenly-mindedness, and transdiagnostic processes. When we are struggling with transdiagnostic processes that seem to weigh us down and distract us from the path ahead, our task as Christians is to pivot from an earthly, time-limited, narrow perspective (focused on what is visible in this world) to a heavenly, spiritual, eternal, broad viewpoint, focusing on an invisible reality with God at the center. As the Puritan John Rowe stated over three hundred years ago,

> Let us contemplate and meditate much of the future life; we should transfer and carry our selves in our thoughts out of this world, and by holy contemplation set our selves down (as it were) in the other world: it were good for us, if now and then we could leave this earth behind us, and climb up to heaven in our thoughts, and consider a little, so far as we may, what the state and condition of the other world is; we should study what God is, and what Christ is.[55]

As we practice shifting our perspective, we are zooming out to see the bigger picture, wherein God is the author of all events and leading us home. In the context of the transdiagnostic processes we have discussed thus far, the distinction between an earthly and heavenly viewpoint may consist of the following:[56]

Earthly-mindedness and transdiagnostic processes

- I focus my attention on visible, temporal things in the present moment.

- I believe that I am on my own to handle adversities (e.g., difficult thoughts, feelings, behaviors, self-perceptions, and relationships).

- I am distracted by daily worries (e.g., failing to secure or maintain adequate resources or material possessions, anticipated catastrophies, a ruined reputation, troubled relationships, rejection by others) because I believe these will be permanent experiences and I will be on my own to handle them.

- I prioritize temporary sources of comfort and happiness (e.g., people, places, possessions, a reputation, safety).

- I struggle to recognize God's role in daily life events, perceiving that he is either distant or absent.

- I have a hard time maintaining an awareness of, and hope in, heaven as a real place and my final destination, wherein I will be free from suffering, meet God face to face, and enjoy fellowshiping with him forever.

Heavenly-mindedness and transdiagnostic processes

- I focus my attention on invisible, spiritual things in the future.

---

[55]Rowe (1672, p. 45).
[56]Adapted from Burroughs (2010, 2014); Jollie (2015); Owen (2016); Rowe (1672).

- I believe that God is with me to handle adversities (e.g., difficult thoughts, feelings, behaviors, self-perceptions, and relationships).

- I am not distracted by daily worries (e.g., failing to secure or maintain adequate resources or material possessions, anticipated catastrophies, a ruined reputation, troubled relationships, rejection by others) because I believe these will be temporary experiences and God will be with me to handle them.

- I prioritize eternal sources of comfort and happiness (e.g., communion with God through union with Christ, heaven as my final destination).

- I recognize God's role in daily life events, perceiving that he is with me to handle my challenges from moment to moment.

- I maintain an awareness of, and hope in, heaven as a real place and my final destination, wherein I will be free from suffering, meet God face to face, and enjoy fellowshiping with him forever.

Ultimately, if we return to the definition of Christian detachment from the previous chapter, shifting from earthly-mindedness to heavenly-mindedness is about "correcting [our] own anxious grasping in order to free [ourselves] for committed relationship with God."[57] In other words, as Christians, effectively responding to our psychological struggles may be about learning to—paradoxically—let go of the temporary things we are convinced we need for our happiness and fulfillment on this side of heaven. Thus, we can learn to shift from perseverative thinking, intolerance of distress, behavioral avoidance, perfectionistic tendencies, and relational struggles to an awareness that God is at the center of our existence and leading us home.[58] Before concluding the chapter, though, I would like to offer an example in Scripture, followed by an exercise to practice meditating on heaven.

SHIFTING FROM EARTHY-MINDEDNESS TO HEAVENLY-MINDEDNESS: AN EXAMPLE IN SCRIPTURE

In the book of Hebrews, the writer provided several examples of biblical figures (e.g., Abel, Enoch, Noah, Abraham) who endured with faith, defining faith as "confidence in what we hope for and assurance about what we do not see" (Heb 11:1). Certainly, these individuals "did not receive the things promised; they only saw them and welcomed them from a distance, admitting that they were foreigners and strangers on earth" as they "[looked] for a country of their own" (Heb 11:13-14). In fact, they were "longing for a better country—a heavenly one" (Heb 11:16).

---

[57]Miles (1983, p. 111).
[58]Knabb and Bates (2020b).

These figures were by no means "thinking of the country they had left" (Heb 11:15) with an earthly-minded perspective; rather, they were looking ahead with faith and hope, recognizing that God's will for their life involved maintaining an awareness of a broader, more transcendent perspective. Given the eternity that awaits us, we barely spend any time in the childhood phase of life.[59] Yet, as we move from infancy to adulthood and beyond, we can certainly struggle with a vast array of troubles in a fallen world, filled with dangers, uncertainties, anxieties, disappointments, and losses, before attaining the security and joy that is our inheritance in heaven.[60] Along the way, maintaining a heavenly-minded perspective takes practice, as it is so easy to be distracted by the immediacy of temporal events in this foreign country. To end this chapter, then, we will be practicing a strategy for maintaining a heavenly, spiritual perspective from moment to moment.

SHIFTING FROM EARTHLY-MINDEDNESS TO HEAVENLY-MINDEDNESS: AN EXERCISE

As Christians, if our ultimate happiness is found in God alone, we must learn to regularly look to him as our source of fulfillment in a fallen world. Of this aim, several centuries ago, the American theologian Jonathan Edwards stated the following:

> Therefore, it becomes us to spend this life only as a journey towards heaven, as it becomes us to make the seeking of our highest end, and proper good, the whole work of our lives; and we should subordinate all the other concerns of life to it. Why should we labor for anything else, or set our hearts on anything else, but that which is our proper end, and true happiness?[61]

With this understanding in mind, for this exercise, please find a quiet environment, free from distractions. Sit in a supportive chair, with your eyes closed. Rest your hands comfortably on your lap. For the next ten minutes, you will be visualizing yourself journeying through a particularly painful life event as a stranger on earth, imagining yourself walking through life with God by your side as you approach your final destination: heaven.

First, visualize yourself walking through your adolescent years, imagining a specific event that was especially difficult for you. You might attempt to remember a major change in life (e.g., parental divorce, moving to a new city), a difficult relationship (e.g., being bullied at school), or any other experience that brought with it some psychological pain. Try to remember what it was like to walk through life

---

[59]Price (1816).
[60]Price (1816).
[61]Stout et al. (2017, p. 508).

during this time period, connecting to some of the thoughts you may have had, emotions you may have felt, and behaviors you may have engaged in. As you connect to the difficult event, try to imagine the loneliness and isolation you may have experienced, along with the sense that the event would last forever. If hopelessness was also present, try to connect to a loss of hope.

Second, begin to reinterpret the event as only temporary, with God walking by your side. In other words, attempt to view the event through the lens of a heavenly-minded perspective, imagining that you are now aware of a broader, more transcendent understanding of reality, wherein God is with you to handle this painful, yet time-limited, occurrence. Rather than focusing exclusively on the event in and of itself (including all of your corresponding thoughts, feelings, and behaviors), try to look up from the situation to see that you are slowly walking to a desired destination (with God as your traveling companion), which will be free from suffering and hardship. In other words, after living a long life fellowshiping with God, you will be able to shed the pain of this temporary experience because you will arrive in heaven.

Third, like the last lap in a long race, try to imagine what it might be like to hold on to a sense of hope that the present pain will eventually be gone, nearing the finish line with confidence because you have run the race with endurance (Heb 12:1). As you do so, anticipate the comfort and happiness you will feel as you move closer to this "country of your own" (Heb 11:14), the familiar territory that will offer the safety and security you have been longing for in the midst of your present pain. In this perfect country, God reigns and there is no hardship or suffering. Rather, he is welcoming you home with outstretched arms (Lk 15:11-32).

Finally, as you slowly walk with God to heaven as your final destination, imagine that he is in complete control, orchestrating this event with his perfect love, wisdom, and power. More specifically, although quite painful, God is directing this current experience in your adolescent years by "[working] for the good" (Rom 8:28).

Once you have concluded this exercise, spend a few minutes journaling by answering the following questions:

How well did you do in shifting from an earthly to heavenly perspective?

_____

_____

_____

_____

What thoughts and feelings emerged as you attempted to do so?

_____

_____

_____

_____

Where was God during the exercise? Did you experience him as with you? What other experiences did you have of God during this time?

_____

_____

_____

_____

What are the strengths of this exercise? What about the limitations? How might this exercise help you to respond differently to unhelpful transdiagnostic processes? How can you continue with this exercise throughout your day?

_____

_____

_____

_____

_____

CONCLUSION

In this chapter, we have reviewed the four-step meditative process you will be utilizing throughout the workbook. In addition, we have explored a shorter, one-step version, which involves shifting from an earthly to heavenly perspective in response to the transdiagnostic processes that may never fully go away on this side of heaven. Whether we are struggling with difficult thoughts, feelings, behaviors, self-perceptions, or relationships, maintaining an awareness of a more transcendent, spiritual reality can help us to press forward, running the race with perseverance as we travel with God to eventually cross the finish line. In the remaining chapters of this workbook, we will be working on applying this four-step meditative model to five transdiagnostic processes, drawing from a rich Christian heritage that offers astute psychological insights on how to travel in this foreign land with hope and perseverance.

TARGETING PROBLEMS
with COGNITION

Christian Meditation for
Repetitive Negative Thinking

God is the most glorious object that our minds could ever fasten upon, the most alluring. Thoughts of Him should therefore swallow up all other thoughts, as they are not worthy to be seen the same day with Him.

Thomas Goodwin

But our thoughts, at best, are like wanton spaniels, they indeed go after their master and come to their journey's end with him, but they run after every bird, they wildly pursue every flock of sheep they see.

Thomas Goodwin

IN THIS FIRST OF FIVE intervention chapters, I review repetitive negative thinking as one of several transdiagnostic processes that may be keeping you stuck in life. To begin, I offer a definition, along with a brief review of its relationship to mental disorders. In turn, I review several of the meditative practices (e.g., desert, Orthodox, medieval, French, Protestant) you can use to work toward relating differently to repetitive negative thinking, offering the background on each meditative exercise, then providing easy-to-follow instructions. Within this chapter, you will have the opportunity to identify and log repetitive negative thinking throughout the day and journal about your experiences. I also offer transcripts and an audio recording for you to follow along with, should you prefer to do so.

Ultimately, because of the fall of humankind, our thinking may not always be fully accurate. Rather than relying on our own understanding of this fallen world, learning to shift from an earthly to a heavenly view is key, inviting God into our thinking process along the way. As we learn to walk with him from moment to moment, we are more likely to understand his will for our lives and find a deeper, more restful contentment in his unwavering, perfect friendship. As a reminder, the four-step process throughout the workbook involves (1) noticing, (2) shifting, (3) accepting, and (4) acting, cultivating a spiritual awareness of God's active, loving presence in the here-and-now.

REPETITIVE NEGATIVE THINKING: A SECULAR PSYCHOLOGICAL UNDERSTANDING

In the secular psychology literature, repetitive negative thinking has received a considerable amount of attention in recent years. Defined as "excessive and repetitive thinking about current concerns, problems, past experiences or worries about the future,"[1] repetitive negative thinking has several key ingredients:[2]

- It involves being preoccupied with the past, such as repeatedly reviewing past conversations, mistakes, or problems.

- It involves dwelling on the present day, such as struggling to come up with a resolution to a dilemma or continuing to think about a current experience.

- It involves concern about the future, such as wondering what will go wrong next (more generally) or anticipating a certain catastrophic outcome (more specifically).

- It is perseverative, such as having a difficult time controlling or stopping a certain line of thinking or repeating certain thoughts over and over again.

- It is unwanted, such as experiencing thoughts as negative and disruptive.

- It is unhelpful, such as repeatedly thinking about a problem without coming up with a useful solution.

- It is distracting, such as particular thoughts taking up vital mental energy or attention.

In recent years, research has revealed that repetitive negative thinking is linked to symptoms of depression and anxiety in both clinical and non-clinical samples.[3] In addition, among a recent sample of adults diagnosed with major depressive disorder, generalized anxiety disorder, or obsessive-compulsive disorder, the length of time

---

[1]Ehring and Watkins (2008, p. 192).
[2]Adapted from Ehring et al. (2011).
[3]Ehring et al. (2011).

engaged in repetitive negative thinking was over twice as long when compared to a non-clinical sample (about 33 minutes versus 16 minutes "per episode," respectively).[4]

In response to these types of findings, mindfulness meditation has emerged as an intervention for repetitive negative thinking, given its role in helping practitioners to nonjudgmentally and nonreactively observe their thoughts.[5] For example, among a sample of college students who were asked to focus on their breath for about twenty minutes, a negative link emerged between mindfully attending to the breath and repetitive negative thinking.[6] As another example, when examining a clinical sample of adults, findings revealed that worry helped to explain the relationship between mindfulness and anxiety, whereas rumination helped to explain the link between mindfulness and depression.[7]

Overall, repetitive negative thinking may play a role in understanding the influence that mindfulness has on mental health outcomes (e.g., depression, anxiety). In other words, mindfulness may change our relationship with rumination and worry (which can lessen the symptoms of depression and anxiety) because of its emphasis on cultivating nonjudgmental awareness and attention in the present moment.[8] When we learn to gently and repeatedly shift our focus from unhelpful thinking processes to other aspects of our unfolding experience, we are able to "take up space" in the mind[9] so that perseverative thinking is no longer at the forefront of our awareness.

In the psychology literature, mindfulness-based cognitive therapy (MBCT) has emerged as a popular treatment option for a variety of psychological problems,[10] teaching different types of meditation to cultivate attention, awareness, and a greater insight into the nature of the human mind. Theoretically, mindfulness meditation may help practitioners to shift from the "doing mode" of the mind to the "being mode" of the mind.[11] With the former, rumination is a common feature, attempting to problem solve by "monitoring 'what is' in relation to what is desired, required, expected or feared with the intention of solving or eliminating the problem,"[12] whereas the latter captures "accepting" and "allowing," letting present-moment experiences naturally unfold, without trying to change them in any way.[13] In a recent review of six mindfulness-based intervention studies, findings revealed

---

[4]Wahl et al. (2019).
[5]Greeson et al. (2014).
[6]Burg and Michalak (2011).
[7]Desrosiers et al. (2013).
[8]Feldman et al. (2007).
[9]Segal et al. (2012, p. 183).
[10]Eisendrath (2016); Segal et al. (2012).
[11]Segal et al. (2012).
[12]Crane (2009, p. 31).
[13]Segal et al. (2012, p. 72).

that repetitive negative thinking helped to explain the relationship between mindfulness and psychological functioning (e.g., depression, anxiety, stress).[14]

In sum, the psychology literature has shed light on an unhelpful, perseverative type of thinking, made up of ruminating about the past, dwelling on the present, and worrying about the future, demonstrating its link to suffering. In addition, this literature has developed helpful interventions, with mindfulness meditation often leading the way, for learning to get unstuck from repetitive thinking. Yet, although there is certainly some overlap, the Christian tradition offers its own understanding of perseverative thinking, often referred to as rumination, likened to a cow chewing cud all day long in a field of grass and utilized in the context of meditating on short passages in Scripture.[15] Therefore, what follows is a brief review of a Christian understanding of repetitive thinking, both positive and negative, before offering the interventions for this chapter. Above all else, Christians are tasked with moving from earthly-mindedness to heavenly-mindedness,[16] meditating on Scripture, rather than our own understanding of a fallen world (Prov 3:5), consistent with the shift from doing to being in the mindfulness literature.[17]

REPETITIVE NEGATIVE THINKING: A CHRISTIAN UNDERSTANDING

In the first few pages of the Old Testament, we read that Adam and Eve ate from the "tree of the knowledge of good and evil," violating a firm boundary that God had previously established (Gen 2:17). In doing so, Adam and Eve chose to look to themselves, rather than God, relying on their own understanding of good and evil; in turn, this decision led to disunion from him, with Adam and Eve no longer relying on God as the center of their existence.[18] Unfortunately, to this very day, we regularly choose to place ourselves, rather than God, at the center, attempting to rely on our own understanding of good and evil, rather than trusting in God's infinite wisdom. When it comes to negative thinking, we may ruminate about a past that cannot be changed, dwell in the present, unilaterally trying to solve a problem, or worry about an unknown future.

Turning to the New Testament, Jesus instructed us to let go of worry, because God will provide (Mt 6:25-34). In this teaching, he pointed to the "birds of the air" and the "lilies of the field," noting that God takes care of his creation. In other words, rather than solely relying on our own efforts, we are to look to God's sovereign will, prioritizing God's plan for our lives as our main focus.[19] In this passage,

---

[14]Gu et al. (2015).
[15]McPherson (2002).
[16]Burroughs (2010, 2014).
[17]Segal et al. (2012).
[18]Bonhoeffer (1955).
[19]France (1985).

the Greek word *merimnan* is used for "worry," meaning "to worry anxiously."[20] Jesus is helping us to understand that worry does not accomplish anything, especially in light of God's providential care for his creation, and that worry can be defeated through (1) accepting and living out God's will, rather than pursuing our own, and (2) living in the moment, rather than in the past or future.[21] Ultimately, "when a man gets so involved in the things of time that he has no time for the things of eternity he is in a dangerous position."[22] Thus, when it comes to worry, being "heavenly-minded," rather than "earthly-minded," is key.[23]

Also in the New Testament, in his letter to the Colossians, the apostle Paul instructs his audience to "set [their] minds on things above, not earthly things" (Col 3:2). Here, we can see the notion that we are to change our perspective, fully identifying with Jesus Christ and organizing our lives around him, rather than the cares of the world, regardless of the obstacles in our way.[24] In his letter to the Philippians, moreover, Paul advocates for thinking about what is "true, . . . noble, . . . right, . . . pure, . . . lovely, . . . admirable, . . . excellent, or praiseworthy" (Phil 4:8). In this verse, the Greek word *logizo* is used, meaning "to carefully take into account" or "mull things over."[25] Above all else, we are to "mull over" what is "excellent" and "praiseworthy," rather than ruminate on an unchangeable past or worry about an unknown future.

Interestingly, Christian monks have long talked about the importance of ruminating in this life, likening it to a cow chewing cud in a field.[26] In other words, as we slowly chew on an idea, we begin to be nurtured by it, repeatedly dwelling on the thought until it is digested. Yet, the content of our rumination is key. Rather than "chewing the cud" of perseverative negative thinking, we can learn to get sustenance from God's special revelation, the Bible, which can help us to "take up the cognitive 'space' in the mind otherwise filled with ruminative thoughts,"[27] futilely revisiting a previous conversation or anticipating a future catastrophe.

One way to do so, as a Christian, is to learn how to meditate, which can help you shift from earthly preoccupations to an awareness of a more transcendent, heavenly reality. In doing so, you are striving to "see the forest for the trees," as the saying goes, recognizing that your own story, including your unique experiences of suffering, is embedded within a meta-narrative revealed in the pages of the Bible.

---

[20]Barclay (2001, p. 295).
[21]Barclay (2001).
[22]Barclay (1974, p. 202).
[23]Burroughs (2010, 2014).
[24]Dunn (1996).
[25]Witherington (2011, p. 256).
[26]Wilhoit and Howard (2012).
[27]Segal et al. (2012, p. 37).

My own research has revealed a negative link between surrendering to God's will (as a positive form of coping) and repetitive negative thinking.[28] In prior research, I have also found that various forms of Christian meditation may help to improve worry, a preoccupation with uncertainty, depression, anxiety,[29] and stress,[30] and repetitive negative thinking.[31] What follows, then, is a range of meditative strategies, emanating from desert, Orthodox, medieval, French, and Protestant spiritual practices, all within the Christian tradition.

Throughout the chapter, my hope is that you will be training your mind to shift from your own knowledge to a more satisfying contentment in God's plan. Remember, the four-step process throughout this workbook involves (1) noticing, (2) shifting, (3) accepting, and (4) acting, all in the context of gaining a more transcendent awareness of God's active, loving presence from moment to moment. As a starting point, you will be working on beginning to notice repetitive negative thinking, slowing down to get to know the nature of the mind with a bit more distance and humility.

MONITORING YOUR THOUGHTS: THE REPETITIVE NEGATIVE THINKING LOG

In the Eastern Orthodox tradition, the Greek word *hesychia* means "inner stillness" and is used to describe a state of rest that is sought by focusing the mind on God.[32] To do so, though, we need to learn to be watchful (*nepsis*, Greek) over intrapsychic experiences.[33] The first step, then, is to sit still for an extended period of time, getting to know the patterns of the fluctuating human mind. Like a spider attempting to feel the "slightest stirring on the web" in order to sense its prey,[34] we are to remain still to get to know the vibrations of the inner world, rather than frantically scurrying about, distracting ourselves from our thoughts and feelings.

In this first exercise, you will be turning inward throughout the day for an entire week, learning to better understand the contents of your mind. In particular, I would like you to especially try to notice when you are engaging in repetitive, perseverating thinking, such as rumination and worry. If possible, notice where in your thinking you spend most of your time—in the past or future.

To begin, simply set aside a few minutes several times per day to slow down, remain still, and ask yourself what you are thinking. You can also choose to do so

---

[28]Knabb et al. (2018).
[29]Knabb et al. (2017).
[30]Knabb and Vazquez (2018).
[31]Knabb, Vazquez, Garzon, Ford, Wang, Conner, Warren, and Weston (2020).
[32]Johnson (2010).
[33]Johnson (2010).
[34]Talbot (2002, p. 113).

when you are feeling anxious or depressed, working backwards by asking, "What am I thinking to myself right now?" "What am I dwelling on?" or "What am I chewing on within my mind?" Remember that we are always thinking about *something*, similar to chewing a piece of gum all day long. As a result, you will be learning to notice *that* you are chewing, along with *what* the proverbial flavor of the gum might be. To get you started, I have filled in an example. Feel free to use additional paper, if you need to.

REPETITIVE NEGATIVE THINKING LOG

Day of the Week	Time of Day	Type of Thinking	Specific Thought Content
Monday	12:00 P.M.	Rumination	I've been dwelling on a conversation from yesterday. My thoughts include, "I can't believe I said that," "What was I thinking?" and "I'm so stupid."
Monday	4:15 P.M.	Worry	I'm worrying about being terminated at work. My thoughts include, "What if I can't pay my bills?" and "What if I can't find another job?"

Day of the Week	Time of Day	Type of Thinking	Specific Thought Content

Day of the Week	Time of Day	Type of Thinking	Specific Thought Content

"STAYING PUT" IN THE CELL: LEARNING TO ENDURE BECAUSE GOD IS PRESENT

Among the early desert Christians, men and women who moved to the deserts of Egypt and Syria in the third and fourth centuries, a famous instruction was to "stay put" in the cell, which was a small room each monk lived in; rather than fleeing the cell to run from problems, monastic life involved living in solitude, facing suffering through endurance.[35] Abba Antony, for example, said the following about the cell:

> Just as fish die if they are on dry land for some time, so do monks who loiter outside their cells or waste time with worldlings release themselves from the tension of *hesychia* [inner stillness and peace]. So we should hasten back to the cell (like the fish to the sea) lest while loitering outside we forget to keep a watch on the inner [self].[36]

Abba Poemen, another early desert Christian, instructed the following: "Let us enter into our cell, and sitting there, remember our sins, and the Lord will come and help us in everything."[37]

Both the cell and wider desert landscape offered very little comfort for these Christian desert-dwellers; still, they chose to live there, "staying put" and recognizing the desert was a place to face their temptations and rely on God for survival, similar to Jesus in Matthew's Gospel (Mt 4:1-11).[38] Instead of being distracted with societal comforts and unhealthy coping strategies, they purposefully migrated to this harsh, silent environment to encounter a loving God via a faithful act of surrender.[39]

"STAYING PUT" IN THE CELL: AN EXERCISE

For this ten-minute exercise, find a quiet place, free from distractions. Close your eyes and say a brief prayer to God. In particular, ask that God will help you rely exclusively on him, recognizing it is just the two of you, alone, in this very moment.

Next, begin to imagine that you are living in the desert, all alone, without any of the societal comforts that have distracted you from fully experiencing God's presence. Imagine how quiet the desert is, with no television, Internet access, or other forms of entertainment.

Now, imagine that you are completely alone with God. As one of the early desert Christians, Abba Alonius, used to teach, "If a man does not say in his heart, in the world there is only myself and God, then he will not gain peace."[40] Really try to sink into the idea that it is just you and God in this desert landscape—you are

---

[35]Harmless (2004).
[36]Wortley (2012, p. 15).
[37]As cited in Burton-Christie (1993, p. 55).
[38]Chryssavgis (2008).
[39]Chryssavgis (2008).
[40]As cited in Keller (2011, p. 28).

utterly dependent on him for survival. There is no need to revisit a past conversation or worry about a distant future because he is with you right now. You are simply "staying put" in your cell, facing your inner experience in solitude and silence.

As a final step, when you are ready, begin to recite the words "There is only myself and God," slowly and gently. Really try to savor these words, recognizing your reliance upon his presence to get you through each unfolding moment, continuing to visualize that you are in a harsh desert landscape. When your mind drifts to rumination or worry, just bring yourself back to the words "There is only myself and God," imagining you are completely and totally alone with him. In other words, allow all of your worldly cares, whether rooted in past or future experiences, to naturally fall away as you focus on God's active, loving presence in the unforgiving desert terrain. There is no one to impress, no task to achieve, no goal to accomplish, and no possession to acquire. Your only job is to rest in his presence, connecting to the reality that he is all you need.

Continue this exercise for ten minutes, repeating the "There is only myself and God" phrase over and over again. Once you are finished, say a quick prayer to God, thanking him for spending this time with you.

After completing the exercise, journal for a few minutes, attempting to answer the following questions:

- What was it like to imagine you were in the desert? What were the benefits? The limitations?

- How well were you able to focus on the words "There is only myself and God"? Were you able to shift from all other distractions to him?

- What, if anything, got in your way? Were you able to overcome the obstacles? If so, how? If not, why not?

- How, if at all, can imagining that it is just you and God in the desert help you with rumination and worry as you move through the rest of your day?

- How, if at all, can imagining that it is just you and God in the desert help you to accept God's loving presence, minute by minute, and act in a manner that is anchored to fellowshiping with, and finding true contentment in, him as you carry out your day?

_____

_____

_____

_____

_____

_____

_____

_____

_____

"TALKING BACK": MEDITATING ON SCRIPTURE TO RESPOND TO RUMINATION AND WORRY

As one of the early desert Christians, Evagrius of Ponticus wrote extensively on the Christian life. One particular writing, *Talking Back*, focuses on strategies for responding to perceived demonic attacks in the desert.[41] In particular, early desert Christians believed that many of their recurrent, tempting, compulsive thoughts (*logismoi*, Greek) came from demons (although they also believed that tempting thoughts are self-generated)[42]; thus, similar to Jesus' temptations in the desert (Mt 4:1-11), they used Scripture as a way to "talk back." For these desert dwellers, this strategy was called *antirrhesis* (in Greek), meaning "the speaking of relevant passages from the Bible that would contradict or . . . cut off demonic suggestions."[43]

Although we cannot be certain about the exact source of rumination and worry (in no way do I, as a Christian psychologist, want to assume these types of thinking patterns come directly from demons, as living in a fallen world means there are all sorts of sources of suffering), Evagrius has provided twenty-first-century Christians with a strategy for interrupting perseverative thinking patterns, drawing on God's word, the Bible. In *Talking Back*, to be more precise, he offered 498 phrases, rooted in the Bible, with over half focusing on tempting, compulsive thoughts.[44] Ultimately, talking back to these unhelpful thinking patterns prevents Christians from living a life guided by rumination and worry: "Every thought that we have, good or bad, can be cut off by a corresponding opposing thought."[45] To be sure, when we get stuck in perseverative thinking, we inevitably come to a fork in the

---

[41]Evagrius (2009).
[42]Harmless (2004); Paintner (2012).
[43]Evagrius (2009, p. 1).
[44]Evagrius (2009).
[45]Evagrius (2009, p. 27).

road—do we continue to head in the direction of rumination and worry or turn toward God and his Word?

For the purpose of this chapter, we will be focusing on Evagrius's use of Psalm 27 to "talk back" to "thoughts of sadness."[46] In Psalm 27:1, David rhetorically asked the following: "The LORD is my light and my salvation—whom shall I fear? The LORD is the stronghold of my life—of whom shall I be afraid?"

God is our source of light and salvation, as well as a stronghold, or fortified, safe location in the midst of a battle. To "talk back" to ruminations about the past and worries about the future, we can begin to recite the above passage, learning to recognize God's role as a stronghold in the midst of battle, which will be practiced in the next exercise.

"TALKING BACK": AN EXERCISE

In this exercise,[47] you will be practicing talking back to your rumination and worry, shifting from unhelpful to helpful thoughts by focusing on Scripture. Find a quiet location, free from distractions, and close your eyes.

Now, begin to recite the verse, "The LORD is my light and my salvation—whom shall I fear? The LORD is the stronghold of my life—of whom shall I be afraid?" Try to do so in a gentle and unhurried manner, slowly sinking into the words and savoring them. Continue doing this for a few minutes.

At a certain point, you will notice your mind going to the past or future, possibly in the form of rumination or worry. When this happens, simply recite the passage again: "The LORD is my light and my salvation—whom shall I fear? The LORD is the stronghold of my life—of whom shall I be afraid?" Similar to interrupting someone else's story because what you have to say is more important, keep interrupting your rumination and worry with Psalm 27:1.

In this passage, you are acknowledging that God is your source of light, salvation, and safety. Although your mind might feel like a battlefield, with rumination and worry seemingly winning the war, God is your stronghold, a place of safety in the midst of the battle.

After ten minutes, thank God for offering you safety and stability in the middle of a fallen world, filled with uncertainty and doubt. In other words, thank God for providing you with his Word, the Bible, to anchor you to a more transcendent reality. As you wrap up, make a commitment to carry this verse with you throughout your day, interrupting the steady flow of rumination and worry that goes on in your head with God's Word.

---

[46]Evagrius (2009).
[47]Adapted from Evagrius (2009).

After completing the exercise, journal for a few minutes, attempting to answer the following questions:

- What was it like to talk back to rumination and worry with Scripture? What were the benefits? The limitations?

- How well were you able to focus on the words from Psalm 27:1? Were you able to shift from all other distractions to an awareness of God as your source of safety?

- What, if anything, got in your way? Were you able to overcome the obstacles? If so, how? If not, why not?

- How, if at all, can talking back with Scripture help you with rumination and worry as you move through the rest of your day?

- How, if at all, can talking back help you to accept God's loving presence, minute by minute, and act in a manner that is anchored to fellowshiping with, and finding true contentment in, him as you carry out your day?

_____

_____

_____

_____

_____

_____

_____

_____

_____

_____

_____

_____

_____

_____

_____

_____

THE JESUS PRAYER: SHIFTING FROM RUMINATION AND WORRY TO JESUS' PRESENCE WITHIN

With possible roots in early desert Christians' use of "monologic prayer" (i.e., repeating a short phrase to focus the mind throughout the day),[48] the Jesus Prayer developed in the first millennium, with the long version consisting of twelve words: "Lord Jesus Christ, Son of God, have mercy on me, a sinner." Consistent with passages in Scripture that involve the instruction to "pray without ceasing" (e.g., 1 Thess 5:17) and individuals asking God for mercy (Lk 18:38), the Jesus Prayer is made up of at least four characteristics, including (1) calling upon Jesus' name, (2) asking Jesus for mercy, (3) slowly repeating the prayer, and (4) cultivating inner peace and stillness (*hesychia*).[49]

In the context of repetitive negative thinking, repeating the Jesus Prayer, both formally and throughout the day, can help cultivate the mental skills of attention, present-moment awareness, and acceptance[50] as we focus our attention on Jesus' name in the present moment and ask for Jesus' loving, compassionate responsiveness in the midst of our struggles. In a way, we are learning to surrender to God in the here-and-now, over and over again. In my research, I found that, overall, college students who practiced the Jesus Prayer experienced less daily stress over a two-week period of time.[51] In a separate pilot study, I found that, in general, community adults who practiced the Jesus Prayer, among several other Christian meditative strategies, experienced less worry over an eight-week period of time.[52]

Overall, this famous Eastern Orthodox prayer may hold promise in allowing you to shift from earthly preoccupations, such as ruminations and worries, to a more transcendent understanding of God's mercy. Essentially, when we call upon Jesus' name, we are saying, "Lord, save me! I am stuck in my own perseverative thinking," similar to Peter crying out to Jesus when attempting to walk on water (Mt 14:30).

In *Our Thoughts Determine Our Lives*, the late Eastern Orthodox monk Thaddeus of Vitovnica said the following about the power of our thoughts:

> Our life depends on the kinds of thoughts we nurture. If our thoughts are peaceful, calm, meek, and kind, then that is what our life is like. If our attention is turned to the circumstances in which we live, we are drawn into a whirlpool of thoughts and can have neither peace nor tranquility.[53]

---

[48]Ware (2014).
[49]Ware (2014).
[50]Feldman et al. (2007).
[51]Knabb and Vazquez (2018).
[52]Knabb et al. (2017).
[53]Thaddeus (2012).

When writing about worry in the Christian life, he went on to note the following:

> The Lord has taken all of our sufferings and cares upon Himself, and He has said that He will provide for all our needs, yet we hold on to our cares so tightly that we create unrest in our hearts and minds, in our families, and all around us.[54]

Again, the Eastern Orthodox practice of the Jesus Prayer can help shift the ruminative and worrying Christian mind toward Jesus, who tells us not to worry because God will provide (Mt 6:24-34). To call on Jesus' name, asking for his perfect mercy, means we are reaching out to him for his loving-kindness, compassion, and empathy during our time of need.[55] What follows is a strategy for filling the mind with Christ, pivoting from earthly preoccupations to a heavenly reality.

THE JESUS PRAYER: AN EXERCISE

To begin this exercise,[56] find a quiet place, free from distractions. Sit up straight in a supportive chair, closing your eyes as you prepare to spend this time with Jesus Christ.[57]

When you are ready, begin to notice your breathing, recognizing that God has given you the "breath of life" (Gen 2:7). There is nothing you need to do to control your breathing; rather, God is caring for you in blessing you with an autonomic nervous system that does all of the work for you. Just spend a few minutes noticing your breath going in and out of your lungs, thanking God for giving you this life.

Next, begin to recite the words of the Jesus Prayer—"Lord Jesus Christ, Son of God, have mercy on me"—aligning them with your breath. Breathe in the first part of the prayer—"Lord Jesus Christ, Son of God"—and breathe out the second half of the prayer—"have mercy on me." As you breathe in, you are filling your mind with Jesus Christ, then breathing out to let go of rumination and worry. In this process, you are cultivating a deeper awareness of Jesus' loving-kindness and compassion in the present moment.

At a certain point, you may notice that your mind is beginning to perseverate again, ruminating about the past or worrying about the future. When this happens, simply acknowledge you are perseverating, then shift toward Jesus' presence, asking him for his merciful reply.

Over and over again, breathe in ("Lord Jesus Christ, Son of God"), then breathe out ("have mercy on me"), sinking into Jesus' loving presence as you develop focused, sustained attention on your Lord and Savior.

Continue this practice for about ten minutes. Whenever you recognize you are ruminating or worrying, simply notice this process unfold with a calm, watchful

---

[54]Thaddeus (2012).
[55]Talbot (2013).
[56]Adapted from Talbot (2013).
[57]You can also follow along with the audio recording (track 1), found at ivpress.com/Knabb1.

vigilance, sinking deeper and deeper into the reality that Jesus' mercy is all that you need in this very moment.

As the practice comes to a close, thank Jesus for being with you, asking him to walk with you for the rest of the day so you can deepen your communion with, and contentment in, him.

After completing the exercise, journal for a few minutes, attempting to answer the following questions:

- What was it like to recite the Jesus Prayer? What were the benefits? The limitations?

- How well were you able to focus on the words "Lord Jesus Christ, Son of God, have mercy on me"? Were you able to shift from all other distractions to Jesus' presence?

- What, if anything, got in your way? Were you able to overcome the obstacles? If so, how? If not, why not?

- How, if at all, can reciting the Jesus Prayer help you with rumination and worry as you move through the rest of your day?

- How, if at all, can reciting the Jesus Prayer help you to accept God's loving presence, minute by minute, and act in a manner that is anchored to fellowshiping with, and finding true contentment in, him as you carry out your day?

APOPHATIC MEDITATION IN THE *CLOUD OF UNKNOWING*

In the *Cloud of Unknowing*, an anonymous medieval English work, the author offered instructions on cultivating an awareness of God's loving presence, arguing for
the limitations of human knowledge in fellowshiping with God.[58] In particular, the
Cloud author advocated for reaching out to God in love in a "cloud of unknowing,"
placing all human knowledge beneath a "cloud of forgetting."[59] The *Cloud* author
further noted:

> This is what you are to do: lift your heart up to the Lord, with a gentle stirring of
> love desiring him for his own sake and not for his gifts. Center all your attention
> and desire on him and let this be the sole concern of your mind and heart. Do all
> in your power to forget everything else, keeping your thoughts and desires free
> from involvement with any of God's creatures or their affairs whether in general or
> in particular.[60]

These instructions emanate from the *apophatic* Christian tradition, which suggests
that, ultimately, God is beyond words; thus, language will fall short when trying to
comprehend God.[61] When it comes to meditation, therefore, an *apophatic* approach
stresses few to no words and no images, in contrast with a *kataphatic* strategy,
which uses words and images.[62] A biblical example of this understanding comes
from Moses' encounter with God in "thick darkness" (Ex 20:21), as well as "the
cloud" (Ex 24:16-18), with the cloud language also used, of course, in the *Cloud of
Unknowing*.[63] Combined, these two ways of knowing God suggest that, although
God is ineffable and never fully known with our fallen, limited human mind, he
has revealed himself to us via the Bible and, thus, we can partially understand him
because of his divine revelation.[64]

Returning to the *Cloud* author's instructions, he recommended using a short
word to focus our attention on God in a "cloud of unknowing," letting go of all other
thoughts (whether perceived as positive or negative).[65] In the context of repetitive
negative thinking, we are cultivating the virtue of detachment, pivoting from earthly
preoccupations to an awareness of God's loving presence in each unfolding moment.

In a recent study among Christian college students, I found a negative link between surrendering to God (as a coping skill) and repetitive negative thinking, with

---

[58]Bangley (2006).
[59]Bangley (2006).
[60]Johnston (2014, p. 35).
[61]McGrath (2011).
[62]Ruffing (2005).
[63]Howells (2005).
[64]Demarest (2011).
[65]Bangley (2006).

"humble detachment" helping to explain this relationship.[66] "Humble detachment," in this study, involved the ability to "let go of the tendency to clutch or push away a preoccupation with inner experiences and the self" and "pivot from a preoccupation with the self and inner experiences to a more transcendent awareness of God's active, loving presence."[67] In theory, then, surrendering life's stressors to God may help with repetitive thinking, explained by the ability to "humbly detach" from an unhealthy preoccupation with unpleasant inner experiences and self-interests.

In our efforts to "humbly detach," we are learning to recognize the limitations of language, consistent with the *apophatic* tradition. The *Cloud* author further explained:

> If you want to gather all your desire into one simple word that the mind can easily retain, choose a short word rather than a long one. A one-syllable word such as "God" or "love" is best. But choose one that is meaningful to you. Then fix it in your mind so that it will remain there come what may. This word will be your defense in conflict and in peace. Use it to beat upon the cloud of darkness above you and subdue all distractions, consigning them to the cloud of forgetting beneath you. Should some thought go on annoying you demanding to know what you are doing, answer with this one word alone.[68]

When it comes to rumination and worry, we are employing this short word to shift from earthly-mindedness to heavenly-mindedness,[69] relying on love, rather than knowledge, in the process. This *apophatic* strategy can help you to let go of your own understanding (Prov 3:5), resting in God's loving arms during formal practice. Then, throughout the day, drawing on a single-syllable word can serve as a reminder to surrender everything to God—even ruminations and worries—recognizing that human knowledge is limited as a medium for fully understanding both reality and God's plan for our life. What follows is a formal, two-step strategy for learning to rest in God's loving presence, practicing letting go of earthly perseverations along the way.

THE *CLOUD OF UNKNOWING*: AN EXERCISE

To begin this ten-minute, two-step exercise, find a quiet location, free from distractions, and sit up straight in a supportive chair. Close your eyes, then begin the two-step process:[70]

Recite. Begin to gently and slowly recite the word *love*, recognizing that "God is love" (1 Jn 4:8). Over and over again, use the word love to capture your desire to lovingly reach out to God in a "cloud of unknowing."

---

[66]Knabb et al. (2018).

[67]Knabb et al. (2018, p. 172).

[68]Johnston (2014, p. 43).

[69]Burroughs (2010, 2014).

[70]Adapted from Bangley (2006).

Return. Whenever you notice you are preoccupied with ruminations and worries, perseverating on earthly matters, compassionately return to the word *love*, which serves as a tool for focusing all of your attention on God, who resides in the "cloud of unknowing," placing your worldly cares beneath a "cloud of forgetting."

After completing the exercise, journal for a few minutes, attempting to answer the following questions:

- What was it like to attempt to reach out to God in love, rather than employing your own knowledge? What were the benefits? The limitations?

- How well were you able to focus on the word *love*? Were you able to shift from all other distractions to God?

- What, if anything, got in your way? Were you able to overcome the obstacles? If so, how? If not, why not?

- How, if at all, can reciting the word *love* help you with rumination and worry as you move through the rest of your day?

- How, if at all, can reciting the word *love* help you to accept God's loving presence, minute by minute, and act in a manner that is anchored to fellowshiping with, and finding true contentment in, him as you carry out your day?

_____

_____

_____

_____

_____

_____

_____

_____

_____

_____

_____

_____

_____

_____

"IN YOU ALONE I HAVE EVERYTHING": JULIAN OF NORWICH AND GOD'S ENDURING LOVE

In fourteenth-century, medieval England, Julian of Norwich reported experiencing over a dozen "showings," or "revelations," from God as she was dying from some sort of severe illness.[71] As one of several themes, she wrote that the love of God is foundational in the Christian life and that Christians can only find true rest in his unwavering, perfect goodness, not earthly things.[72] Of God's goodness, Julian of Norwich stated as follows:

> For as the body is clad in cloth, and the flesh in the skin, and the bones in the flesh, and the heart in the chest, so are we, soul and body, clad and enclosed in the goodness of God. Yes, and more inwardly, for all these may decay and wear away. God's goodness is always complete, and incomparably closer to us, for truly our lover, God, wants our souls to cling to him with all their might, and always to be clinging to his goodness. For of all the things that the heart can think, this pleases God most and helps us soonest. For our soul is so especially loved by him who is highest that it surpasses the knowledge of all created things—that is to say, there is no being made who can know how much and how sweetly and how tenderly our maker loves us.[73]

What is more, according to Julian of Norwich, God takes "very great pleasure" in Christians crying out to God with a prayer such as the following:

> God, of your goodness, give me yourself; you are enough for me, and anything less that I could ask for would not do you full honor. And if I ask anything that is less I shall always lack something, but in you alone I have everything.[74]

In this prayer we see the importance of finding true contentment in God, resting in his immutable love. In the context of rumination and worry, we may struggle with fellowshiping with God in the present moment and allowing his love to be enough in the here-and-now. Nevertheless, we can learn to turn toward the "being mode of the mind" and away from unhelpful rumination and worry in the "doing mode of the mind"[75] by meditating on God's perfect goodness. What follows, then, is a simple meditation[76] for learning to rest in God's loving arms, recognizing that he is all we need in this very moment.

---

[71]McGinn (2006).
[72]McGinn (2006).
[73]Windeatt (2015, p. 47).
[74]McGinn (2006, p. 242).
[75]Segal et al. (2012).
[76]Adapted from McGinn (2006).

"IN YOU ALONE I HAVE EVERYTHING": AN EXERCISE

For this next ten-minute meditative exercise,[77] try to find a quiet location, resting in a comfortable chair with your eyes closed. Now, imagine that you have God's full attention in this very moment. In other words, he is waiting for you to share your heart with him. Just spend a minute sinking into this reality—God is with you and listening to your heartfelt cry. In fact, you are "soul and body, clad and enclosed in the goodness of God."

Next, begin to identify some of the ruminations and worries you have been struggling with over the last week. Recognize the themes that have emerged, along with the fact that they are rooted in a past that is irreversible and a future that has yet to materialize. Spend a minute noticing these perseverative thoughts, bringing them to God in this very moment. As you do so, imagine handing them to God, with God receiving the thoughts that have weighed you down in the last week. Because you are "enclosed in the goodness of God," he is with you, gladly receiving everything you have to offer.

Now, when you are ready, say the words, "God, of your goodness, give me yourself; you are enough for me, and anything less that I could ask for would not do you full honor," before shortening this phrase to the simple words, "God, give me yourself; you are enough for me." Get into the rhythm of repeating these words over and over again, gently and steadily, "God, give me yourself; you are enough for me." Imagine handing God your ruminations and worries from the previous week, replacing them with nothing short of God himself, given you are "enclosed in the goodness of God." In other words, God is now filling up your mind, rather than your ruminative and worrying thoughts.

Spend a few minutes repeating these words, "God, give me yourself; you are enough for me," again and again. Whenever you notice you are ruminating about the past or worrying about the future, hand your perseverative thoughts to God, then simply return to these words. Try to let go of the past, as well as the future, resting in God's perfect love in this very moment, given God is taking up all the space in your mind in the here-and-now. In this instance, you are "enclosed in the goodness of God."

In transitioning to the second half of the meditation, begin to recite the phrase, "God, in you alone I have everything," dwelling on these words with an awareness that God's perfect, unending love is available to you as the seconds pass by in this very instance. "God, in you alone I have everything." Repeat these words in a steady, unhurried manner, savoring them as you commune with God in the here-and-now. "God, in you alone I have everything." Remember, you are "enclosed in the goodness

---

[77]Adapted from McGinn (2006); Windeatt (2015).

of God" in this very instance, which means there is nothing else you need, nothing you need to fix, and nowhere else to be.

Again, when you notice your mind perseverating on the past or the future, hand your ruminations and worries to God, then return to his presence, slowly chewing on the phrase "God, in you alone I have everything." Continue to do so for several minutes, resting in God's perfect goodness, which you are "enclosed in." "God, in you alone I have everything." There is no need to go over a past that is unchangeable or a future that is in God's loving hands; instead, just rest in the phrase "God, in you alone I have everything."

As this meditative practice comes to an end, thank God for giving you his perfect love, asking him to remind you throughout the rest of your day of the goodness that only comes from him.

After completing the exercise, try to journal for a few minutes, attempting to answer the following questions:

- What was it like to hand your ruminations and worries to God? What were the benefits? What were the limitations?

- What was it like to repeat Julian of Norwich's phrase "God, in you alone I have everything," rather than ruminating about the past or worrying about the future? What were the benefits? The limitations?

- How well were you able to focus on Julian of Norwich's phrase "God, in you alone I have everything"? Were you able to shift from ruminations and worries to God's perfect goodness?

- What, if anything, got in your way? Were you able to overcome the obstacles? If so, how? If not, why not?

- How, if at all, can reciting Julian of Norwich's phrase "God, in you alone I have everything" help you with rumination and worry as you move through the rest of your day?

- How, if at all, can reciting Julian of Norwich's phrase "God, in you alone I have everything" help you to accept God's loving presence, minute by minute, and act in a manner that is anchored to fellowshiping with, and finding true contentment in, him as you carry out your day?

"THE METHOD OF PRAYER": JEANNE GUYON AND FRENCH SPIRITUALITY

In seventeenth-century France, Jeanne Guyon[78] wrote the famous book *A Short and Easy Method of Prayer*. In this simple work, she outlined several strategies for drawing closer to God, employing the medium of prayer. Defining prayer as "the application of the heart to God, and the internal exercise of love," she argued that "nothing is so easily obtained as the possession and enjoyment of God."[79] Among the different methods for drawing closer to God, Guyon offered the following on meditation:

> When, by an act of lively faith, you are placed in the Presence of God, recollect some truth wherein there is substance and food; pause gently and sweetly thereon, not to employ the reason, but merely to calm and fix the mind: for you must observe, that your principal exercise should ever be the Presence of God; your subject, therefore, should rather serve to stay the mind, than exercise the understanding. From this procedure, it will necessarily follow, that the lively faith in a God immediately present in our inmost soul, will produce an eager and vehement pressing inwardly into ourselves, and a restraining all our senses from wandering abroad: this serves to extricate us speedily from numberless distractions, to remove us from external objects, and to bring us nigh unto our God, Who is only to be found in our inmost centre, which is the Holy of Holies wherein He dwelleth.[80]

---

[78]Guyon (2010).
[79]Guyon (2010).
[80]Guyon (2010).

Here, we can see that Christian meditation appears to involve several key ingredients:[81]

- *Remember.* "Recollect some truth" of "substance."

- *Focus.* "Calm and fix the mind" by "pausing gently and sweetly."

- *Maintain.* Maintain an awareness of the "Presence of God . . . inwardly."

- *Let go.* Let go of the tendency to overly rely on "the reason."

Given the tendency for perseverative, ruminative, and worrying thinking to involve the idea that the past or future is not quite right, you will be practicing meditating on the simple truth that God is a perfect source of contentment, even in the midst of an unstable, uncertain world. In other words, although the fall has led to hardship and suffering, including the reality that daily living is not quite right, we have the ability to rest in God's presence, even in the middle of suffering.

In fact, in the apostle Paul's letter to the Ephesians, he emphasized that Christians are an *actual* dwelling place for God:

> Consequently, you are no longer foreigners and strangers, but fellow citizens with God's people and also members of his household, built on the foundation of the apostles and prophets, with Christ Jesus himself as the chief cornerstone. In him the whole building is joined together and rises to become a holy temple in the Lord. And in him you too are being built together to become a *dwelling* in which God lives by his Spirit. (Eph 2:19-22, italics added)

From Paul's letter we see that (1) Jesus holds the entire temple together, and (2) we are the temple that God dwells in.[82] Because of our union with Christ, we are able to commune with God, who actually lives within us.

In reconciling this passage with Jeanne Guyon's instructions for meditation, we learn to recognize God's loving presence within us as his dwelling place. To be sure, as God's temple, we can cultivate a deeper awareness of his perfect love, readily available from moment to moment. When we struggle with ruminative and worrying thinking, we can shift toward this awareness, recognizing that God's love is always available in the here-and-now. What follows, then, is a meditative exercise for recognizing God's loving presence, shifting from perseverative thinking to his enduring goodness within the depths of our being.

"THE METHOD OF PRAYER": AN EXERCISE

In this exercise,[83] if you are able, try to go on a ten-minute walk outside. Find a location that is relatively free from distractions and noise. Next, begin to walk with

---

[81]Guyon (2010).
[82]Snodgrass (1996).
[83]Adapted from Guyon (2010).

God, recognizing that you are his dwelling place. In this very moment, God is loving you from the inside out, meaning he is residing in the depths of your soul.

Continue to walk at a slow pace, turning inward by visualizing God's loving presence. In this very instance, he is available to you, residing within as you place one foot after the other. As best you can, keep your awareness on God's goodness, recognizing that he is with you, reminiscent of someone you are going on a walk with. Yet, instead of a neighborhood friend or family member, it is God himself who is with you, living within you and offering you his perfect love.

Over and over again, "recollect [this] truth," namely that God is loving you from the inside out. "Fix [your] mind" on God's love, "pausing gently and sweetly" every few seconds to bask in this reality. Keep this awareness of the presence of God by inwardly maintaining your focus, letting go of the tendency to overthink God's presence.

As soon as you notice you are ruminating about the past or worrying about the future, gently return to focusing on God as you walk, "pausing gently and sweetly" on his love as he dwells within you. Again and again, pause to recognize this reality, relinquishing any effort on your part to use reason to understand his presence. Instead, as you walk, just notice the fact that he dwells within you, offering his love as you take each and every step on this short journey with him.

When this walk comes to an end, thank God for living within you, offering his love as you move through life. Ask him to continue to dwell inside, loving you as the rest of your day unfolds.

After completing the exercise, try to journal for a few minutes, attempting to answer the following questions:

- What was it like to walk with God and attempt to maintain an awareness of his presence within? What were the benefits? What were the limitations?

- What was it like to attempt to "fix [your] mind" on God's love, rather than ruminating about the past or worrying about the future? What were the benefits? The limitations?

- How well were you able to "[pause] gently and sweetly" to maintain an awareness of the presence of God inwardly? Were you able to shift from ruminations and worries to God's loving presence within?

- What, if anything, got in your way? Were you able to overcome the obstacles? If so, how? If not, why not?

- How, if at all, can practicing these steps, whether walking or doing some other simple task, help you with rumination and worry as you move through the rest of your day?

● How, if at all, can practicing these steps, whether walking or doing some other simple task, help you to accept God's loving presence, minute by minute, and act in a manner that is anchored to fellowshiping with, and finding true contentment in, him as you carry out your day?

_____

_____

_____

_____

_____

_____

_____

_____

_____

_____

_____

_____

"THE VANITY OF THOUGHTS" IN THE PURITAN TRADITION

In the 1600s, the Puritan author Thomas Goodwin wrote *The Vanity of Thoughts,*[84] in which he argued that "it is not what thoughts are in your hearts, or what passes through them, but it is what lodging you give to them that makes the difference." More specifically, he defined thoughts, which are ultimately vain because of our fallen nature, as follows: "Those more simple conceits, apprehensions that arise; those fancies and meditations which the understanding (with help from the imagination) frames within itself of things; those on which your minds ponder and pore and muse."[85]

Unfortunately, we tend to chase after unhelpful thoughts and avoid helpful thoughts, given our shortcomings as imperfect human beings:[86]

God is the most glorious object that our minds could ever fasten upon, the most alluring. Thoughts of Him should therefore swallow up all other thoughts, as they

---

[84]Goodwin (2015).
[85]Goodwin (2015).
[86]Goodwin (2015).

are not worthy to be seen the same day with Him. But I appeal to your experience, are not your thoughts of Him the most unsteady? Do you not have as much trouble holding your thoughts on Him as you would holding a telescope on a star with a palsy-shaking hand? . . . So when we are at our business, which God commands us to do with all our might [Eccles 9:10], our minds, like truant children . . . will go out of the way to see any sport, will run after every hare that crosses the way, will follow after every butterfly buzzing about us.

In the context of perseverative thinking, we tend to ruminate about a past we cannot change and a future we cannot know, struggling to stay connected to an awareness of God's presence in each unfolding moment. Unfortunately, we end up giving our mind too much credit, overly relying on our thought stream as if it were *always* factual and accurate.

Yet, according to Goodwin,[87] we need to view our own thoughts with a healthy dose of humility, given our fallen nature:

As wanton boys sometimes scribble broken words which make no sense, so our thoughts sometimes are—and if you could but read over what you have thought, as you can what you have written, you would find as much nonsense in your thoughts as you will find in madmen's speeches.

Interestingly, researchers within the mindfulness-based cognitive therapy (MBCT) literature have suggested that the mere act of identifying and labeling unhelpful thoughts, that is, "decentering" or "distancing," can be effective, given we are cultivating meta-cognitive awareness.[88] In other words, instead of trying to fully eradicate rumination and worry, simply recognizing the limitations of our thinking process can help to gain a wider perspective, that is, a "birds-eye," "balcony," or "helicopter" view.

From a Christian perspective, recognizing our own mental limitations because of the fall can help us to rely less on our own understanding (Prov 3:5) and, instead, learn to trust in God, meditating on his attributes and actions to fill our mind with Jesus Christ. Of course, as mentioned by Goodwin,[89] this is easier said than done, and we often drift toward cognitive material that is less than fully edifying.

In response to such unhelpful thinking patterns, or "words of the mind," Goodwin[90] recommends that we (1) maintain a sense of humility toward our thoughts, and (2) attempt to shift our mind toward God by meditating on his attributes and fellowshiping with him. In this next exercise, then, you will be working on conversing with God by meditating on him. To do so, you will be using the metaphor of traveling with two companions.

---

[87]Goodwin (2015).
[88]Segal et al. (2012).
[89]Goodwin (2015).
[90]Goodwin (2015).

"THE VANITY OF THOUGHTS": AN EXERCISE

In this ten-minute meditative exercise,[91] you will be developing a deeper awareness of the "vanity of thoughts" with a metaphor, learning to shift from listening to the words of an unwise traveling companion toward a trusted friend. Begin by finding a quiet location, free from unnecessary distractions. Sitting in a supportive chair, close your eyes and begin to imagine you are walking down a long dirt road.

On each side of you is a traveling companion. To the left, you have an unwise, rambling fellow traveler who simply will not stop talking. This person gives unhelpful advice and is frequently wrong about matters that are important to you. In fact, you tend to notice that you are irritated and annoyed whenever this person begins to speak.

To the right side of you, however, is a very different traveling companion. This person is wise, considerate, and supportive. On a regular basis, you notice that you are drawn to this person, who offers comfort as you travel together.

Although the person to the left of you is much louder and more distracting, you find that you naturally want to spend all your time with the person to the right of you. Thus, you have a decision to make—should you focus your attention and energy on the person to the left or to the right of you?

Of course, the person to the left of you represents your own mind, often unreliable and notoriously inaccurate. To the right, however, is God, with his attributes and actions already revealed to you in the pages of the Bible.

As a next step, see if you can simply notice your ruminative, worrying mind, reminiscent of an "annoying traveling companion." Then, turn your attention to a "wise traveling companion," God, like you would in simply shifting your attention from the person walking to your left to the person walking to your right. In this process, gently repeat the phrase, "I will trust in you, not my own understanding" (see Prov 3:5).

Continue to practice this two-step exercise for several minutes, noticing the annoying traveling companion, shifting to the wise traveling companion, and repeating the phrase, "I will trust in you, not my own understanding." Again and again, notice and shift by saying, "I will trust in you, not my own understanding."

As this exercise comes to a close, thank God for traveling with you and offering you his perfect wisdom from moment to moment. Ask for his help in shifting your attention from your own thinking process to his infinite wisdom as you go about your day.

After completing the exercise, journal for a few minutes, attempting to answer the following questions:

---

[91]Adapted from Goodwin (2015); Hayes et al. (2012).

- What was it like to get to know each "traveling companion"? What were the benefits? What were the limitations?

- What was it like to attempt to shift from focusing on the annoying traveling companion to the wise traveling companion? What were the benefits? The limitations?

- How well were you able to focus on the adapted verse, "I will trust in you, not my own understanding"? Were you able to shift from ruminations and worries, that is, your "own understanding," to trusting in God?

- What, if anything, got in your way? Were you able to overcome the obstacles? If so, how? If not, why not?

- How, if at all, can practicing these steps help you with rumination and worry as you move through the rest of your day?

- How, if at all, can practicing these steps help you to accept God's loving presence, minute by minute, and act in a manner that is anchored to fellowshiping with, and finding true contentment in, him as you carry out your day?

THE USE OF SILENCE: QUAKER MEDITATION

Among the Quakers, a Christian group dating back to the 1600s who advocate for the importance of an inner encounter with God, silent worship in church service, and peace and nonviolence in daily living,[92] the use of silence is foundational for fellowshiping with the triune God and allowing for spiritual spontaneity in each unfolding moment.[93] In other words, silence serves as a vehicle through which we can deepen a loving intimacy with God,[94] letting go of more scripted attempts to dictate each step in our relationship with him. As the Quaker Isaac Penington noted, "So, be still and quiet, and silent before the Lord, not putting up any request to the Father, nor cherishing any desire in thee."[95] What is more, the Quaker George Fox offered the following:

> Be still and cool in thy own mind and spirit from thy own thoughts, and then thou wilt feel the principle of God to turn thy mind to the Lord God, whereby thou wilt receive his strength and power from whence life comes, to allay all tempests, against blusterings and storms. That is it which moulds up into patience, into innocency, into soberness, into stillness, into stayedness, into quietness, up to God, with his power.[96]

Here, we can see an emphasis on stillness and silence, aspects of daily living that are commonly lacking in the twenty-first century. In fact, a recent review of the psychology of silence explicated a variety of benefits,[97] suggesting the use of silence may produce more fruit than we realize in our noisy Western culture.

From a Christian perspective, silence before God is important in order to hear his "gentle whisper" (1 Kings 19:11-13). What is more, as the psalmist David revealed, "Truly my soul finds rest in God; my salvation comes from him," with some translations using the word *silence* to capture the importance of "waiting in silence" upon God (Ps 62:1).

Interestingly, within the mindfulness-based stress reduction (MBSR) program, which is highly popular in the psychology literature and applicable to a wide variety of psychological problems, participants attend a silent retreat toward the end of the eight-week intervention. Writing about the benefits of doing so, two MBSR authors offered the following:

> Silence helps our minds to rest. Just as sand stirred in a tumbler of water gradually settles to the bottom and leaves the water clear if we let it rest for a while, so the agitation of our minds and stressful thoughts can gradually settle as well. Our

---

[92]Brinton (2018); Dandelion (2008).
[93]Bill (2016).
[94]Bill (2016).
[95]Steere (1984, p. 156).
[96]Steere (1984, p. 99).
[97]Valle (2019).

minds generally become calmer, clearer, and more open.[98]

In the context of repetitive negative thinking, silence and stillness before God can help us to begin to settle the mind, letting go of the tendency to "throw gasoline on the fire." Just like the best way to let the snow settle in a snow globe is to simply keep it in one place (e.g., on a bookshelf) for a period of time, we can learn to settle our perseverative thinking by remaining still and silent before God, attempting to hear from him, rather than our own endless inner chatter.

To do so, consistent with the Quaker tradition, we can practice three steps:[99]

1. *Expect.* Develop a confident expectation that God is present in the silence and will commune with you as you rest in him.

2. *Be still.* Remain still in the silence, letting go of all other expectations.

3. *Focus.* Focus on a short passage in Scripture that captures the importance of silence, meditating on this verse to focus your attention on God in the here-and-now.

These three steps will be practiced next in the final exercise for the chapter.

THE USE OF SILENCE: AN EXERCISE

For this final exercise in the chapter,[100] please find a quiet location to spend the next ten minutes. Because of the importance of allowing your ruminating and worrying mind to settle, time is of the essence. Thus, please be prepared to rest in silence and in God's presence.

To begin, close your eyes, sit up straight in a supportive chair, and spend a few minutes developing a confident expectation that God is actually with you in the *silence.* In other words, let go of the expectation that you will hear an audible voice from God over the next ten minutes. Although God can certainly move in any way he so chooses, learning to hear from God in the silence is especially important during this time. Rather than viewing God as distant or absent, begin to assume he is with you and just as excited as you are to spend this time together.

Next, take a few minutes to really settle into your position, remaining as still as possible and letting go of the tendency to fidget, move around, or make any slight adjustments in this time with him. As you remain still before the Lord, relinquish all of your expectations about what will happen in the silence, only holding on to the expectation that God is showing up and spending this time with you now.

Finally, spend the remainder of the time meditating on the English Standard

---

[98]Lehrhaupt and Meibert (2017, p. 150).
[99]Adapted from Bill (2016).
[100]Adapted from Bill (2016); Lehrhaupt and Meibert (2017).

Version (ESV) version of Psalm 62:1, "For God alone my soul waits in silence; from him comes my salvation," aligning the verse with your breathing. With the in-breath, silently say to yourself, "For God alone my soul waits in silence," and with the out-breath say, "from him comes my salvation." Again and again, repeat the verse, "For God alone my soul waits in silence" as you breathe in, then "from him comes my salvation" as you breathe out.

Continue to sink further and further into this reality as you fellowship with God in the silence. Since God is offering you salvation in this very moment, your only job is to wait on him in silence.

Whenever you notice you are ruminating about the past or worrying about the future, allow your perseverative thoughts to run their natural course, settling into the silence because you are remaining still before the Lord and pivoting toward the verse, "For God alone my soul waits in silence; from him comes my salvation," aligning it with the natural rhythm of your breathing.

As you conclude this meditation, thank God for the time spent with him, asking God to continue to show up in these instances of silence throughout your day by offering you his "gentle whisper."

After completing the exercise, journal for a few minutes, attempting to answer the following questions:

- What was it like to sit in silence with God? What were the benefits? What were the limitations?

- What was it like to remain still in your silent time with God? What were the benefits? The limitations?

- How well were you able to focus on the verse, "For God alone my soul waits in silence; from him comes my salvation"? Were you able to shift from ruminations and worries to silently waiting on God?

- What, if anything, got in your way? Were you able to overcome the obstacles? If so, how? If not, why not?

- How, if at all, can practicing these steps help you with rumination and worry as you move through the rest of your day?

- How, if at all, can practicing these steps help you to accept God's loving presence, minute by minute, and act in a manner that is anchored to fellowshiping with, and finding true contentment in, him as you carry out your day?

_____

_____

_____

_____

_____

_____

_____

_____

_____

_____

REFLECTING ON THE PRACTICE

In this chapter, we have focused on repetitive negative thinking, including ruminating about the past and worrying about the future. From a psychological perspective, perseverative thinking is linked to the symptoms of both depression and anxiety,[101] whereas a biblical understanding of rumination and worry can be traced back to the fall of humankind, captured in the first few pages of the Bible. In either case, by shifting from our own thinking patterns to a focus on God, we are moving in the direction of finding a deeper rest in him and fellowshiping with him as we walk along the roads of life. To do so, we have been focusing on a variety of meditative strategies, rooted in desert, Orthodox, medieval, French, and Protestant spiritual practices, to (1) notice perseverative thinking, (2) shift from earthly preoccupations to a heavenly, spiritual reality, (3) accept God's presence and focus on him in each unfolding moment, and (4) act based on a deeper communion with, and contentment in, God. Before concluding this chapter and moving on to the next transdiagnostic processes in this workbook—impaired emotional clarity and distress intolerance—I would like you to reflect on your recent meditative experiences with a final journaling activity.

REFLECTING ON THE CHAPTER: A JOURNALING ACTIVITY

To conclude this chapter, spend a few minutes journaling about your experience with relating differently to rumination and worry through the use of Christian meditation. Please use additional paper, if necessary. A few questions to consider:

- What was it like for you to begin to identify rumination and worry? How well were you able to do so? Were you able to step back and see these perseverative

---

[101]Ehring et al. (2011).

thought patterns in the moment? What can you do to continue to work on watching your ruminative and worrying thoughts?

- How well were you able to shift from repetitive negative thinking to God? What went well? What do you still need to work on?

- Which exercises, if any, were most helpful in allowing you to get unstuck from perseverative thinking and shift toward God? How can you build these exercises into daily life?

- How, if at all, did Christian meditation help you to pivot from an earthly perspective to a more transcendent, heavenly reality? What can you do to strengthen this daily practice?

- How did you do with developing the mental skills of attention, present-moment awareness, and acceptance in the context of your relationship with God?

- How, if at all, did your relationship with God change as you spent more time meditating on his word, the Bible?

- How, if at all, did your ability to commune with God change? How about your ability to find a deeper contentment in him as you made decisions throughout the day?

TARGETING PROBLEMS
with AFFECT

Christian Meditation for
Impaired Emotional Clarity and
Distress Intolerance

*The one who does most to avoid suffering is, in
the end, the one who suffers most.*

THOMAS MERTON

*Although the people of God meet with many seeming rubs and set-backs
on their way to heaven, which are like contrary winds to a ship; yet they
are from the day of their conversion to the day of their complete
salvation, never out of a trade-wind's way to heaven.*

JOHN FLAVEL

IN THIS CHAPTER, I focus on impaired emotional clarity[1] and distress
intolerance,[2] including their foundations in the secular psychology literature, link
to mental disorders, and relationship with mindfulness meditation. In addition, I
discuss impaired emotional clarity and distress intolerance in the context of the
Christian tradition, offering a biblical understanding and intervention strategies.
Along the way, you will be able to track these transdiagnostic processes with a daily
log, as well as practice a wide variety of meditation strategies grounded in several

---

[1]Vine and Aldao (2014).
[2]Zvolensky et al. (2010).

bodies of Christian spiritual writings (e.g., desert, Orthodox, Jesuit), all in an effort to recognize God's providential care in the midst of the full gamut of emotions—both "positive" and "negative"—that you experience in this fallen, broken world.

Throughout the chapter, more specifically, I explain each exercise, offer transcripts for ease of use, provide corresponding journaling exercises to reflect on each practice, and include one audio recording to listen to, should you prefer to do so. Ultimately, my aim in this chapter is to help you gain more insight into the relationship between impaired emotional clarity and distress intolerance, focusing on God (including his providential care) and deepening your contentment in, and communion with, him. As a reminder, the four-step process throughout this workbook involves (1) noticing, (2) shifting, (3) accepting, and (4) acting, cultivating a spiritual awareness of God's active, loving presence in the here-and-now.

IMPAIRED EMOTIONAL CLARITY: A SECULAR PSYCHOLOGICAL UNDERSTANDING

In daily life, the ability to connect to, and understand, our emotional world is helpful for an array of tasks, such as managing our emotions, maintaining well-being, giving life meaning and purpose, navigating relationships, and making life decisions.[3] On a basic level, our emotions serve as signals, revealing salient information to us on a minute-by-minute basis about objects within our awareness.[4] As a quick review, sadness reveals that we have experienced the loss of something valuable, fear alerts us to present-moment danger, anxiety points to an anticipated future catastrophe, frustration reveals an unmet expectation, anger reveals a perceived injustice, and guilt illuminates that we have wronged someone else and need to reconcile with the person we have offended. Therefore, there is a cognitive component to our emotional world—our emotions offer us meaning. To be sure, in being able to identify and understand these emotional experiences, we are in a better position to make effective decisions, deepen relationships, and pursue salient goals in life.

However, impaired emotional clarity involves struggling to pinpoint the emotions we are feeling at any given time.[5] In other words, we may have a hard time identifying, understanding, and differentiating emotions like sadness, fear, anxiety, anger, guilt, or shame. More specifically, impaired emotional clarity involves (1) struggling to make sense of our current feelings, (2) having a hard time accurately identifying and distinguishing our current feelings, and (3) confusion about our

---

[3]Lischetzke and Eid (2017); Park and Naragon-Gainey (2019).
[4]Elliott (2006); Hareli and Hess (2012); Knabb, Johnson, Bates, and Sisemore (2019); Oatley and Johnson-Laird (1996).
[5]Vine and Aldao (2014).

current feelings.[6] When this happens, we may be unable to effectively manage the frequency or duration of difficult emotional experiences, given identifying basic emotions is a starting point for more long-term approaches to regulation.[7] To date, research has consistently revealed that impaired emotional clarity is linked to a range of psychiatric symptoms,[8] whereas mindfulness meditation may help with impaired emotional clarity.[9] Thus, strategies to better recognize emotions, categorize emotions, and understand their source is key for healthy psychological functioning.[10]

Impaired emotional clarity and psychopathology. In a study among college students, impaired emotional clarity was linked to symptoms of both depression and anxiety.[11] What is more, research has revealed that impaired emotional clarity is higher in women with major depressive disorder and social anxiety disorder in comparison to women without a mental disorder.[12] With this body of research in mind, we can see that identifying and understanding our emotions is important for psychological health in daily life, whereas struggling to do so can result in added suffering. As a result, strategies are needed to gain clarity when it comes to our inner experiences.

Impaired emotional clarity and mindfulness meditation. Since emotional clarity is important for psychological health and impaired emotional clarity is linked to psychopathology, researchers have investigated a variety of interventions to improve emotional clarity. In recent years, mindfulness-based approaches have emerged in the psychology literature, given their emphasis on gaining insight into the inner workings of a variety of psychological processes (e.g., thinking, feeling). Stated differently, mindfulness meditation may help practitioners to develop the ability to nonjudgmentally and flexibly "hold in awareness" whatever inner experiences emerge in the present, rather than attempt to numb the pain with avoidance strategies.[13] Theoretically, then, "open awareness" meditative practices,[14] such as mindfulness meditation, may be a useful starting point for developing key skills for improving emotional clarity. Research-wise, although further empirical investigations are still needed, a recent review of seventeen studies revealed that mindfulness-based approaches may be helpful for improving impaired emotional clarity.[15]

---

[6]Gohm and Clore (2000); Gratz and Roemer (2004).
[7]Gratz and Roemer (2004); Vine and Aldao (2014).
[8]Vine and Aldao (2014).
[9]Cooper et al. (2018).
[10]Thompson et al. (2017).
[11]Vine and Aldao (2014).
[12]Thompson et al. (2017).
[13]Kabat-Zinn (1994).
[14]Kok et al. (2013).
[15]Cooper et al. (2018).

Ultimately, because mindfulness meditation can help practitioners to (1) develop an attitude of openness and nonjudgment toward emotions, and (2) maintain an awareness of present-moment experiences, mindfulness-based interventions may hold promise for increasing emotional clarity among those who struggle to identify and understand their emotional world.[16] Yet, from a Christian perspective, it is important to better understand what the Bible says about our God-given emotions, including the relationship between our feelings and Christian spiritual practices.

IMPAIRED EMOTIONAL CLARITY: A CHRISTIAN UNDERSTANDING

From a Christian perspective, living in a fallen world means we are vulnerable to all sorts of suffering, including mental disorders that impair daily living. With emotional disorders (e.g., major depressive disorder, panic disorder, social anxiety disorder, generalized anxiety disorder), a main feature is impairment in the ability to manage emotions, including sadness, fear, and anxiety, along with efforts to avoid these unpleasant experiences.[17] Along the way, as noted above, we may struggle to identify and understand our emotional world, which can have a negative impact on our functioning.

Unfortunately, as Christians, we sometimes develop an unhealthy relationship with our emotions, believing we should only experience "positive" emotional states, such as joy and peace, and avoid "negative" emotional states, including sadness and fear. Of course, the fruit of the Spirit (e.g., love, joy, peace; Gal 5:22-23) are foundational to Christian living. Yet, in that we live in a fallen, broken world, we may also experience "negative" emotions from time to time, such as those mentioned previously. When this happens, how are we, as Christians, to make sense of these experiences, including God's presence within them? Are our "negative" emotions helpful to us? Do "negative" emotions somehow serve as signals, offering us vital cognitive, physiological, and motivational information to effectively navigate the roads of life,[18] with God at the center? Can we "find God in *all* things," as the famous Jesuit saying goes, including painful feelings? Similarly, like the Puritans, can we find God in "afflictive providences," such as our most difficult emotions?[19] To answer these questions, I would like to make the case that the Bible offers us a glimpse into the God-given role of our emotions, including both "positive" and "negative" emotional experiences in daily life.

Impaired emotional clarity and the Bible. One way to conceptualize emotions, whether perceived to be "negative" (e.g., anger, anxiety, fear, sadness, guilt) or "positive"

---

[16]Cooper et al. (2018).
[17]Barlow et al. (2011).
[18]Krystal (1988); Stolorow et al. (1995).
[19]Cosby (2012).

(e.g., joy, happiness), is to view them as God-given signals.[20] In other words, our emotions are physiologically grounded, with cognitive and motivational themes,[21] alerting us to a range of salient experiences about a particular object.[22] More specifically, our emotions include bodily states, revealing the need to take action; attitudes surrounding a particular situation, relationship, or topic; and deeper concerns in the immediate moment about what is most salient.[23] Or, put more succinctly, our emotions help us to discern what is important and motivate us to take action.[24] Within both the Old and New Testament, references to the heart offer an integrated understanding of humans, with both cognitive and emotional components.[25]

Our emotions, moreover, are spiritual, not just physiological and psychological.[26] In fact, there are a wide variety of emotions—perceived to be both "positive" and "negative"—documented in the pages of the Bible. For instance, God experienced a range of emotions throughout Scripture, including delight (Is 42:1)[27] and sadness (Gen 6:6).[28] The psalmists expressed heartfelt emotions, such as joy (Ps 95) and sadness (Ps 42), as did Jesus (Jn 11:35), and the fruit of the Spirit include emotions such as love and joy (Gal 5:22-23).

With these examples, we can clearly see that emotions convey rich meaning throughout Scripture. For instance, emotions such as joy are plainly expressed in the context of dancing and worshiping, whereas sadness is often linked to weeping, wailing, lamenting, and mourning.[29] Conversely, when we struggle to understand our emotions, we may fail to recognize the signals that God is sending our way. To be sure, if God is governing all of life's events, and we can "find God in all things," consistent with the famous Jesuit saying, God is communicating to us in even our most difficult emotional experiences.[30] Sadness, as an example, can serve as a signal that tells us we have lost something we value. If God is present in our experience of sadness, he may be revealing to us that we are attempting to cling to something we really need to be letting go of, like the rich young ruler (Mk 10: 17-27). Or, in our frustration, God may be revealing to us that we have an unmet expectation we need to surrender to him. To offer one more example, with anxiety, God might be helping us to see that we are anticipating some sort of danger ahead and

---

[20]Knabb, Johnson, Bates, and Sisemore (2019).
[21]Krystal (1988).
[22]Elliott (2006).
[23]Roberts (2007).
[24]Roberts (2007).
[25]Elliott (2006).
[26]Roberts (2007).
[27]Borgman (2009).
[28]Borgman (2009).
[29]Elliott (2006).
[30]Saint-Jure and Colombiere (1983).

need to instead trust in him for protection and comfort. In sum, in each of these emotional experiences, we may struggle to recognize that God is communicating to us, especially if we expect that the Christian life consists solely of the pursuit of pleasure and avoidance of pain. But how, exactly, can we cultivate emotional clarity in order to better discern God's active, loving presence in daily life?

Impaired emotional clarity and Christian meditation, prayer, and contemplation. Although Christian meditation, prayer, and contemplation for emotional clarity will be presented in more detail in the second half of this chapter, for now, I would like to offer an introduction on the role that these classic Christian practices can play in helping us to better understand our emotional world, along with God's active, loving presence, as we learn to endure psychological pain with hope and stability.

With Christian meditation, we may ponder a short passage in Scripture in order to connect to a certain emotion, such as joy, sadness, and so forth. Meditating on the Psalms, for instance, can help us to deepen our awareness of the seasons of life, whether periods of thanksgiving and celebration; loss, hardship, and suffering; or surprise and renewed hope.[31] In meditating on these powerful words, we are able to connect to our own inner world, given many of the psalms capture common human experiences throughout the lifespan.

As another example, we may utilize prayer as a way to converse with God, using our God-given senses (i.e., sight, sound, taste, touch, smell) to become part of a story in Scripture.[32] In this practice, referred to as "prayer of the senses" in the Jesuit tradition, we have the opportunity to feel our way into a passage in the Bible, joining God as we experience him by conversing with him in the present moment. Along with the prayer of the senses, we can practice the examen, also from the Jesuit tradition, which involves delving into the inner world, wherein a variety of painful emotions reside (e.g., guilt, shame, sadness).[33] With the examen, we engage in five steps—thanking God for his enduring love, asking God to reveal himself to us, reflecting on our psychological experiences throughout the day and recognizing God's presence within them, asking for God's forgiveness, and preparing for the day ahead by attempting to discern God's will for tomorrow—which can help us to recognize God's presence in each and every moment of the day.[34]

Finally, contemplation can help us to learn to simply rest in God, regardless of the difficult inner experiences that are emerging in the here-and-now. By slowing down to focus on God with loving attention, we are cultivating a deeper appreciation for

---

[31]Brueggemann (1984).
[32]Endean (1990); Hansen (2012).
[33]Gallagher (2006); Ignatian Spirituality (n.d.).
[34]Gallagher (2006); Ignatian Spirituality (n.d.).

his active presence, which means we can relate differently to unpleasant emotions because God is by our side. In slowly reciting a prayer word (e.g., "Jesus," "God"), we develop the habit of noticing painful emotions, then gently shifting our focus to God, over and over again.[35] With time, we begin to gain insight into the reality that our emotions cannot harm us, as well as the stability to endure them, given they are temporary and God is with us to handle them.[36] Before turning to the various exercises in this chapter, though, I would like us to review another transdiagnostic process that resides under the umbrella of "problems with affect," distress intolerance.

DISTRESS INTOLERANCE: A SECULAR PSYCHOLOGICAL UNDERSTANDING

In recent years, the psychology literature has increasingly focused on distress intolerance as a transdiagnostic process. With distress tolerance, we are able to endure emotional or physical states that are perceived to be negative; on the other hand, distress intolerance involves the struggle to withstand these types of discomfort.[37] More specifically, there may be several types of intolerance of distress, including intolerance of uncertainty and ambiguity, frustration and negative emotional states, and physical discomfort and pain.[38]

With intolerance of uncertainty, we may have a hard time accepting an uncertain future,[39] holding negative views of uncertainty in and of itself (e.g., "Uncertainty is unfair and spoils everything"), along with its corresponding impact on the self and behavior.[40] In a similar vein, intolerance of ambiguity relates to the struggle to accept vague or complex situations, leading to increased emotional distress in these often-common scenarios.[41] For intolerance of frustration, we may have a hard time accepting unmet expectations and other goals in life, and intolerance of negative emotion involves struggling to accept inner distress.[42] Similar to challenges with enduring emotional pain, intolerance of physical sensations captures the inability to accept different types of physical discomfort (e.g., feeling dizzy or light-headed).[43]

In each of these struggles, we may be unwilling or unable to allow the distress to run its natural course, developing an unhealthy fear of the current or anticipated psychological experience and expectation that we should be free from it. In turn,

---

[35]Laird (2006).
[36]Laird (2006).
[37]Zvolensky et al. (2010).
[38]Zvolensky et al. (2010).
[39]Dugas and Robichaud (2007).
[40]Sexton and Dugas (2009, p. 176).
[41]Zvolensky et al. (2010).
[42]Zvolensky et al. (2010).
[43]Zvolensky et al. (2010).

we may choose to avoid the pain, which may make matters worse in the long run. Over time, we may become especially sensitive to discomfort, so much so that we are preoccupied with uncertainty, ambiguity, emotional distress, and physical discomfort, to the point of struggling to fulfill daily life obligations or maintain relationships. Overall, there is evidence to suggest that, although there may be several subtypes, including those mentioned above,[44] one general type of distress intolerance exists.[45] In fact, distress intolerance may be linked to a range of psychiatric symptoms and disorders.[46]

Distress intolerance and psychopathology. In recent research, results have revealed that distress intolerance is related to symptoms of depression and anxiety.[47] In addition, distress intolerance is associated with a greater likelihood of having a mood or anxiety disorder over the course of a lifetime.[48] In sum, these emerging results in the psychology literature suggest that the inability or unwillingness to withstand distressing emotional and physiological experiences is related to both psychiatric symptoms and disorders. As a result, researchers have started to investigate interventions to help those who struggle with distress intolerance, focusing on mindfulness meditation as a strategy for improving the ability to endure distress in life. With mindfulness, practitioners are cultivating nonjudgmental, present-moment awareness, which may allow them to relate differently to experiences of distress.

Distress intolerance and mindfulness meditation. Because mindfulness meditation helps practitioners to develop several key mental skills (e.g., attention, present-moment awareness, acceptance),[49] researchers have recently explored the use of mindfulness-based approaches for improving distress tolerance. As an example, university students learned a brief mindfulness exercise with several components (e.g., mindfulness of breathing), then completed a range of stress-inducing activities (e.g., placing a hand in a bucket of ice), with results revealing the mindfulness group was able to do a better job in persisting with the required task when compared to a control group.[50] To offer one more example, a study examining the effects of an eight-week mindfulness-based program for adults revealed that the mindfulness group outperformed the wait-list control group when examining improvements in distress tolerance.[51]

---

[44]Bebane et al. (2015).
[45]McHugh and Otto (2012).
[46]Leyro et al. (2010).
[47]Macatee et al. (2016).
[48]Bernstein et al. (2011).
[49]Feldman et al. (2007).
[50]Carpenter et al. (2019).
[51]Nila et al. (2016).

These accumulating results suggest that mindfulness-based approaches may be helpful for improving distress tolerance, possibly due to the aforementioned mental skills that are cultivated during formal practice. Yet, similar to prior discussions in this workbook, a Christian conceptualization of the problem (i.e., distress intolerance) and solution (i.e., a deeper communion with God through Christian meditation, prayer, and contemplation) may be at least somewhat different from the secular perspectives emanating from the psychology literature. Therefore, what follows is a brief discussion on a Christian view of distress intolerance, followed by several exercises to help you cultivate distress tolerance from within the Christian tradition.

DISTRESS INTOLERANCE: A CHRISTIAN UNDERSTANDING

Distress intolerance and the Bible. Throughout the pages of Scripture, biblical figures were tasked with enduring distress in the service of a greater purpose. For example, God called Moses to deliver an extremely difficult message to Pharaoh, then help rescue the Israelites from slavery in Egypt, despite likely being anxious about fulfilling this designated role and "slow of speech and tongue" (Ex 3–4). Also, Jesus' disciples were called to leave their old life behind to follow Jesus over the course of several years, learning from him, emulating him, and, ultimately, risking their life in the process (Mt 4:18-22; 16:24-26). Moreover, the apostle Paul suffered greatly to serve God (2 Cor 11:16-33). Finally, as the Suffering Servant (Is 53), Jesus yielded to God's will while on this planet, fulfilling the Father's purpose for him in the midst of extreme sorrow (Mt 26:38-39).

In each of these examples, God called his servants to withstand hardship and suffering in order to fulfill his purposes. In other words, they followed the will of God, despite the corresponding distress. Whether they were faced with uncertainty and ambiguity, frustration and emotional pain, or physical discomfort, they pressed forward with endurance and hope, since they had a final destination in mind.

Interestingly, the biblical equivalent of distress tolerance may be *hypomone*—used about thirty times in the New Testament—which is commonly translated as "patience," capturing the ability to endure suffering with hope, faith, joy, courage, and perseverance.[52] As Christians, we are able to endure with hope—*hypomone*—because we have a future glory, being face-to-face with God in heaven, in mind.[53] As noted in the previous chapter, for the early desert Christians staying in their cells, *hypomone* was paramount because God was with them.[54] Within this framework, they exercised patience and endurance, recognizing the importance

---

[52]Barclay (1974).
[53]Barclay (1974); Boersma (2018).
[54]Chryssavgis (2008).

of stability in their efforts to simply be with their inner world.[55] Conversely, when we try to escape the proverbial cell of the inner world through avoidance strategies, we may end up making matters worse, because there is nowhere to run and hide from our emotional experiences. As an anonymous early Christian stated, "If a trial comes upon you in the place where you live, do not leave that place when the trial comes. Wherever you go, you will find that what you are running from is there ahead of you."[56]

Distress intolerance and psychopathology among Christians. In the last several years, I have conducted several studies on the relationship between the ability to accept difficult experiences and other forms of psychological functioning among Christians. With a sample of Christian college students, I found a link between distress endurance—the ability to continue to press on to achieve what matters most in life in spite of distress[57]—and religious commitment and faith maturity.[58] Among a different sample of Christian college students, I found a relationship between experiential avoidance—the struggle to accept unpleasant inner experiences[59]—and symptoms of depression, anxiety, and stress.[60] Finally, with both college and community samples of Christian adults, I found an association between intolerance of uncertainty and worry.[61] With this correlational research, we can see that whether we accept or avoid life's distress can play a role in both psychological and spiritual functioning. Building on this understanding, I would like for us to explore the theoretical relationship between distress intolerance and Christian spiritual practices, before turning to some of the actual exercises in this chapter.

Distress intolerance and Christian meditation, prayer, and contemplation. To withstand the distress that naturally emerges on a daily basis in a fallen, broken world, Christian meditation, prayer, and contemplation can help us deepen our ability to fellowship with God and find contentment in him. In other words, although the pain of life may not fully go away, we can learn to press forward, tolerating our most difficult experiences because God is right by our side. In this relational understanding, we have a traveling companion on the treacherous roads of life, slowly walking home with God to our final destination—heaven—to be with him forever.[62]

---

[55]Paintner (2012).
[56]Paintner (2012, p. 23).
[57]Gamez et al. (2011).
[58]Knabb et al. (2014).
[59]Gamez et al. (2011).
[60]Knabb and Grigorian-Routon (2014).
[61]Knabb et al. (2017).
[62]Knabb and Bates (2020b).

For example, with meditation, we can ponder God's promises[63] in order to remind ourselves that he is with us in our most difficult moments. By reciting short passages in Scripture, we are able to notice our inner distress, then shift toward a more transcendent perspective as we walk with God through—not around—the experience. Moreover, with prayer, we can recite the name of Jesus, calling on him when we are wary of pressing on in order to experience his presence within the depths of our inner world.[64] Finally, with contemplation, we can learn to simply sit at the feet of Jesus, without needing to do anything, reminiscent of Mary in Luke's Gospel (Lk 10:38-42). Mary, representing the contemplative life, looked upon Jesus in the here-and-now, whereas Martha, capturing the active life, struggled to connect to the immediacy of the moment, erroneously prioritizing anxious activity.[65] Certainly, as Christians, we can learn to attend to God's presence from moment to moment with a simple, loving attentiveness, rather than engaging in driven behavior that fails to provide what we need.

Ultimately, with these Christian spiritual practices, we are learning to persevere with faith and hope, recognizing that God is leading us along the paths of life with his purpose in mind. In other words, in (1) noticing the different areas of distress we are struggling with in life, (2) shifting toward a more transcendent, spiritual reality, (3) accepting and enduring life's distress with hope because God is with us, and (4) fellowshiping with God and finding a deeper contentment in him, we are gradually learning to relate differently to distressing life experiences.

To offer an example of what this actually looks like, grounded in the research literature, I recently completed a pilot study among a dozen or so Christian adults who struggled with daily worry, targeting their intolerance of uncertainty to help them relate differently to a variety of difficult symptoms.[66] For eight weeks, these chronic worriers practiced Christian meditation, prayer, and contemplation, learning to shift from worrying to trusting in God's providential care in response to the uncertainties of daily life.[67] At the conclusion of the study, in general, participants reported a reduction in intolerance of uncertainty, worry, depression, anxiety, and stress.[68] Here, we can see that daily spiritual practices, anchored to the Christian tradition, can help us to relate differently to distress, especially when spending time with God through key spiritual disciplines. Now, I would like you to consolidate this understanding, then begin to practice monitoring your daily emotions, since simply noticing the fluctuations within your inner world is the first step in this workbook's four-step meditative practice.

---

[63]Byfield (2013).
[64]Gillet (1985).
[65]Butler (1926).
[66]Knabb et al. (2017).
[67]Knabb et al. (2017).
[68]Knabb et al. (2017).

IMPAIRED EMOTIONAL CLARITY, DISTRESS INTOLERANCE, AND GOD'S PROVIDENCE: AN INTEGRATED CHRISTIAN UNDERSTANDING

Taking the above review into consideration, our emotions are God-given signals that help us to better understand God's will for our lives. In fact, in returning to the third chapter of this workbook and the Heidelberg Catechism, if "all things come not by chance, but by [God's] fatherly hand,"[69] God is revealing himself from moment to moment in our full spectrum of emotional experiences, what the Puritans called "afflictive providences."[70] In a similar vein, in the Jesuit Tradition, one particular work, *Trustful Surrender to Divine Providence*, made the case that the "secret to peace and happiness" is recognizing and surrendering to God's providential care in all of life's occurrences, including our emotional struggles.[71] Ultimately, if "in all things God works for the good of those who love him" (Rom 8:28)[72] and if God's attributes include a unique combination of his perfect power, presence, love, and wisdom (i.e., the four "omnis"), we can trust that, in our emotional pain, God is (1) in control, (2) with us, (3) loving us, and (4) choosing the best possible outcome for us.

Understandably, though, because many of our emotions cause quite a bit of pain, we may end up viewing them in an adversarial manner, as experiences to eradicate. When this happens, we may rely on avoidance as an ineffective coping skill, striving to eliminate the very experiences that God is using to communicate with us. Yet, if God is the author of *all* events and his providential care extends to all of creation from moment to moment, our distressing experiences can help us to better understand his will for our life. Therefore, learning to (1) notice life's distress, (2) shift toward a broader, more transcendent understanding of life's distress, (3) accept life's distress because God is governing all of our experiences (in both the inner and outer world), and (4) act in life in a manner that is anchored to fellowshiping with God and finding a deeper contentment in him is key. As a first step, let us now turn to monitoring life's distress, practicing with a daily log in order to strengthen the ability to "see the forest for the trees," as the saying goes.

NOTICING YOUR FEELINGS: A DAILY LOG FOR EMOTIONAL CLARITY AND DISTRESS TOLERANCE

In this first exercise, you will be turning inward throughout the day for an entire week, learning to better identify and understand your emotional experiences. In particular, I would like you to especially try to notice when you are experiencing

---

[69]Ursinus (1852, pp. 146-47).
[70]Cosby (2012).
[71]Saint-Jure and Colombiere (1983).
[72]See also Flavel (1754).

more difficult emotions, such as sadness, fear, anxiety, anger, guilt, and shame. If possible, try to notice which emotions you experience most throughout the day, then attempt to understand the meaning behind each emotion, given your emotions serve as signals.

To begin, simply set aside a few minutes, several times per day, to slow down and ask yourself what you are feeling in the moment, as well as connect to any other type of distress (e.g., uncertainty, ambiguity, physical discomfort). Next, attempt to identify the meaning behind the emotion, since our emotions serve as God-given signals. Simple questions to connect to your emotions include the following: *What am I feeling right now? What thoughts am I having that are linked to the feeling and reveal its meaning? What might God be revealing to me in this feeling (or other type of distress)?* To get you started, I have filled in two examples. Feel free to use additional paper, if you need to.

At the end of the week, see if you can notice any specific patterns in your emotional world, along with the possible meaning and God's role in the experiences. Also, reflect on whether you have been able to get better at slowing down to simply notice your feelings, as well as the meaning behind them, since they function as signals, especially in our relationships with other people[73] and God. With this first step, noticing, in mind, I would like to transition to the rest of the four-step meditative process with an exercise—lamenting to God with the Psalms—that can help you to express your emotions to him during the most difficult seasons of life.

"COME QUICKLY, LORD, TO HELP ME": LAMENTING TO GOD FOR EMOTIONAL CLARITY AND DISTRESS TOLERANCE

Among the early desert Christians, the Psalms were often memorized and recited as a way to manage compulsive thoughts.[74] More specifically, these monks of the desert would meditate on short passages in Scripture as a psychological strategy for responding to inner temptations, which often emanated from troubling memories throughout the day.[75] Rather than trying to fully rid themselves of their most difficult thoughts and memories, however, these desert dwellers would shift their mind toward the words of the Bible, dually focusing on Scripture and calling on God to help them as they surrendered themselves to him.[76]

The early desert Christians often meditated on Psalms 70:1 for this very purpose: "Hasten, O God, to save me; come quickly, LORD, to help me."[77] In fact, according

---

[73]Hareli and Hess (2012).
[74]Gillingham (2012).
[75]Burton-Christie (1993).
[76]Burton-Christie (1993).
[77]Burton-Christie (1993).

EMOTIONAL CLARITY AND DISTRESS TOLERANCE LOG

Day of the Week	Time of Day	Type of Thinking	Specific Thought Content
Monday	1:00 P.M.	Sadness/ thoughts of worthlessness	I'm really sad that I didn't get the promotion at work and experiencing a sense of worthlessness, which tells me the promotion was really important to me and wrapped up in who I am as a person. Maybe God is revealing to me that I need to rely on him for my self-worth.
Monday	5:30 P.M.	Anxiety/ thoughts of uncertainty	I'm experiencing a lot of anxiety right now, which tells me I'm uncertain about whether or not my boss will fire me next week. Maybe God is helping me learn to lean on, and trust in, him when I am uncertain.

Day of the Week	Time of Day	Type of Thinking	Specific Thought Content

to one of these desert monks, Abba Isaac, Psalm 70:1 captured quite the amalgam of human experiences and emotions, such as reaching for God in the midst of daily struggles, humility, watchfulness and attentiveness, a realization of human weakness, confidence that God hears Christians' plea for help, a sense of safety, and love for God, among others.[78] In other words, in response to our tempting, compulsive thoughts (e.g., worry, self-doubt) and corresponding emotional pain (e.g., sadness, fear, anxiety, guilt, shame), we are to reach for God, crying out to him for help as we acknowledge our utter powerlessness and total dependency. Throughout Christian history, to be sure, a common practice in monastic life has been to meditate on the Psalms throughout the day, linking them with prayer.[79] In sum, in this daily practice, we are (1) focusing on God and (2) connecting to a range of human emotions, all in an effort to deepen our fellowship with him.

Within this famous book of the Bible, more precisely, psalms of lament document "seasons of disorientation," capturing the emotional pain that these biblical writers experienced in life.[80] In many of these lament psalms, an overarching, multi-step pattern emerges, including (1) a plea to God to help remedy the present state, and (2) praise toward God, thanking him for listening to the petition.[81] In more detail, the psalmist is (1) personally calling on God, (2) presenting a specific problem to God, (3) asking God to intervene, (4) expressing the reason for the request, (5) confidently stating God has heard the request, and (6) concluding by thanking and praising God, regardless of whether the often-dire situation has been resolved.[82] But what, exactly, allows these biblical writers to psychologically shift from the immediacy of the problem toward praising God, even though the external circumstances may not have changed?

First, the psalmists express a range of heartfelt emotions, which may have helped them to experience catharsis as they pivoted from the "complaint" to the "praise" phase of each psalm.[83] Second, the bridge between "complaint" and "praise" may have involved some sort of recognition of God's sovereignty, based on God's promises in the Bible (see, e.g., Jer 30:10-11),[84] capturing the safety and comfort that can only come from God. Building on this two-step process, I would like us to review one particular psalm, then practice lamenting to God, since expressing our problems to God and thanking him can allow us to gain emotional clarity and distress tolerance.

---

[78]Cassian (1997).
[79]Dyer (1999).
[80]Brueggemann (1984).
[81]Brueggemann (1984).
[82]Brueggemann (1984).
[83]Brueggemann (1984).
[84]Brueggemann (1984).

LAMENTING TO GOD: AN EXERCISE

In this exercise, you will read a lament psalm, then practice writing your own lament to God. To start, slowly read through the below passage, before lamenting to God with a current situation in your own life:

> How long, LORD? Will you forget me forever?
>> How long will you hide your face from me?
> How long must I wrestle with my thoughts
> and day after day have sorrow in my heart?
>> How long will my enemy triumph over me?
> Look on me and answer, LORD my God.
>> Give light to my eyes, or I will sleep in death,
> and my enemy will say, "I have overcome him,"
>> and my foes will rejoice when I fall.
> But I trust in your unfailing love;
>> my heart rejoices in your salvation.
> I will sing the LORD's praise,
>> for he has been good to me. (Ps 13)

In this famous psalm, notice that the author, David, personally calls on God ("LORD"), offering a problem ("Will you forget me forever?"), petition ("Look on me and answer, LORD my God"), reason for the request ("I will sleep in death," "my foes will rejoice when I fall"), and gratitude ("I will sing the LORD's praise"). David combined emotional clarity and the acknowledgment of distress with gratitude to God, something that is difficult to do. Yet, his sorrow seemed to be offering him a better understanding of his immediate experience—feeling alone and abandoned by God—which helped him go to God with his request for God's light. In fact, his emotional pain may have served as a catalyst for boldly reaching to God, then thanking God for God's "unfailing love," "salvation," and goodness. Ultimately, David modeled the healthy expression of emotions, which can help us to dually achieve catharsis and commune with God, despite the inevitable distress that naturally emanates from our fallen, broken state. To offer a "complaint" and "praise," to be sure, is about recognizing the role that our emotional world plays in drawing us closer to God when we need him most. In other words, in times of difficulty, we do not want to "cut off the branch we are sitting on," as the saying goes. Rather, we want to walk with God in the midst of psychological suffering, recognizing he is our source of hope and salvation on the treacherous and unpredictable roads of life.

Now that you have reviewed an example, if possible, work on writing your own lament to God, focusing on exploring a recent problem as the "complaint," then offering gratitude to God as a form of "praise."[85] In doing so, you are cultivating the

---

[85]Adapted from Brueggemann (1984).

LAMENTING TO GOD

Step	Lament
Situation	
Provide details on the who, where, when, what, and why of the situation.	
"Complaint" to God	
Call out to God by name.	
Provide God with the details of the problem.	
Ask for God's help.	
Offer the reason for the request.	
"Praise" to God	
Acknowledge that God has heard you in your complaint and request.	
Thank God for his perfect love and presence, praising him for being with you during this difficult time, regardless of the outcome.	

ability to (1) understand your emotions as signals that provide vital information about your current situation and relationship with God and (2) tolerate distress, given God is right by your side and you are thanking him for his loving presence.

After completing the exercise, journal for a few minutes, attempting to answer the following questions:

- What was it like to lament to God? What were the benefits? What were the limitations?

- What was it like to connect to your emotions in your time with God? What were the benefits? The limitations?

- How well were you able to lament to God? Were you able to gain emotional clarity and cultivate distress tolerance?

- What, if anything, got in your way? Were you able to overcome the obstacles? If so, how? If not, why not?

- How, if at all, can practicing these steps help you with emotional clarity and distress tolerance as you move through the rest of your day?

- How, if at all, can practicing these steps help you to accept God's loving presence, minute by minute, and act in a manner that is anchored to fellowshiping with, and finding contentment in, him as you carry out your day?

_____

_____

_____

_____

_____

_____

_____

_____

_____

_____

_____

_____

_____

THE "INVOCATION OF THE NAME": CALLING ON THE NAME OF JESUS FOR EMOTIONAL CLARITY AND DISTRESS TOLERANCE

In the New Testament, Jesus taught his followers to pray in his name (Jn 14:13-14). Therefore, over the last two millennia, Christians have faithfully called on Jesus' name to help them with a variety of struggles in daily life. As a spiritual practice, Christians can slowly and deliberately recite the name of Jesus, either formally in solitude and silence or informally during a variety of tasks throughout the day.[86] In doing so, as Christians, we are surrendering our whole self to God, reciting Jesus' name within the depths of our being.[87] In other words, we are asking Jesus to be with us in our inner world, depending on him for comfort because we trust in his ability to soothe our wounds in our time of need.

In the Eastern Orthodox tradition, calling on the name of the Jesus serves as the foundation for the Jesus Prayer: "Lord Jesus Christ, Son of God, have mercy on me."[88] Although there are different versions of this famous prayer, reciting "Jesus" is the simplest form.[89] By calling on Jesus' name and requesting his mercy, we are asking him to console us in our vulnerable, broken state. Here, the Greek word for mercy, *eleos*, means to direct compassion and kindness to someone who is suffering, with a similar Greek word, *elaion*, meaning olive oil.[90] Olive oil in Jesus' time was used for healing wounds; thus, in Eastern Orthodox Christianity, asking for Jesus' mercy is to ask for his soothing comfort.[91] In the context of our emotional world, we can call on the name of Jesus to be with us when we are struggling with difficult feelings, such as sadness, fear, anxiety, anger, guilt, and shame.

Indeed, the medieval author Bernard of Clairvaux powerfully advocated for calling on the name of Jesus with the following:

> Does one of us feel sad? Let the name of Jesus come into his heart, from there let it spring to his mouth, so that shining like the dawn it may dispel all darkness and make a cloudless sky. Does someone fall into sin? Does his despair even urge him to suicide? Let him but invoke this life-giving name and his will to live will be at once renewed. . . . And where is the man, who, terrified and trembling before impending peril, has not been suddenly filled with courage and rid of fear by calling on the strength of that name? Where is the man who, tossed on the rolling seas of doubt, not quickly find certitude by recourse to the clarity of Jesus' name? Was ever a man so discouraged, so beaten down by afflictions, to whom the sound of this name did not bring new resolve? In short, for all the ills and disorders to which

---

[86]Gillet (1985).
[87]Gillet (1985).
[88]Ware (1986).
[89]Gillet (1985).
[90]Strong (2001b).
[91]Ware (2014).

flesh is heir, this name is medicine. . . . For when I name Jesus I set before me a man who is meek and humble of heart, kind, prudent, chaste, merciful, flawlessly upright and holy in the eyes of all; and this same man is the all-powerful God whose way of life heals me, whose support is my strength.[92]

Jesus' name is psychological and spiritual medicine for our soul, soothing us in our time of need. If this is the case, we can learn to better understand our emotional world, accepting unpleasant inner experiences in the process because Jesus is present.

Interestingly, in the mindfulness-based stress reduction (MBSR) program, the body scan is used to help practitioners relate differently to difficult psychological experiences, including emotional pain.[93] With the body scan, practitioners are quite literally scanning their body over a period of time—from the toes to the head—breathing into each bodily region, then "letting go" as a sort of "purification" or "detoxification" process.[94] As a mindfulness-based exercise, the aim of the body scan, of course, is to accept whatever inner experiences (e.g., thoughts, feelings, sensations) emerge in the present moment, cultivating an attitude of nonjudgmental, curious "non-striving."[95] Over time, this approach can help practitioners to be more comfortable in their own skin, as well as lessen the tendency to avoid unpleasant feelings and sensations. Along the way, practitioners are learning to accept, with compassion, whatever emerges, leaning into the experience in order to mindfully rest in the present moment. Of course, because mindfulness comes from the Buddhist tradition and lacks a relational conceptualization of a personal God in the here-and-now, a Christian-distinctive alternative incorporates Jesus Christ, who holds everything together and has reconciled us with God (Col 1:15-20).

As a Christian-sensitive replacement, then, we can learn to be with our most difficult emotions and sensations because Jesus is at the center, soothing and comforting us with his enduring, perfect love and unending, merciful compassion. To be certain, because Jesus lived a fully human life and understands our vulnerabilities, he is a trustworthy companion as we learn to accept our inner world with a newfound courage and hopeful perseverance (Heb 4:14-16). Ultimately, instead of accepting the emotions and sensations that emanate from our body for merely pragmatic purposes (e.g., the alternative, avoidance, does more harm than good in the long run), we can learn to breathe in and out as we recognize Jesus' soothing, comforting presence in our bodily experiences. Certainly, if he is psychological and spiritual medicine for our pain (as Bernard of Clairvaux revealed) and olive oil for our deeper wounds (as explicated by the Eastern Orthodox tradition), we can get into the habit of recognizing his presence within the inner world.

---

[92]Bernard (2016, p. 72).
[93]Kabat-Zinn (2013).
[94]Kabat-Zinn (2013).
[95]Kabat-Zinn (2013).

THE "INVOCATION OF THE NAME": AN EXERCISE

For this next exercise,[96] try to set aside ten minutes, finding a quiet environment that is free from distractions. During this time, you will be practicing a three-step process as you slowly scan your body with an attitude of acceptance, nonjudgment, and compassion: (1) breathe in Jesus' presence in the here-and-now, inviting him into the center of whatever emotion or sensation emerges by pairing the name Jesus with your in-breath; (2) breathe out whatever emotion or sensation you experience, recognizing that Jesus is in control and offering you his loving compassion and soothing comfort in the present moment, by pairing the act of letting go with your out-breath; and (3) whenever a distracting thought emerges, simply return to the exercise, breathing in Jesus' soothing presence, then letting go of whatever emotion or sensation emerges. If you are able, lay on the ground or a comfortable bed, then slowly complete the following steps (offered in more detail):

1. First, with your eyes closed, say a brief prayer to God, asking Jesus to be with you in this very moment, offering you his perfect compassion as a psychological ointment for your most difficult emotions and sensations.

2. Second, begin to notice that you are breathing, recognizing that God is giving you the gift of breath in this very moment, with no effort of your own. Just notice your breath cycle with gratitude and awe, without attempting to do anything else.

3. Third, start to breathe into the various regions of your body, one at a time, imagining that Jesus is present to soothe you, no matter what emotion or sensation arises. To do so, slowly say the name Jesus as you breathe in. For example, you may want to start with your left foot, envisioning that Jesus is with you to provide comfort to this region of your body. Rather than necessarily taking away the sensation, though, he is offering you his presence, which means you can endure whatever emerges in this very moment. As another example, when you get to your chest region, breathe in Jesus' presence to whatever emotion emerges, imagining that he is at the center. Continue with this scanning of the body, slowly going over (and breathing into) each region with an awareness that Jesus is present, offering you his loving kindness and mercy.

4. Fourth, after breathing into each region, combining the in-breath with Jesus' merciful presence, breathe out by imagining you are letting go of the experience by handing it over to him. As you breathe out, only Jesus remains, who is soothing and comforting you in the moment. In this process, imagine that Jesus is providing psychological ointment for your soul.

---

[96]Adapted from Bernard of Clairvaux (2016); Gillet (1985); Kabat-Zinn (2013).

5. Fifth, continue to practice this exercise for the full ten minutes, breathing into the designated region of your body and imagining Jesus is right there, at the center, then accepting whatever emotion or sensation emerges and letting go by giving control to Jesus. Overall, imagine that he is soothing and comforting your experiences, offering medicine and olive oil, psychologically speaking, to your present distress.

6. Sixth, say a prayer to God, thanking him for his loving presence during this activity and asking him to be with you throughout the rest of your day.

After completing the exercise, journal for a few minutes, attempting to answer the following questions:

- What was it like to breathe in Jesus' presence into the emotion or sensation, then breathe out by letting go and handing over the experience to him? What were the benefits? The limitations?

- How well were you able to accept your emotions and sensations during the exercise?

- What, if anything, got in your way? Were you able to overcome the obstacles? If so, how? If not, why not?

- How, if at all, can inviting Jesus into your emotions and sensations help you with emotional clarity and distress tolerance as you move through the rest of your day?

- How, if at all, can breathing in Jesus' presence help you to accept his loving action, minute by minute, and act in a manner that is anchored to fellow-shiping with, and finding contentment in, him as you carry out your day?

THE PRAYER OF THE SENSES: USING SCRIPTURE FOR EMOTIONAL CLARITY AND DISTRESS TOLERANCE

In the Jesuit tradition, the prayer of the senses is included in Ignatius Loyola's *Spiritual Exercises*, employing several overarching steps to help Christians experientially converse with God and discern his will:[97]

1. Pray to God, asking him to be present during the exercise and reveal his will.

2. Use our God-given senses to feel our way into a chosen biblical story.

3. With the five senses, converse with Jesus in the biblical story by asking a salient question and waiting on an answer, paying particular attention to both the pleasant (i.e., "consolations") and unpleasant (i.e., "desolations") emotions that emerge.

4. Pray to God in order to conclude the exercise.

More specifically, this prayer involves using each of the five senses to literally embed ourselves in a biblical story (commonly a Gospel account of Jesus' life so as to directly interact with him), starting with imagining what the scene might look like with our sense of sight (e.g., the faces and clothing of the biblical figures, the surrounding landscape), followed by imagining the possible sounds with our sense of sound (e.g., comments from biblical figures, sounds in the environment) and smells and tastes with our senses of smell and taste.[98] Finally, we are to use our sense of touch to imagine what it might be like to "[embrace] and [kiss] the places where these persons tread and sit."[99] This process ends with us asking Jesus an important question, anchored to our deeper feelings (i.e., consolations and desolations) that reflect the current status of our relationship with him, then waiting for his reply.[100] To be sure, an important part of this prayer involves relying on perceived "positive" (e.g., joy, happiness) and "negative" (e.g., sadness, fear) emotions in our exchange with Jesus, which can reveal insights into our relationship with him, given he is active and present "in all things."[101]

Ultimately, this prayer is meant to bring to life our interactions with biblical stories, especially as we feel what it might be like to converse with characters in the text.[102] Along the way, we are emotionally and physically experiencing the designated narrative in Scripture, not just studying the Bible in an abstract, detached

---

[97]Adapted from Endean (1990); Ivens (1998); Hansen (2012).
[98]Ivens (1998).
[99]Ivens (1998, p. 98).
[100]Endean (1990).
[101]Endean (1990); Manney (2011).
[102]Hansen (2012).

manner.[103] As we use our God-given imagination to experience the Gospels in new ways, we are striving to love and follow Jesus in the here-and-now.[104]

To apply this prayer to emotional clarity and distress tolerance, we are interacting with God in the Gospels in fresh ways, recognizing that our emotions and senses can serve as important signals in our time spent with him. What is more, we are learning to endure difficult inner experiences, given Jesus is with us and revealing his will for our life. Over time, we are recognizing that God is active and present "in all things," as the Jesuit saying goes, including our emotional world. As a result, rather than attempting to disavow these desolations, we are cultivating the ability to locate God's will in them.[105] With this understanding in mind, I would like for us to turn to an actual example from the Gospels in order to develop greater emotional clarity and distress tolerance.

THE PRAYER OF THE SENSES: AN EXERCISE

In this ten-minute exercise,[106] you will be imagining that you are joining Jesus on the Mount of Olives, shortly before his crucifixion (Lk 22:39-44). Find a quiet environment, free from distractions, sitting in a supportive chair. Close your eyes, resting your hands comfortably in your lap with your palms faced upward to symbolize receptivity and acceptance of God's will. Now, follow along with the below steps:

1. First, say a brief prayer to God, asking him to be with you during this time and reveal his will for you through the use of this Gospel account.

2. Second, slowly read through Jesus' interaction with God the Father in Luke's Gospel, imagining that you are there to observe this exchange:

   > Jesus went out as usual to the Mount of Olives, and his disciples followed him. On reaching the place, he said to them, "Pray that you will not fall into temptation." He withdrew about a stone's throw beyond them, knelt down and prayed, "Father, if you are willing, take this cup from me; yet not my will, but yours be done." An angel from heaven appeared to him and strengthened him. And being in anguish, he prayed more earnestly, and his sweat was like drops of blood falling to the ground. (Lk 22:39-44)

3. Third, use your senses to imagine that you are there with Jesus, experiencing his interaction with God the Father.

   a. *Sight*. Take a look around, using your sense of sight to envision the scenery. Are there trees around? What does the ground look like? Are there rocks,

---

[103]Hansen (2012).
[104]Endean (1990).
[105]Manney (2011).
[106]Adapted from Endean (1990); Ivens (1998); Hansen (2012); Knabb (2018); Knabb and Frederick (2017).

large or small? What about the surrounding landscape? Is the Mount of Olives well-lit or dark? Where is Jesus located? How is he dressed? What are you observing as you watch him pray to God the Father? Does he look upset and "in anguish"? Is he sweating because of the distress he is in? What other visible signs can you observe to capture his "anguish"?

b. *Sound.* Is it quiet? Are there noises in the background? Do you hear insects in the distance or other particular sounds reflective of night? As Jesus is praying to his Father, what do you hear in his voice? What is the pitch and pace? Are there pauses? What is Jesus' tone of voice? Is he emphasizing certain words? What is the volume?

c. *Smell.* What do you smell within the scene? Is there an aroma of fresh olives? Are there other distinct scents that you are experiencing in this famous scene?

d. *Touch.* Imagine what it might be like to touch the ground, with your feet firmly planted on the Mount of Olives. What might it be like to walk around? Are you leaning on a tree? If so, what is the texture?

4. Fourth, imagine what it might be like to walk up to Jesus after he has concluded his prayer to God the Father. Connect to what you are feeling in this very moment. Are you sad, afraid, or anxious? Are you at peace or content? What are these feelings revealing to you? As you start to talk to Jesus, what are you feeling as you notice that he is in anguish, clearly distressed about the task he is about to accomplish? In seeing Jesus in anguish, connect to your own feelings. What are they revealing to you? What is God telling you in this very moment, elucidated through your emotional experience?

5. Fifth, ask Jesus a question, rooted in what you are feeling in the present moment. With this step, try to dig deep, asking a question in a vulnerable manner that captures your willingness to yield to him and faithfully follow him on the roads of life.

6. Sixth, patiently wait for Jesus' reply. If possible, stay connected to your inner experiences, including the emotions that emerge in the present moment.

7. Seventh, pray to God to conclude the prayer, asking him to be with you throughout your day by revealing himself to you in both your perceived "positive" and "negative" emotions.

After completing the exercise, journal for a few minutes, attempting to answer the following questions:

- What was it like to imagine that you were with Jesus on the Mount of Olives, sharing the encounter with him and asking him a question that is tethered to your senses and emotional experiences? What were the benefits? The limitations?

- How well were you able to connect to (and accept) your emotions during the exercise?

- What, if anything, got in your way? Were you able to overcome the obstacles? If so, how? If not, why not?

- How, if at all, can embedding yourself in a Gospel story and conversing with Jesus, utilizing your senses and emotions, help you with emotional clarity and distress tolerance as you move through the rest of your day?

- How, if at all, can praying with your God-given five senses help you to accept his loving presence, minute by minute, and act in a manner that is anchored to fellowshiping with, and finding contentment in, him as you carry out your day?

THE EXAMEN: REFLECTING ON THE DAY FOR EMOTIONAL CLARITY AND DISTRESS TOLERANCE

In addition to the prayer of the senses in Ignatius's *Spiritual Exercises*, the examen is utilized to examine our day and "find God in all things," including *all* of the situations, conversations, and psychological experiences we have encountered over the course of a twenty-four-hour period of time, whether we perceive them to be major events or mundane activities. More specifically, with the examen, we take several distinct steps, all in an effort to dually (1) recognize the ways in which God is moving from moment to moment, revealing himself to us in our emotional experiences, and (2) assess how well we are following (and emulating) Jesus Christ:[107]

Give thanks. First, we thank God for his active, loving presence in daily life, cultivating a sense of gratitude for God's perfect, generous gifts from moment to moment.

Request God's presence. Second, we ask God to reveal himself to us, including his will, in *all* of our daily experiences, especially our emotions. In other words, we are requesting that God help us to view the world through his eyes, not our own.

Reflect on the day. Third, we reflect on our day, carefully reviewing our experiences to discern all the ways in which God is at the center.

Ask for forgiveness. Fourth, we ask God for forgiveness for coming up short in our efforts to emulate Jesus Christ. In this confession of our struggles throughout the day, we are remaining aware of the corresponding emotional distress, which should propel us to take action as we anticipate the next day. To be sure, because God loves us and forgives us, we need to accurately diagnose the problem, before looking ahead to the solution—pressing forward as we walk with Jesus and try to be more like him, step by step.

Look to tomorrow. Fifth, we look to the next day with hope and a renewed conviction to faithfully follow him wherever he asks us to go.

Threaded throughout the practice, we are connecting to both our perceived "positive" (i.e., consolations, such as joy and happiness) and "negative" (i.e., desolations, such as sadness, fear, anxiety, and anger) emotional experiences so as to better understand God's activity within them.[108]

With this understanding of the daily examen in mind, practice the exercise, attempting to "find God" in your emotional experiences and inner distress. In other words, whether you are struggling with uncertainty and ambiguity, frustration or other painful emotions, or physical pain, God is communicating to you, offering his loving presence at the center of these psychological difficulties. To reframe these struggles in this manner, to be sure, is no easy task. Yet, in considering the psychology literature—including impaired emotional clarity and distress intolerance as transdiagnostic vulnerabilities—learning to recognize your emotions and accept the inevitable distress that emanates from daily life is key. Beyond a purely secular understanding of the pragmatic benefits of emotional clarity and distress tolerance, though, you have a loving God who is with you, so much so that he took on human form, entered the world, and experienced the full gamut of human experiences in order to reconcile you to himself so you can walk with him in an enduring, unbreakable friendship.

---

[107]Adapted from Gallagher (2006); Ignatian Spirituality (n.d.); Manney (2011).
[108]Manney (2011).

THE EXAMEN: AN EXERCISE

For this exercise,[109] find a quiet environment, free of distractions, and sit up straight in a supportive chair. Try to set aside ten minutes, twice per day, to slowly move through the below five steps, paying particular attention to your consolations and desolations throughout the day, including God's role in your emotional experiences:

Give thanks. First, thank God for his active, loving presence in all of today's encounters, including his perfect grace and the abundance of gifts he has given to you. In this first step, also thank God for revealing himself to you with his gift of emotions, whether perceived to be "negative" or "positive." In other words, offer gratitude to God for communicating to you through your emotions, which serve as signals and help you to better discern his presence and will for your life.

Request God's presence. Second, ask God to reveal himself to you, including his will, in all of your emotional experiences throughout the day. Specifically, request that God help you to view the world through his eyes, not your own, doing so by illuminating his active, loving presence in both your "positive" (e.g., happiness, joy) and "negative" (e.g., sadness, fear, anxiety, anger, guilt, shame) emotions.

Reflect on the day. Third, reflect on your day, carefully reviewing the full spectrum of your emotional experiences to discern the ways in which God is at the center, revealing his presence and perfect will for your life. Pay particular attention to specific emotions (e.g., happiness, joy, sadness, fear, anger, guilt, shame) and what God may be revealing to you in them, attempting to interpret these emotions as signals that help you to better discern God's will for your moment-by-moment communion with him.

Ask for forgiveness. Fourth, ask God for forgiveness for coming up short in your efforts to emulate Jesus Christ. In other words, anchoring yourself to the awareness that you are already reconciled to God through your union with Jesus Christ and that God is offering you his perfect love in this very moment, try to identify the ways in which you have turned away from God throughout the day. In this time of acknowledgment, attempt to connect to the corresponding emotional distress, which serves as a useful signal for you to begin to follow Jesus Christ again as you look to the next day. Stated differently, since God loves you and forgives you, strive to accurately diagnose the problem before looking ahead to the solution—pressing forward as you walk with Jesus and try to be more like him, step by step.

Look to tomorrow. Fifth, look to the next day with hope and a renewed conviction to faithfully follow him wherever he asks you to go.

After completing the exercise, journal for a few minutes, attempting to answer the following questions:

---

[109]Adapted from Gallagher (2006); Ignatian Spirituality (n.d.); Manney (2011).

- What was it like to examine your day, paying particular attention to your emotions, including God's role in them? What were the benefits? The limitations?

- How well were you able to accept your emotions during the exercise?

- What, if anything, got in your way? Were you able to overcome the obstacles? If so, how? If not, why not?

- How, if at all, can "finding God in all things," including your emotional experiences, help you with emotional clarity and distress tolerance as you move through the rest of your day?

- How, if at all, can "finding God in all things," including your emotional experiences, help you to accept his loving presence, minute by minute, and act in a manner that is anchored to fellowshiping with, and finding contentment in, him as you carry out your day?

_____

_____

_____

_____

_____

_____

_____

_____

_____

_____

_____

_____

_____

_____

BREATH PRAYERS: PAIRING SCRIPTURE WITH BREATHING
FOR EMOTIONAL CLARITY AND DISTRESS TOLERANCE

Throughout Christian history, Christians have been meditating on Scripture and other sayings as a way to focus their mind on God. As revealed in the fourth chapter of this workbook, the Jesus Prayer—"Lord Jesus Christ, Son of God, have mercy on me"—is often recited in a slow and deliberate manner, aligning the first half of the prayer with the in-breath ("Lord Jesus Christ, Son of God") and the second half with the out-breath ("have mercy on me"). In doing so, we are attempting to fill ourselves with God's presence, then surrender to him and let go of everything short of God.[110] In this process, whenever another thought or feeling emerges, we simply notice the experience, then gently return to meditating on the words of the prayer. With this method, we are indirectly learning to relate differently to our thoughts and feelings, given we are noticing and shifting, over and over again.[111]

Beyond the Jesus Prayer, though, we can employ a wide variety of these breath prayers[112] in order to gain emotional clarity and distress tolerance, albeit indirectly. More specifically, with breath prayers, we are breathing in the name of God, followed by breathing out a request to God, often anchored to a short passage in Scripture.[113] With these steps, we are learning to call on God when we are struggling with emotional clarity and distress (e.g., uncertainty and ambiguity, frustration and other difficult emotions, physical pain),[114] then petition God to be with us in our struggles. Rather than asking for God to take away our pain, though, which may quickly lead to an ineffective avoidance strategy, we are developing the ability to lean on God in the midst of suffering, walking with him through life as we deepen our communion with, and contentment in, him.

In the context of the four-step process threaded throughout this workbook, we are (1) noticing when we are struggling with emotional clarity and distress intolerance, (2) shifting toward an awareness of God by calling on his name, (3) accepting his active, loving presence as a remedy for our inner and outer struggles, and (4) making decisions throughout the day that are Christlike because we are fellowshiping with God, moment by moment, and leaning on him for a more enduring contentment.

Possible examples of breath prayers for emotional clarity and distress tolerance include the following (slightly adapted from passages in Scripture):

- Psalm 3:3: "You, LORD, are a shield around me."

- Psalm 4:8: "For you alone, LORD, make me dwell in safety."

---

[110]Talbot (2013).
[111]Ware (2000).
[112]Calhoun (2015).
[113]Calhoun (2015).
[114]Zvolensky et al. (2010).

- Psalm 6:2: "Have mercy on me, Lord, for I am faint."
- Psalm 7:1: "Lord my God, I take refuge in you."
- Psalm 9:1: "I will give thanks to you, Lord, with all of my heart."
- Psalm 9:10: "For you, Lord, have never forsaken those who seek you."
- Psalm 10:14: "You, God, see the trouble of the afflicted."
- Psalm 12:7: "You, Lord, will keep the needy safe."
- Psalm 16:1: "Keep me safe, my God, for in you I take refuge."
- Psalm 18:1: "I love you, Lord, my strength."
- Psalm 70:1: "Hasten, O God, to save me."
- Psalm 70:1: "Come quickly, Lord, to help me."

As you can see from the above select passages, popular themes include God as a source of strength, who we can choose to love and thank in the midst of life's challenges. Although this is certainly not an exhaustive list, each passage is concise so you can breathe in God's name and breathe out your request to God. Or, you can simply give thanks to God in the midst of the difficult experience. In either case, you are learning to notice your emotional world, then invite God into the experience. In doing so, you are slowly developing the ability to recognize the full gamut of emotions you feel in any given moment, as well as connecting to a more transcendent understanding of the present, wherein God is at the center. Next, see if you can select your own breath prayer, then practice for ten minutes in order to gain emotional clarity and tolerate whatever distressing experiences emerge in your time spent with God.

BREATH PRAYERS: AN EXERCISE

For this exercise,[115] select a short passage in Scripture that includes God's name and a statement or request (e.g., "I love you, Lord, my strength," "Come quickly, Lord, to help me"). Try to set aside ten minutes, finding a quiet environment that is free from distractions. Sit in a supportive chair, with your hands gently resting on your lap and palms facing up to symbolize your willingness to surrender to God's providential care over the course of the next several minutes.[116] Once you are ready, slowly move through the below steps:

Notice. First, with your eyes closed, begin to notice you are breathing. In that God is governing all of life's events, he is giving you the "breath of life" (Gen 2:7) in this very moment. In other words, recognize that you do not need to control your

---

[115]Adapted from Calhoun (2015).
[116]You can also follow along with the audio recording (Track 2), found at ivpress.com/Knabb2.

breathing in any way, given God has provided you with an autonomic nervous system that naturally allows you to breathe in and out without any effort of your own.

Recite. Second, begin to slowly and gently recite your chosen verse, which may be a passage in Scripture that you have personally selected or one of the verses listed in the previous section. Get into the rhythm of softly repeating the verse in your mind, over and over again in a focused, deliberate manner.

Breathe. Third, start to align the verse with your breath, inhaling God's name, then exhaling your request. Over and over again, simply inhale God's name (e.g., LORD), recognizing that God is active and present within your inner world. In other words, he is sovereign over your emotions, whether you experience them as positive or negative. Then, simply exhale your request, letting go of your own efforts to unilaterally control your inner experiences. Right now, God is extending his providential care to even the impermanent, passing emotions that you are experiencing in this very moment.

Return. Fourth, whenever you get distracted by a thought or feeling, gently return to the breath prayer, anchored to the passage in Scripture, by inhaling God's name to call on him for his all-encompassing presence, then petition him with your request or praise. Continue this step—noticing and shifting—over and over again until the exercise has concluded.

Praise. Fifth, give praise to God, expressing gratitude for being with you in this time spent with him. Ask him to reveal himself to you throughout your day, helping you to recognize his providential care in each passing emotion and find a deeper contentment in him.

After completing the exercise, journal for a few minutes, attempting to answer the following questions:

- What was it like to call on God's name, then present your request (or a statement) to him, doing so in the midst of difficult emotional experiences? What were the benefits? The limitations?

- How well were you able to accept your emotions during the exercise?

- What, if anything, got in your way? Were you able to overcome the obstacles? If so, how? If not, why not?

- How, if at all, can calling on God's name and inviting him into your emotional experiences help you with emotional clarity and distress tolerance as you move through the rest of your day?

- How, if at all, can calling on God's name and inviting him into your emotional experiences help you to accept his loving presence, minute by minute, and act in a manner that is anchored to fellowshiping with, and finding contentment in, him as you carry out your day?

_____

_____

_____

_____

_____

_____

_____

_____

_____

_____

_____

_____

_____

THE TRUSTFUL SURRENDER OF EMOTIONS TO GOD: LETTING GO FOR EMOTIONAL CLARITY AND DISTRESS TOLERANCE

Returning to the Jesuit writing *Trustful Surrender to Divine Providence* that was mentioned earlier in this chapter, the authors centrally argue that the "secret to peace and happiness" is to recognize that God governs everything in the universe with his perfect will.[117] In fact, in this work, the authors argue that we are to even attribute the very life experiences, relational encounters, and inner struggles that we *cannot* make sense of to God, given he is infinitely powerful, wise, and loving.[118] More specifically, in *Trustful Surrender to Divine Providence*, we read the following:

> To remain indifferent to good fortune or to adversity by accepting it all from the hand of God without questioning, not to ask for things to be done as we would like them but as God wishes, to make the intention of all our prayers that God's will should be perfectly accomplished in ourselves and in all creatures is to find the secret of happiness and content.[119]

[117]Saint-Jure and Colombiere (1983).
[118]Saint-Jure and Colombiere (1983).
[119]Saint-Jure and Colombiere (1983, chap. 2, sect. 1, para. 6).

From this Christian viewpoint, we can find a deeper peace in knowing that God is "willing and allowing" all of life's events.[120] This perspective may especially come in handy when we struggle to understand the "why" and "what if" questions that emanate from psychological suffering.[121] Certainly, if the secular version of acceptance can be embraced for pragmatic purposes (e.g., to lessen psychological suffering by cultivating the "being mode of the mind"),[122] Christians can find a more transcendent purpose for life's difficulties that is tethered to a Christian worldview.[123] In fact, as we learn to trust in God's providential care and recognize his active, loving presence in "all things," we are developing the ability to find a deeper contentment in life, which is a central component of Christian mental health.[124] If contentment is about an enduring inner satisfaction, regardless of the struggles we may face in life, learning to accept the ups and downs of our emotional world is key.[125] With this understanding in mind, I would like you to practice surrendering to God's providence in the here-and-now, doing so with a three-step process from *Trustful Surrender to Divine Providence*.

THE TRUSTFUL SURRENDER OF EMOTIONS TO GOD: AN EXERCISE

In this exercise,[126] try to set aside ten minutes, settling into a quiet environment, free from distractions. Sit in a supportive chair, with your hands resting in your lap and palms up to symbolize your willingness to yield to God's providential care in this very moment, regardless of the emotions that arise. When you are ready, follow along with the below three steps to meditate on faith in God's providence, hope in God's providence, and love for God's providence:

Faith. Because God's perfect, loving care extends to all of creation, he is present within all of your emotional experiences, whether you perceive them to be "positive" (e.g., joy, happiness) or "negative" (e.g., sadness, fear, anxiety, anger, guilt, shame). Therefore, accept your current emotions without judgment, recognizing that God is revealing himself to you through them in this very moment.

Hope. Since God is infinitely powerful, wise, and loving, he knows what you need, has your best interests in mind, and is in control of your inner world, all in the here-and-now. Because of this, accept your current emotions without judgment, trusting that God is communicating to you through each and every feeling that emerges in the present moment. In other words, the emotional experiences you

---

[120]Saint-Jure and Colombiere (1983, chap. 1, sect. 1, para. 1).
[121]Knabb, Vazquez, and Pate (2019).
[122]Segal et al. (2004).
[123]Knabb, Johnson, Bates, and Sisemore (2019).
[124]Knabb, Vazquez, and Wang (2020); Knabb and Bates (2020b).
[125]Knabb, Vazquez, Garzon, Ford, Wang, Conner, Warren, and Weston (2020).
[126]Adapted from Saint-Jure and Colombiere (1983).

have, day after day, are part of God's plan for your life, with God working everything out for his good (Rom 8:28).

Love. In that "God is love" (1 Jn 4:8), thank him for his providential care, even if you are uncertain about what life may bring, surrendering to his perfect care in this very moment. Stated differently, accept your current emotions without judgment by loving God right now, given his care extends to each passing emotional experience, whether you perceive it to be "positive" (e.g., joy, happiness) or "negative" (e.g., sadness, fear, anxiety, anger, guilt, shame).

After completing the exercise, journal for a few minutes, attempting to answer the following questions:

- What was it like to surrender your emotions to God in the present moment, placing your faith, hope, and love in his perfect care? What were the benefits? The limitations?

- How well were you able to accept your emotions without judgment during the exercise?

- What, if anything, got in your way? Were you able to overcome the obstacles? If so, how? If not, why not?

- How, if at all, can surrendering to God's providence help you with emotional clarity and distress tolerance as you move through the rest of your day?

- How, if at all, can surrendering to God's providence help you to accept his loving presence, minute by minute, and act in a manner that is anchored to fellowshiping with, and finding contentment in, him as you carry out your day?

REFLECTING ON THE PRACTICE

In this chapter, we have focused on impaired emotional clarity and distress intolerance. From a psychological perspective, impaired emotional clarity and distress intolerance can get in the way of optimal functioning, quickly leading to avoidance as an ineffective coping strategy in daily life. Alternatively, acceptance (without judgment) has been promoted in the psychology literature of late, given the ability to relate differently to the inevitable distress of life can help us to live with purpose and values.[127] A biblical understanding of distress intolerance, however, can be linked to the fall of humankind, with humans struggling with a variety of ailments, diseases, and disorders in this broken, fragmented world. As the antidote to suffering, for Christians, trusting in God's providential care is key, "finding God" even in emotional struggles. Along the way, we are deepening our ability to rest in God and find a more fulfilling contentment in him, knowing he is active and present in the full spectrum of distressing life experiences.

By shifting from being preoccupied and alone in our distress to an awareness of God's active, loving presence, we are moving in the direction of finding a deeper rest in him and fellowshiping with him as we walk along the roads of life. To do so, we have been focusing on a variety of meditative strategies, rooted in Jesuit and Orthodox spiritual practices, among others, to (1) notice distress intolerance, (2) shift from earthly preoccupations to a heavenly, spiritual reality, (3) accept God's presence and focus on him in each unfolding moment, and (4) act based on a deeper communion with, and contentment in, God. Before concluding this chapter and moving on to the next transdiagnostic processes in this workbook—behavioral avoidance—reflect on your meditative experiences thus far with a final journaling activity.

REFLECTING ON THE CHAPTER: A JOURNALING ACTIVITY

To conclude this chapter, spend a few minutes journaling about your experience with relating differently to your emotions through the use of Christian meditation. Please use additional paper, if necessary. A few questions to consider:

- What was it like for you to begin to identify the emotions you experience on a daily basis? How well were you able to do so? Were you able to step back and see these emotional patterns in the moment? What can you do to continue to notice your most difficult emotions?

- How well were you able to shift from distress intolerance to God? What went well? What do you still need to work on?

---

[127]Hayes et al. (2012).

- Which exercises, if any, were most helpful in allowing you to get unstuck from your most difficult emotions and shift toward God? How can you build these exercises into daily life?

- How, if at all, did Christian meditation help you to pivot from an earthly perspective to a more transcendent, heavenly reality? What can you do to strengthen this daily practice?

- How did you do with developing the mental skills of attention, present-moment awareness, and acceptance in the context of your relationship with God?

- How, if at all, did your relationship with God change as you spent more time meditating on his word, the Bible?

- How, if at all, did your ability to commune with God change? How about your ability to find a deeper contentment in him as you made decisions throughout the day?

TARGETING PROBLEMS
with BEHAVIOR

Christian Meditation for
Behavioral Avoidance

*You cannot be Christ's servant if you are not willing to follow him,
cross and all. What do you crave? A crown? Then it must be
a crown of thorns if you are to be like him. Do you want to
be lifted up? So you shall, but it will be upon a cross.*

Charles Spurgeon

IN THIS CHAPTER, I focus on behavioral avoidance,[1] including its foundations in secular psychology, link to mental disorders, and relationship with mindfulness meditation. In addition, I discuss behavioral avoidance in the context of the Christian tradition, offering a biblical understanding and intervention strategies. Along the way, you can track this transdiagnostic process with a log, as well as practice a wide variety of meditation strategies grounded in several bodies of Christian spiritual writings (e.g., Jesuit, desert, Celtic, medieval). Throughout the chapter, I explain each exercise, offer transcripts for ease of use, provide journaling exercises, and include an audio recording to follow along with, if you choose to do so.

Ultimately, my aim in this chapter is to help you gain more insight into the relationship between behavioral avoidance, focusing on God (including following Jesus Christ and becoming more like him), and deepening your contentment in, and communion with, him. What follows, then, is a range of meditative strategies, all housed within the Christian tradition. These practices are offered in an effort to help you more confidently follow Jesus, wherever he asks you to go.

---

[1]Gamez et al. (2011).

As a reminder, the four-step process throughout this workbook involves (1) noticing, (2) shifting, (3) accepting, and (4) acting, cultivating a spiritual awareness of God's active, loving presence in the here-and-now. For this chapter, more specifically, the emphasis is on *acting*, as in noticing behavioral avoidance, shifting toward a more heavenly, transcendent perspective, accepting God's active, loving presence, and becoming more like Jesus Christ as you surrender to him, fellowship with him, live out his teachings, and find a deeper, more enduring contentment that only he can provide.

BEHAVIORAL AVOIDANCE: A SECULAR PSYCHOLOGICAL UNDERSTANDING

In daily living, we experience a wide variety of difficult thoughts, feelings, and sensations in the inner world, as well as a range of distressing events, people, tasks, and so forth in the outer world.[2] In the context of these inner and outer events, we may employ avoidance as an often ineffective coping strategy (whether attempting to avoid the experience before it happens or withdraw from the experience once it has already commenced), choosing a short-term solution that seemingly eliminates the psychological difficulties that arise in the moment. Yet, over time, daily living may become unmanageable and we may end up avoiding life altogether, unable to live out the values that are most important to us as we sit on the proverbial sidelines of life as a spectator, rather than actually playing the game.[3]

In the psychology literature, we call this ineffective coping strategy *behavioral avoidance*, defined generally as "refraining from, or escaping from, an action, person or thing."[4] In such efforts, we may *actively* avoid, as is the case when we actually withdraw from a problem, event, or activity or replace the distressing experience with an alternative source of distraction.[5] Or, we may *passively* avoid, consistent with procrastinating or deliberately sidestepping the problem, eschewing a direct attempt to solve the challenge before us.[6] With both our active and passive attempts to avoid, the actual experiences (e.g., celebrations, events, activities, tasks) may involve either interpersonal exchanges or activities and goals that we would normally pursue alone.[7]

Unfortunately, when we avoid as a behavioral coping strategy, we are commonly only thinking about a short-term solution (i.e., reducing or eliminating psychological

---

[2]Hayes et al. (2012); Ottenbreit and Dobson (2004).
[3]Hayes et al. (2012).
[4]Ottenbreit and Dobson (2004, p. 293).
[5]Ottenbreit and Dobson (2004).
[6]Ottenbreit and Dobson (2004).
[7]Ottenbreit and Dobson (2004).

pain), rather than the bigger picture.[8] In other words, in avoiding, we may miss out on living out our values, which include the most salient principles we believe in that guide life and help us create purpose and meaning on a daily basis (e.g., loving others, serving within a local community).[9] By "hitting the pause button on life," we may end up continuing to experience the original symptoms, with added suffering because our life lacks the vitality and richness that naturally flow from value-based daily living.[10]

Behavioral avoidance and psychopathology. In the current edition of the *Diagnostic and Statistical Manual of Mental Disorders* (DSM-5), avoidance is a common component of a variety of psychiatric diagnoses.[11] For instance, with major depressive disorder, many symptoms may lead to behavioral avoidance, including a loss of interest in previously enjoyable activities and hobbies, decreased energy, overwhelming guilt, and thoughts of worthlessness or uselessness.[12] With anxiety disorders, too, a common theme is to avoid the anxiety-inducing situation, whether it relates to having a panic attack, socializing with others, interacting with a specific type of feared object, or catastrophizing about a broad range of anticipated future experiences.[13] As one final example, in response to a traumatic event, we may avoid any reminder of the experience, as is the case with posttraumatic stress disorder (PTSD).[14] Threaded across these disorders, avoidance may be the default coping strategy, although it can end up, in the long run, doing more harm than good. Undoubtedly, as we avoid the unwanted experience, life may pass us by, and we may be unable to live out a set of values that contribute to a fulfilling, meaningful life.[15]

In support of this understanding, in the twenty-first century, empirical research has revealed that behavioral avoidance (both social and nonsocial) is positively related to symptoms of depression and anxiety among college students.[16] In addition, behavioral avoidance is positively linked to symptoms of depression, situational phobias, and obsessive-compulsive disorder (OCD) symptoms, as well as negatively linked to purpose in life, life satisfaction, and quality of life among psychiatric patients.[17] With this line of research, we can see that efforts to avoid, in general, may not produce the intended outcome. Rather than actually eliminating life's difficulties, behavioral avoidance may end up exacerbating the very symptoms

---

[8]Hayes et al. (2012).
[9]Harris (2011).
[10]Harris (2009).
[11]American Psychiatric Association (APA; 2013).
[12]APA (2013).
[13]APA (2013).
[14]APA (2013).
[15]Harris (2009); Hayes et al. (2012).
[16]Ottenbreit and Dobson (2004).
[17]Gamez et al. (2011).

we are looking to eradicate. On the other hand, meditative strategies may help us to more effectively engage with, rather than avoid, difficult daily experiences.

Behavioral avoidance and mindfulness meditation. Since mindfulness meditation helps practitioners to nonjudgmentally accept unpleasant inner experiences (e.g., thoughts, feelings, sensations), this type of daily practice may allow us to engage more directly with the world, rather than allowing our thoughts and feelings to determine our course of action throughout the day.[18] By mindfully relating to our world with open, flexible curiosity, we are decreasing the tendency to be on automatic pilot, struggling to be fully present because we are lost in our head in a sea of thoughts that distract us from leaning into the here-and-now.[19] With automatic pilot, we may almost robotically engage in rumination and worry, unaware that these perseverative thoughts can lead to avoidance behaviors.

As a quick example, we may get stuck in a pattern of worry, anticipating that one doomsday prediction after the next will come true. In turn, we may attempt to avoid these catastrophic expectations by avoiding the people, places, and things that we believe will lead to our eventual downfall. Yet, if we can begin to mindfully notice—on a meta-level—our thought patterns, then engage more directly with our world by using the five senses (not merely relying on cognition as the only medium through which we relate to the environment), we are able to fully experience the life that is unfolding before us. So, mindfully eating a raisin (which may seem, upon first glance, like a silly activity) can help us to use our five senses to get out of automatic pilot to directly engage with life again.[20]

In a recent empirical study, twenty minutes per day of mindfulness meditation over a six-week period of time among a French sample of community adults led to a reduction, pre- to post-intervention, in experiential avoidance.[21] This study shows that mindfulness-based practices may help participants to improve the tendency to avoid life (including avoiding the pursuit of personal values that are meaningful) because of difficult thoughts, feelings, and memories. In fact, the opposite of avoidance is acceptance, with well-defined values (i.e., principles for living, or "chosen life directions")[22] serving as the proverbial map for navigating the roads of life, not fluctuating thoughts and feelings. Yet, to live out our values, behaviorally speaking, we must be willing to bring psychological pain along for the ride, by no means an easy task.

Behavioral avoidance, willingness, and values. In acceptance and commitment therapy (ACT), clients are encouraged to accept (with nonjudgment) difficult

---

[18]Greeson et al. (2014); Hayes et al. (2012).
[19]Segal et al. (2012).
[20]Segal et al. (2012).
[21]Antoine et al. (2018).
[22]Harris (2009, p. 189).

thoughts and feelings in order to live out a set of well-defined values (e.g., being a loving spouse, being kind to coworkers, being generous to family members, being an adventurous friend, being curious about learning new things, being healthy and physically fit, being friendly and compassionate when meeting people, being honest in every area of daily life).[23] In other words, when we try to avoid, through our behaviors, unpleasant inner or outer experiences, we may end up doing more harm than good, given we likely will continue to struggle with the very symptoms we are trying to avoid (e.g., low mood, worry), *as well as* miss out on living a life of purpose and meaning.[24] Conversely, to live out our values, we need to make room for uncomfortable experiences, whether emanating from the inner (e.g., thoughts, feelings, sensations) or outer (e.g., conversations, events, activities) world, which requires a willingness to do so. With willingness, we are deliberately facing (not behaviorally avoiding) unpleasant inner and outer experiences in an all-or-nothing manner because we are choosing to prioritize living out our values, irrespective of whether or not we want these difficult experiences to persist.[25]

Consistent with this understanding, recent research among both student and psychiatric samples revealed that distress endurance—the ability to continue to pursue values in spite of difficult inner experiences—was negatively correlated with symptoms of depression, phobias in specific situations, and obsessive-compulsive symptoms, as well as positively correlated with having a purpose in life and overall life satisfaction and quality of life.[26] Therefore, in contrast with behavioral avoidance, distress endurance as a strategy for effectively responding to difficult inner and outer experiences in life may actually lead to better mental health outcomes. However, for Christians, we are called to endure distress (whether difficult thoughts, feelings, and sensations in the inner world or relationships, circumstances, and activities in the outer world) because Jesus has invited us to follow him on the roads of life, doing so with his famous declaration, "Come, follow me" (Mt 4:19).

BEHAVIORAL AVOIDANCE: A CHRISTIAN UNDERSTANDING

Ever since the fall (Gen 3), humankind has struggled with turning away from God, prioritizing ourselves above him in daily life. If sin in the Christian tradition is succinctly defined as "idolatry,"[27] to this day, we continue to place our own unilateral pursuit of possessions, relationships, life goals, and so forth before worshiping God at the center of existence. With Adam and Eve, more specifically, they

---

[23]Harris (2009, 2011).
[24]Hayes et al. (2012).
[25]Hayes et al. (2012).
[26]Gamez et al. (2011).
[27]Keller (2016b).

prioritized attempting to be "like God," rather than relying on him, then quickly hid in the garden when they realized the colossal mistake they just made (Gen 3). Because of this mistake, of course, suffering entered the world, with Adam and Eve being banished from their perfect safety in the garden, as well as experiencing a ruptured relationship with God. Since then, we continue to struggle with focusing on ourselves, not God, and prioritizing our own will above God's design for our life, which sometimes includes avoiding, behaviorally speaking, actions that are Christlike and honoring to God.

With widespread brokenness and suffering in this world, we are subject to a plethora of hardships, linked to both inner and outer experiences. Unfortunately, when we experience the inevitable pain of life, we often turn away from God, avoiding the very source of comfort that we need when we are struggling. Rather than reaching for God when we are in pain, we commonly avoid, reminiscent of Adam and Eve in the garden.

What follows is a brief review of behavioral avoidance in the Bible, along with the link between avoidance and psychopathology among Christians, the relationship between behavioral avoidance, obedience to God, and Christian virtues, and the association between behavioral avoidance and classic Christian spiritual practices. In this discussion, my aim is to convey that behavioral avoidance seldom works in the long run. Behavioral avoidance also prevents us from confidently following Jesus to be more like him as we walk day to day with him toward heaven as our final destination.[28]

Behavioral avoidance and the Bible. Although by no means an exhaustive list, I would like to provide two examples of behavioral avoidance in the Bible, demonstrating that—from a Christian perspective—we can never truly run from God. Rather, if the purpose of the Christian life is to cultivate Christlikeness,[29] avoiding his will only makes matters worse in the end. In other words, the contentment we long for on this side of heaven—an enduring, inner psychological satisfaction in spite of difficult life events[30]—is found in surrendering to God's will, not our own. When we notice we are avoiding God's will, therefore, our best option is to quickly realign ourselves with his plan, similar to Jonah in the Old Testament and Peter in the New Testament.

For Jonah, God told him to "go to the great city of Nineveh and preach against it," but Jonah "ran away from the LORD" (Jon 1:1-3). Although we do not exactly know what thoughts and feelings Jonah was experiencing when he turned from God's plan and prioritized his own wishes, he may have had concerns for his own

---

[28]Knabb and Bates (2020b).
[29]Wilken (2003); Willard (2002).
[30]Knabb, Vazquez, Garzon, Ford, Wang, Conner, Warren, and Weston (2020).

life, anxiously anticipating danger in traveling to Ninevah, or he may have been angry about having to carry out an order he did not wish to fulfill.[31] Nevertheless, although there ended up being several other exchanges in the story, while trapped inside the famous fish, Jonah cried out to God, asked for God's help, and praised God (Jon 2:1-10). Although Jonah attempted to avoid God's plan, upon reaching for God in his estranged state, God showed Jonah mercy.[32]

With Peter, he denied that he knew Jesus three times (Lk 22:54-62), possibly because of the uncertainty and anxiety that surrounded Jesus' arrest and crucifixion. Although Peter had followed Jesus for several years as one of Jesus' disciples, boldly proclaiming that he was "ready to go with [Jesus] to prison and to death" (Lk 22:33), Peter quickly denied knowing his Lord.

As a parallel, because of the fall, we often turn away from God in daily life, sometimes because of the unpleasant inner or outer experiences that are linked to following Jesus on the proverbial roads of life. Still, as soon as we recognize we have wandered away and looked to ourselves, rather than God, we can get back on the right path, choosing to follow Jesus wherever he would have us go. Beyond these two famous examples in Scripture, I have conducted recent research among Christians that has revealed some interesting insights into the link between behavioral avoidance, distress endurance, and Christian living.

Behavioral avoidance and psychopathology among Christians. In a study among Christian college students, I found that distress endurance was positively correlated with both religious commitment and faith maturity.[33] With both religious commitment and faith maturity, the emphasis is on living out a set of religious values and practices (e.g., helping underserved populations, serving the church, praying, worshiping).[34] Therefore, this research reveals that being willing to persevere in the midst of distress may help Christians to more effectively live out our faith, which includes becoming more like Jesus Christ, the Suffering Servant (Is 53). In other words, because Jesus suffered, we, too, can expect to suffer in this world. Yet, in the midst of suffering, we are cultivating a deeper contentment, in that we are fellowshiping with God and carrying out his perfect will for our life.

Behavioral avoidance, surrender, and virtues. Consistent with ACT in the psychology literature, as Christians, we must be willing to endure, behaviorally pressing forward with courage and hope in order to live out our purpose on this planet, which is to become more like Jesus Christ and fulfill God's will. In other words, we are moving from behavioral avoidance (based on our own plan in life),

---

[31]Henry (2005).
[32]Henry (2005).
[33]Knabb et al. (2014).
[34]Knabb et al. (2014).

to surrender (yielding to God's plan in life), to virtues (living out a set of patterns of living that are modeled to us by Jesus Christ).

In emulating Jesus Christ and yielding to his will, we are cultivating virtues, or habitual dispositions (e.g., kindness, compassion, forgiveness), made up of an amalgam of deeply rooted thoughts, feelings, and behaviors.[35] To do so, for Christians, "surrender" may be the equivalent to ACT's "willingness," in that we are prioritizing God's plan above our own as we develop habitual patterns that are shaped after Jesus' life, reminiscent of Jesus in the Garden of Gethsemane: "My Father, if it is possible, let this cup pass from Me; yet not as I will, but as You will" (Mt 26:36-46). In the psychology literature, in fact, surrender has recently been researched as a form of religious coping, placing God's will above our own as we behaviorally respond to stressful life events.[36]

In my own research, as an example, I have found that surrendering to God (e.g., following God's plan, carrying out God's direction) is positively linked to positive views about God's providence (e.g., believing that God is in control and will intervene when problems arise) and negatively linked to worry among both student and community samples of Christian adults.[37] What is more, I conducted a recent pilot study on the use of Christian spiritual practices (e.g., meditation, prayer, contemplation) for Christian adults with chronic worry, with results revealing that daily practice over an eight-week period of time resulted in an increase in positive views of God's providence and the ability to surrender to God as a form of religious coping.[38]

To summarize, in the Christian life, we are called to align our will with God's will, as well as become more like Jesus Christ by emulating his behavior, since only God knows what is best for us in this fallen, broken world. To become more Christlike, we have a plethora of examples in Scripture of these "habitual dispositions," or "spiritual characteristics," commonly called virtues.[39] In fact, since our "dispositions" are "patterns or ways of thinking, feeling, and behaving that have become so embedded into the fabric of [our] being that they seem to come naturally,"[40] we must have a solid grasp of them when attempting to impact behavioral change. Common virtues in the New Testament include the fruit of the Spirit (Gal 5:22-23) and other Christlike, habitual, enduring characteristics (e.g., faith, hope, love, joy, peace, patience, kindness, gentleness, mercy, compassion, gratitude, humility, forgiveness, detachment, solitude, tolerance, persistence).[41] To cultivate

---

[35]Kloepfer (2003).
[36]Wong-McDonald and Gorsuch (2000).
[37]Knabb et al. (2017).
[38]Knabb et al. (2017).
[39]Kloepfer (2003); Koessler (2003).
[40]Kloepfer (2003, p. 86).
[41]Kloepfer (2003).

these "dispositions," the Christian tradition has a variety of spiritual disciplines (e.g., meditation, prayer, contemplation, Bible reading, worship) for those who wish to mimic Jesus Christ, both internally and externally.[42]

Behavioral avoidance, surrender, virtues, and Christian meditation and contemplation. If spiritual disciplines are about developing Christlikeness and Christian virtues through a variety of practices, rather than avoiding life, we are learning to emulate Jesus and become more like him by surrendering to God's will and pressing forward, reminiscent of Jesus in the Garden of Gethsemane (Mt 26:36-46). In this famous biblical scene, Jesus by no means engaged in "refraining from, or escaping from, an action, person or thing," as is the case with behavioral avoidance.[43] Instead, he endured suffering in order to carry out God's plan, something we are tasked with doing as his followers (Mt 16:24-26). Therefore, rather than actively (or passively) avoiding life's most difficult conversations, activities, goals, and so forth, with inner practices (e.g., meditation, prayer, contemplation) in the inner world we are preparing to carry out outer practices (e.g., simplicity, surrender, service, self-sacrifice) in the outer world,[44] all in line with God's will.

Through daily meditation, as an example, we can internalize God's Word, shifting from ruminating on our own concerns to ruminating on God's promises, attributes, and actions in Scripture. In doing so, we are preparing ourselves to take Christlike behavioral action, anchored to a biblical, transcendent understanding of the human condition.[45] Along the way, we are learning to surrender our will to God, replacing our unilaterally derived wishes with his perfect plan, then live out God's will through a variety of "spiritual dispositions" that were modeled to us by Jesus Christ (e.g., love, detachment, mercy).

With daily contemplation, moreover, we are learning to surrender to God, detaching from our own preoccupations in order to attach to, and commune with, God,[46] living life in accordance with his perfect plan. In this process, we are cultivating a simpler, Christlike love, given we are gazing upon God with loving attentiveness,[47] letting go of distractions that get in the way of following Jesus on the roads of life. In simply sitting at the feet of Jesus, like Mary (Lk 10:38-42), we are learning to recognize his presence, focus on him, and live like he lived, guided by a set of "spiritual dispositions" for cultivating a meaningful, vibrant life.

In applying the four-step process in this workbook to the transdiagnostic process of behavioral avoidance, we are working toward (1) noticing when we avoid and

---

[42]Chandler (2014); Foster (2018); Kloepfer (2003); Willard (2002).
[43]Ottenbreit and Dobson (2004, p. 293).
[44]Foster (2018).
[45]Foster (2018).
[46]Foster (2018).
[47]Francis (2011).

withdraw from life, (2) shifting toward an awareness of God's plan for our life (i.e., Christlikeness and the cultivation of Jesus' "spiritual dispositions"), (3) accepting God's plan for our life by developing key mental skills (i.e., focusing our attention on God, maintaining an awareness of God in the here-and-now, accepting God's providential plan), and (4) acting in life based on a set of "spiritual dispositions" (e.g., love, forgiveness, kindness, gentleness, mercy, perseverance) that emanate from a deeper fellowship with, and contentment in, God. With this understanding in mind, I would like you to transition to noticing when you behaviorally avoid (whether actively or passively) social and nonsocial situations,[48] before moving on to actually practicing a variety of exercises for preparing the inner world for Christlike behavioral action in the outer world.

NOTICING YOUR BEHAVIORS: A DAILY LOG

In this first exercise,[49] you will be examining your behavior throughout the day for an entire week, learning to better identify and understand instances that involve avoiding some sort of difficulty, whether a social (e.g., meeting, event, activity) or nonsocial (e.g., goal, task) experience.[50] More specifically, I would like you to notice when you decide to avoid a particular event, activity, relationship, appointment, and so forth, then document the possible consequences in doing so. To get you started, I have filled in two examples. Feel free to use additional paper, if you need to.

NOTICING YOUR BEHAVIORS LOG

Day of the Week	Time of Day	Type of Avoidance Behavior	Reason for Avoidance Behavior	Consequences of Avoidance Behavior
Sunday	8:00 a.m.	Staying home from church	I feel really anxious today and don't want to interact with anyone. I'm afraid I'll be judged.	I don't get to fellowship with other Christians, sing to God during the worship service, or hear God's word in the weekly message.

---

[48] Ottenbreit and Dobson (2004).
[49] Adapted from Harris (2009).
[50] Ottenbreit and Dobson (2004).

Day of the Week	Time of Day	Type of Avoidance Behavior	Reason for Avoidance Behavior	Consequences of Avoidance Behavior
Monday	3:45 P.M.	Canceling lunch with a friend	I don't want to have a difficult (albeit needed) conversation with my friend to let her know she is doing something immoral in her life. I'm afraid she will hate me because of it and there will be added stress in our relationship.	I don't get to display Christlike love in helping my friend to live a life that is more honoring to God.

Day of the Week	Time of Day	Type of Avoidance Behavior	Reason for Avoidance Behavior	Consequences of Avoidance Behavior

VIRTUOUS LIVING IN THE CHRISTIAN TRADITION: CULTIVATING CHRISTLIKENESS

Now that you have tracked some of your patterns of avoidance, let's look at the virtues, or Christlike habitual dispositions of action, you would like to live out as a Christian,[51] in place of the strategies that may be keeping you dually stuck in life and walking away with regret, reminiscent of the rich ruler in the Gospels (Mk 10:17-27). If we are to follow Jesus on the roads of life and become more like him from moment to moment, we need to look to him as an example of the enduring, virtuous behaviors we need to practice.

In fact, within the Christian spiritual disciplines literature, Christlikeness is a central aim,[52] which includes the following (overlapping and by no means exhaustive) list of virtues (Gal 5:22-23):[53]

Faith	Peace	Humility
Hope	Compassion	Solitude
Love	Kindness	Detachment
Courage	Gentleness	Diligence
Endurance	Gratitude	Wisdom
Patience	Mercy	
Tolerance	Forgiveness	

With the above examples, which consist of an amalgam of habitual patterns of thoughts, feelings, and actions,[54] we are striving to become more like Jesus Christ, emulating him as we walk and talk with him throughout the day. Similar to Jesus' disciplines, we are learning to live life this way because we are spending crucial time with him, anchored to a wide variety of spiritual disciplines that help us cultivate Christlike behavioral action, in contrast with behavioral avoidance. Next, I would like you to clarify the virtuous, Christlike behaviors you would like to live out in your own life, in place of the avoidance strategies that may be preventing you from following God's will.

VIRTUOUS LIVING IN THE CHRISTIAN TRADITION: AN EXERCISE

In this exercise,[55] please fill in each section so as to gain more insight into the possible ways in which virtuous, Christlike behavioral action can change your life for the better, replacing the behavioral avoidance that may be getting in the way of fulfilling God's will. (Of note, I have filled in the first row to provide an example.)

---

[51]Kloepfer (2003).
[52]Whitney (2014).
[53]Adapted from Austin and Geivett (2012); Kloepfer (2003).
[54]Kloepfer (2003).
[55]Adapted from Harris (2011).

VIRTUOUS LIVING

Area of Life	Virtues I Would Like to Live Out by Following Jesus and Becoming More Like Him	Christlike Behavioral Action	Positive Results	Steps to Take (e.g., Bible Reading, Meditation, Prayer, Contemplation)
Family	Kind, compassionate, loving, forgiving	I will strive to be a better wife and mother. I will talk to my children in a softer, gentler voice when I need to redirect them. I will be more forgiving and compassionate when my husband makes a mistake by listening to him and letting him know I understand where he is coming from.	I will be more honoring to God by displaying the love of Christ in my family. I will improve my relationships within my family.	I will meditate on Galatians 5:22–23 each morning before getting up for the day. I will pray to God each morning, asking that his Holy Spirit guide me in each of my exchanges with my husband and children and give me strength.
Work				
Church				

Area of Life	Virtues I Would Like to Live Out by Following Jesus and Becoming More Like Him	Christlike Behavioral Action	Positive Results	Steps to Take (e.g., Bible Reading, Meditation, Prayer, Contemplation)
Community				
Marriage/ Romantic Relationship				
Hobbies				
Education/ Learning				

Now that you have documented a range of virtuous, Christlike habitual behaviors that you would like to live out in daily life, I would like you to begin to imagine— through a contemplative, imaginative exercise from the Jesuit tradition—what it might be like to literally follow Jesus on the trails, roads, and highways of life, reminiscent of his first-century disciples.

"COME, FOLLOW ME": FOLLOWING JESUS THE RABBI

In the Gospels, Jesus famously proclaimed, "Come, follow me" (Mt 4:19), capturing the first-century Jewish dynamic of a student choosing a rabbi to learn from, study under, and follow.[56] However, here, Jesus is the one choosing his disciples, asking them to give up their former way of life, trade, and identity, all rooted in their family of origin.[57] In other words, *he* called *them* to find their identity in *him*, embracing his teachings and way of life as a permanent replacement.[58]

For twenty-first-century Christians, we have the opportunity to let go of our old ways, replacing them with Christlike behavioral action that is often inconsistent with the surrounding secular culture. In making this shift, we may experience a wide variety of difficult thoughts and feelings in the inner world and encounters in the outer world. Because of this, the Jesuit practice of imaginative contemplation[59] may be helpful in holding on to what matters most in the midst of perceived psychological barriers in both the inner and outer world, especially when it comes to envisioning that we are actually following Jesus where he would have us go. In fact, because, as Christians, he has called each of us personally and by name, our entire way of life is grounded in following *him* (Jn 10:3-5).

"COME, FOLLOW ME": AN EXERCISE

For this next exercise,[60] set aside ten minutes, finding a quiet location that is free from distractions. Sit up straight in a supportive chair, closing your eyes and resting your hands comfortably in your lap. When you are ready, follow along with the below steps:

Read. First, slowly read the following passage in Scripture:

As Jesus was walking beside the Sea of Galilee, he saw two brothers, Simon called Peter and his brother Andrew. They were casting a net into the lake, for they were fishermen. "Come, follow me," Jesus said, "and I will send you out to fish for people." At once they left their nets and followed him. Going on from there, he saw two

---

[56]Keller (2016a).
[57]Keller (2016a).
[58]Keller (2016a).
[59]Gallagher (2008).
[60]Adapted from Gallagher (2008).

other brothers, James son of Zebedee and his brother John. They were in a boat with their father Zebedee, preparing their nets. Jesus called them, and immediately they left the boat and their father and followed him. (Mt 4:18-22)

Imagine. Second, use your imagination to experience this scene by looking around, picturing being there at the exact location—the Sea of Galilee. Imagine what it might be like to see Jesus walking on the shoreline, calling to Peter and Andrew as they are fishing. Picture Peter and Andrew dropping what they are doing in a radical fashion and beginning to follow Jesus, turning from their old way of life, along with James and John, who left behind their father, Zebedee, in the immediacy of the moment. Imagine how exciting the scene must have been, with these brothers simply letting go of their previous occupation and identity. Also, try to hear the words coming out of Jesus' mouth: "Come, follow me" (Mt 4:19). Listen to the volume and tone as he confidently commanded them to follow him to where he was going.

Follow. Third, use your imagination to picture that you, too, have the opportunity to follow Jesus in this famous Gospel scene. Envision that you are completing one of your daily tasks that captures—at least in part—who you know yourself to be. In doing so, imagine what it might be like to simply let go of what you are doing, spontaneously in the present, to respond to Jesus' call. Try to connect to the thoughts and feelings you might have (both "positive" and "negative"), as well as any possible outer barriers that might emerge (e.g., needing to get the task done because of a deadline). Now, confidently leave what you are doing to, behaviorally speaking, follow Jesus wherever he wants you to go. Listen to him calling you, personally and directly, as he looks in your direction: "Come, follow me" (Mt 4:19). Hear the unwavering confidence in his voice as he matter-of-factly tells you to come with him to his destination.

Pray. Fourth, pray to God, asking him to help you carry this imagery throughout your day, turning from behavioral avoidance to Christlike behavioral action whenever you notice you are declining to follow Jesus on the shores of life. Ask God to give you the ability to accept difficult inner and outer experiences so as to boldly walk with him where he would have you go, displaying Jesus' "spiritual dispositions" (e.g., love, compassion, mercy, forgiveness) as you fellowship with, and find your contentment in, him and him alone.

After completing the exercise, journal for a few minutes, attempting to answer the following questions:

- What was it like to imagine following Jesus the rabbi, regardless of the thoughts and feelings that emerged? What were the benefits? The limitations?

- How well were you able to accept your thoughts and feelings during the exercise?

- What, if anything, got in your way? Were you able to overcome the obstacles? If so, how? If not, why not?

- How, if at all, can learning to follow Jesus the rabbi help you with behavioral avoidance as you move through the rest of your day?

- How, if at all, can following Jesus the rabbi help you to accept his loving presence, minute by minute, and act in a manner that is anchored to fellowshiping with, and finding contentment in, him as you carry out your day?

VIRTUES IN THE DESERT: EMULATING JESUS CHRIST IN DAILY LIFE

Like Jesus in the desert responding to the devil's temptations (Mt 4:1-11), when we are faced with tempting, compulsive thoughts, we can (1) notice their presence, as well as what they are and where they come from, (2) respond with Scripture, and (3) live out a set of corresponding virtues that emanate from God's Word, continuing to follow God's will in the process.[61] In a similar manner, the early desert Christians attempted to face their tempting, compulsive thoughts (*logismoi,* Greek) while in the harsh desert terrain, reminiscent of Jesus' direct interaction with the

---

[61]Harmless (2008).

devil.[62] Over time, they identified eight types of thoughts, which distracted them from following Jesus, becoming more like him, and living out a set of virtues.[63]

Below are these eight thoughts, along with corresponding virtues to combat the compulsive, tempting thoughts:[64]

- Gluttony = love of God (i.e., charity) and self-control (i.e., temperance)

- Lust/fornication = love of God (i.e., charity) and self-control (i.e., temperance)

- Money/material possessions = love of God (i.e., charity) and self-control (i.e., temperance)

- Sadness = patience and courage

- Anger = patience and courage

- Boredom/discouragement/restlessness = patience and courage

- Vanity/fame = good judgment (i.e., prudence), understanding, and wisdom

- Pride = good judgment (i.e., prudence), understanding, and wisdom

As the proverbial bridge between our inner thoughts and virtuous behavior, one of the early desert Christians, Evagrius, recommended talking back to these tempting, compulsive thoughts.[65] Therefore, building on the "Talking Back" exercise in the fourth chapter, see if you can identify verses in Scripture to shift from tempting, compulsive thoughts (*logismoi*) to virtuous, Christlike behavior, consistent with the four-step meditative process offered throughout this workbook.

VIRTUES IN THE DESERT: AN EXERCISE

In this exercise,[66] please fill in the required information below, identifying your specific thoughts related to Evagrius's eight tempting, compulsive thoughts, Scripture to talk back to your thoughts, and specific Christlike actions that demonstrate the corresponding virtues. In this practice, think of your tempting, compulsive thoughts as obstacles to following Jesus. In the below process, you are (1) recognizing your thoughts (including their corresponding category), (2) talking back with Scripture, and (3) engaging in Christlike behavioral action by living out a specific virtue that was modeled by Jesus and helps you to more confidently follow him on the roads of life:

---

[62]Evagrius (2009); Harmless (2004).
[63]Harmless (2004); Konstantinovsky (2016).
[64]Adapted from Brakke (2006); Harmless (2004, 2008).
[65]Brakke (2006); Evagrius (2009).
[66]Adapted from Brakke (2006); Evagrius (2009); Harmless (2004, 2008).

VIRTUES IN THE DESERT

Category (*Logismoi*)	Thought	Scripture to Talk Back	Virtue	Christlike Behavioral Action
Sadness	I'm never going to get the job. I'm worthless and my future is hopeless.	"Trust in the LORD with all your heart and lean not on your own understanding; in all your ways submit to him, and he will make your paths straight" (Prov 3:5–6); "Do not let your hearts be troubled. You believe in God; believe also in me" (Jn 14:1).	Patience and courage	I'm going to demonstrate patience and courage by pursuing a college degree, even when I feel down, and wait patiently for an opportunity to present itself because I trust in God's plan.
Anger			Patience and courage	
Boredom/ discourage- ment/ restlessness			Patience and courage	

Category (Logismoi)	Thought	Scripture to Talk Back	Virtue	Christlike Behavioral Action
Vanity/fame			Good judgment (i.e., prudence), understanding, and wisdom	
Pride			Good judgment (i.e., prudence), understanding, and wisdom	
Gluttony			Love of God (i.e., charity) and self-control (i.e., temperance)	
Lust/ fornication			Love of God (i.e., charity) and self-control (i.e., temperance)	
Money/ material possesions			Love of God (i.e., charity) and self-control (i.e., temperance)	

Now that you have identified the link between your thoughts and behaviors, including the Christlike virtues that emanate from your relationship with him, practice preparing for a day of behavioral action by putting on your "breastplate," consistent with the Celtic Christian tradition.

PREPARING FOR THE DAY WITH A BREASTPLATE PRAYER: JESUS' PROTECTION IN THE CELTIC CHRISTIAN TRADITION

In the Celtic Christian tradition, breastplate prayers (*lorica*, Latin) are prayers of protection, inspired by the armor of Roman soldiers, which help us to call on the name of Christ, who is present in each unfolding moment, especially when we need to press on during difficult circumstances.[67] Patrick, who lived in fifth-century Ireland, offered the following breastplate prayer, which famously captures Jesus' presence as we endure the challenges of life:

> Christ beside me, Christ before me; Christ behind me, Christ within me; Christ beneath me, Christ above me; Christ to right of me, Christ to left of me; Christ in my lying, my sitting, my rising; Christ in heart of all who know me, Christ on tongue of all who meet me, Christ in eye of all who see me, Christ in ear of all who hear me.[68]

In this powerful prayer, we can see Jesus' omnipresence, with this recollection helping us to directly face life's most challenging circumstances, whether internal or external. With this breastplate prayer in mind, practice pairing meditation with Christlike behavioral action, recognizing that Jesus is with you each step of the way as you trek along the roads of life. Rather than avoiding inner or outer challenges, though, you can continue on, knowing Jesus Christ is strengthening you and protecting you, reminiscent of the armor worn by a Roman soldier.

PREPARING FOR THE DAY WITH A BREASTPLATE PRAYER: AN EXERCISE

To begin this exercise,[69] find a quiet environment, free from distractions and excessive noise. Sit in a supportive, comfortable chair, with your back straight to symbolize strength in the midst of hardship. Fold your hands in your lap as you prepare to begin.[70] Now, when you are ready, follow along with the steps below in order to set out on your daily journey with an awareness that Jesus is walking by your side:

Notice. First, notice the inner and outer experiences that lead to behavioral avoidance in your life, whether distressing thoughts and feelings or challenging activities, events, or interactions with others.

---

[67]Earle (2011); Earle and Maddox (2004).
[68]Earle and Maddox (2004, p. 17).
[69]Adapted from Earle (2011); Earle and Maddox (2004).
[70]You can also follow along with the audio recording (Track 3), found at ivpress.com/Knabb3.

Shift. Second, shift your focus from these inner and outer distractions to an awareness of Jesus Christ's active, loving, powerful presence all around you. Slowly pray Patrick's prayer:

> Christ beside me, Christ before me; Christ behind me, Christ within me; Christ beneath me, Christ above me; Christ to right of me, Christ to left of me; Christ in my lying, my sitting, my rising; Christ in heart of all who know me, Christ on tongue of all who meet me, Christ in eye of all who see me, Christ in ear of all who hear me.[71]

Envision that Jesus is your armor, protecting you in this very moment. In fact, he is below you and above you, to the right and left of you, and inside you and outside of you. Moreover, imagine that he is even in control of the people, events, and so forth in your life in each unfolding moment. Because of this, you can trust that he will walk with you *through*, not *around*, your most difficult moments throughout the day.

Accept. Third, accept Jesus' protection in this very moment, focusing on him as you envision carrying out your day. Because he is with you, there is no need to avoid life. Rather, with Jesus' presence all around, you can confidently walk forward, accepting whatever inner and outer struggles emerge in the moment.

Act. Fourth, act in life in a Christlike manner, living out the teachings of Jesus in a way that brings honor to him in your social and nonsocial activities throughout the day.

After completing the exercise, journal for a few minutes, attempting to answer the following questions:

- What was it like to envision Jesus surrounding and protecting you? What were the benefits? What were the limitations?

- What was it like to accept your inner and outer experiences, knowing Jesus is by your side? What were the benefits? The limitations?

- How well were you able to confidently pray the breastplate prayer? Were you able to envision displaying Christlike behavioral action in response to the prayer?

- What, if anything, got in your way? Were you able to overcome the obstacles? If so, how? If not, why not?

- How, if at all, can practicing these steps help you with behavioral avoidance as you move through the rest of your day?

---

[71]Earle and Maddox (2004, p. 17).

● How, if at all, can practicing these steps help you to accept God's loving presence, minute by minute, and act in a manner that is anchored to fellowshiping with, and finding contentment in, him as you carry out your day?

_____

_____

_____

_____

_____

_____

_____

_____

_____

_____

_____

_____

_____

THE PRACTICE OF THE PRESENCE OF GOD: WALKING WITH GOD IN DAILY LIFE

Beyond breastplate prayers, we can practice God's presence throughout the day in order to confidently walk with him on the proverbial trails of life, rather than relying on behavioral avoidance as an ineffective coping strategy. In the Middle Ages, Brother Lawrence,[72] a monk who apparently lived a simple, humble life as a cook and sandal maker, engaged in a simple practice to maintain an awareness of God's presence during the day, regardless of the task before him. In other words, he advocated for practicing God's presence in even the simplest of activities, such as washing the dishes or carrying out other seemingly mundane responsibilities. According to Brother Lawrence,

> The holiest, most ordinary, and most necessary practice of the spiritual life is that of the presence of God. It is to take delight in and become accustomed to his divine company, speaking humbly and conversing lovingly with him all the time,

---

[72]Lawrence (2015).

at every moment, without rule or measure, especially in times of temptation, suffering, or weariness.[73]

Psychological and spiritual health involves developing a deeper friendship with God, one in which we regularly talk to him and enjoy spending time with him, even during instances of suffering. To do so, as per Brother Lawrence, we are to "perform all our actions carefully and deliberately, not impulsively or hurriedly, for such would characterize a distracted mind. We must work gently and lovingly with God, asking him to accept our work."[74]

As we "carefully," "deliberately," "gently," and "lovingly" combine the assigned activity with God's presence, we can recite a short phrase to remember God in the here-and-now, such as the following:[75]

- "My God, I am completely yours."
- "God of love, I love you with all my heart."
- "Lord, fashion me according to your heart."

In this interaction with God, we are learning to honor him by recognizing he is with us, regardless of the task we are engaged in. In our behaviors throughout the day, we can either turn toward or away from God, actively choosing, second by second, whether or not to "find God in all things." Thus, to practice these instructions, begin by applying a simple saying, "God of love, I love you with all my heart," as you engage in a basic activity, washing the dishes.

Although mindfulness-based approaches advocate for practitioners to "mindfully wash the dishes" so as to cultivate attention, present-moment awareness, and acceptance,[76] as Christians, instead, we can *worshipfully* wash the dishes, giving glory to God in the process. In doing so, we are learning to invite God into our most difficult activities throughout our day, rather than relying on behavioral avoidance as an ineffective coping strategy. Yet, we are not actually *inviting* God anywhere, given he is omnipresent:

> Where can I go from your Spirit?
>   Where can I flee from your presence?
> If I go up to the heavens, you are there;
>   if I make my bed in the depths, you are there.
> If I rise on the wings of the dawn,
>   if I settle on the far side of the sea,
> even there your hand will guide me,
>   your right hand will hold me fast. (Ps 139:7-10)

---

[73]Lawrence (2015, p. 38).
[74]Lawrence (2015, p. 38).
[75]Lawrence (2015, p. 44).
[76]Feldman et al. (2007); Nhat Hanh (1976).

Rather, we are simply acknowledging God's presence, recognizing that he is at the center of our experiences, wherever we choose to go throughout the day.

THE PRACTICE OF THE PRESENCE OF GOD: AN EXERCISE

In this ten-minute exercise,[77] you will be practicing the common activity of washing the dishes, coupling this task with maintaining an awareness of God's presence. Try to wash the dishes during a time when no one else is in the kitchen so you can be alone with God, then follow along with the two steps below for the full amount of time. In the following two steps, your job is to spend time with God in what seems to be the most boring of activities, which can help you to practice God's presence when you engage in other behaviors and tasks throughout the day (e.g., conversations, work-related assignments, chores):

"Slowly," "carefully," "deliberately," "gently," and "lovingly" complete the designated activity. As you complete the activity, "interiorly" say to yourself "God of love, I love you with all my heart." When your mind wanders to something else, gently return to pairing the activity and phrase.

After completing the exercise, journal for a few minutes, attempting to answer the following questions:

- What was it like to attempt to practice God's presence while washing the dishes? What were the benefits? What were the limitations?

- What was it like to know that God was with you during this seemingly boring activity? What were the benefits? The limitations?

- How well were you able to practice God's presence throughout the duration of the activity?

- What, if anything, got in your way? Were you able to overcome the obstacles? If so, how? If not, why not?

- How, if at all, can practicing these steps help you with behavioral avoidance as you move through the rest of your day?

- How, if at all, can practicing these steps help you to accept God's loving presence, minute by minute, and act in a manner that is anchored to fellowshiping with, and finding contentment in, him as you carry out your day?

---

[77]Adapted from Lawrence (2015).

_____

_____

_____

_____

_____

_____

_____

_____

_____

_____

REFLECTING ON THE PRACTICE

In this chapter, we have focused on behavioral avoidance. With behavioral avoidance, we are "refraining from, or escaping from, an action, person or thing," whether active or passive and social or nonsocial.[78] As a healthy alternative, the psychology literature advocates for living out our values as a way to cultivate a fulfilling, impactful life, which is not necessarily synonymous with happiness.[79]

A biblical understanding of behavioral avoidance can be traced back to the fall of humankind (Gen 3), with humans struggling to prioritize God above our own self interests. Fast-forward to the New Testament, and Jesus taught us to follow him (Mt 4:19; 16:24), live out a set of Christian virtues as a way to love God and neighbor (Mk 12:30-31), and share the gospel message of hope and restored communion with God (Mt 28:19-20). To follow Jesus and become more like him, thus, is about emulating him, internalizing his teachings, and walking with him wherever he would have us go on the roads of life.

By shifting from behavioral avoidance to a willingness to follow Jesus, we are learning to fellowship with him from moment to moment and draw from a deeper, more fulfilling contentment. To practice doing so, we have focused on a variety of meditative strategies, rooted in desert, Jesuit, Celtic, and medieval spiritual practices, to (1) notice behavioral avoidance, (2) shift from earthly preoccupations to a heavenly, spiritual reality, (3) accept God's presence and focus on him in each unfolding moment, and (4) act based on a deeper communion with, and contentment in, God. Before concluding this chapter and moving on to the next transdiagnostic

_____

[78]Ottenbreit and Dobson (2004, p. 293).
[79]Hayes et al. (2012).

processes in this workbook—perfectionism—I would like you to reflect on your meditative experiences thus far with a final journaling activity.

REFLECTING ON THE CHAPTER: A JOURNALING ACTIVITY

To conclude this chapter, spend a few minutes journaling about your experience with decreasing avoidance behaviors through the use of Christian meditation. Please use additional paper, if necessary. A few questions to consider:

- What was it like for you to begin to follow Jesus on the roads of life? How well were you able to do so? Were you able to step back and recognize your avoidance behaviors in the moment? What can you do to continue to notice when you are utilizing avoidance behaviors as an ineffective coping strategy for responding to difficult thoughts, feelings, and sensations?

- How well were you able to shift from behavioral avoidance to following Jesus? What went well? What do you still need to work on?

- Which exercises, if any, were most helpful in allowing you to begin to follow Jesus again? How can you build these exercises into daily life?

- How, if at all, did Christian meditation help you to pivot from an earthly perspective to a more transcendent, heavenly reality? What can you do to strengthen this daily practice?

- How did you do with developing the mental skills of attention, present-moment awareness, and acceptance in the context of following Jesus on the roads of life?

- How, if at all, did your relationship with Jesus change as you spent more time meditating on God's Word, the Bible?

- How, if at all, did your ability to fellowship with Jesus change? How about your ability to find a deeper contentment in him as you made decisions throughout the day?

TARGETING PROBLEMS
with the SELF

Christian Meditation for Perfectionism

The law humbles, grace exalts. The law works fear
and wrath; grace works hope and mercy.

MARTIN LUTHER

For it is by grace you have been saved, through faith—and this is not from
yourselves, it is the gift of God—not by works, so that no one can boast.

EPHESIANS 2:8-9

But [God] said to me, "My grace is sufficient for you, for my power is
made perfect in weakness." Therefore I will boast all the more gladly
about my weaknesses, so that Christ's power may rest on me.

2 CORINTHIANS 12:9

Let us then approach God's throne of grace with confidence, so that we
may receive mercy and find grace to help us in our time of need.

HEBREWS 4:16

IN THIS CHAPTER, I explore perfectionism,[1] including its foundations in secular psychology, link to mental disorders, and relationship with mindfulness

---

[1]Egan et al. (2011); Limburg et al. (2017).

meditation. In addition, I discuss perfectionism in the context of the Christian tradition, offering a biblical understanding and intervention strategies. Although the fall of humankind resulted in brokenness entering the world, as Christians, we can rely on God's grace from moment to moment as the remedy to our imperfections and shortcomings, given we can fellowship with God because of our union with Jesus Christ.

Within this chapter, you will be able to track this transdiagnostic process with a log, practice a wide variety of strategies that are grounded in several bodies of Christian spiritual writings (e.g., medieval, Protestant), and explore your progress with journaling exercises. Along the way, I explain each exercise, then offer a transcript for ease of use. I also include one audio recording to listen to, should you prefer to do so.

Ultimately, my aim in this chapter is to help you gain more insight into the relationship between perfectionism, focusing on God, and deepening your contentment in, and communion with, him. What follows, then, is a range of meditative strategies, all housed within the Christian tradition. As a reminder, the four-step process throughout this workbook involves (1) noticing, (2) shifting, (3) accepting, and (4) acting, cultivating a spiritual awareness of God's active, loving presence in the here-and-now.

PERFECTIONISM: A SECULAR PSYCHOLOGICAL UNDERSTANDING

In the psychology literature, perfectionism consists of a variety of characteristics, including the following:[2]

- Establishing and maintaining extremely high standards

- Being preoccupied, dissatisfied, and disappointed with unmet standards

- Engaging in self-judgment and self-criticism when personal standards are not met

- Being preoccupied with, and distracted by, perceived mistakes

- Doubting the adequacy and success of personal performances (e.g., tasks, activities)

- Striving to be extremely neat, tidy, and organized in most environments (e.g., work, home)

Put more succinctly, perfectionism that is problematic and may impair daily living involves "maladaptive evaluative concerns."[3] These "evaluative concerns"

---

[2]Adapted from Egan et al. (2011); Limberg et al. (2017); Slaney et al. (2001).
[3]Bieling et al. (2004, p. 1373).

can be applied to ourselves, others, or relationships, with perfectionism rising to a clinical level when we continue to pursue extremely high standards, despite negative consequences in daily life.[4] In other words, although life may be falling apart because of our unrealistic standards and corresponding self-criticism, we may continue to pursue perfectionistic tendencies. To date, research has revealed a link between the self-criticism and self-judgment that sometimes emanates from "missing the mark," perfectionistic strivings, and a variety of psychiatric symptoms, reviewed below.

Perfectionism and psychopathology. In establishing and pursing extremely high standards, we may end up criticizing and judging ourselves when we fall short of our unrealistic expectations. In fact, recent research among adults has revealed a positive correlation between a preoccupation, dissatisfaction, and dissapoinment with unmet standards and symptoms of depression, anxiety, social phobia, and obsessive-compulsive disorder.[5] What is more, a review of almost three hundred studies elucidated that both "perfectionistic concerns" (e.g., a preoccupation with perceived mistakes, doubts about the proper completion of tasks, actions, and so forth) and "perfectionistic strivings" (e.g., the pursuit of organization and neatness; attempting to meet high personal standards) were positively associated with depression, anxiety, social phobia, worry, obsessive-compulsive symptoms, binge eating, and suicidal thoughts.[6] In response to these findings, authors have attempted to develop and empirically confirm a variety of interventions for perfectionism, often housed within the cognitive behavioral therapy (CBT) literature.[7] Along the way, mindfulness meditation has emerged as an intervention for perfectionism, based on its emphasis on nonjudgmental awareness in the present moment.[8]

Perfectionism and mindfulness meditation. Given unhealthy forms of perfectionism may involve rigid, unrealistic standards, self-criticism and self-judgment, and a preoccupation with neatness and organization, mindfulness meditation may help practitioners to simply notice their perfectionistic thinking, then shift toward another object within their awareness.[9] Therefore, in a recent eight-week pilot study of college students with self-reported perfectionism, the intervention group practiced different types of mindfulness meditation (e.g., mindful breathing), whereas the control group simply read a self-help book on perfectionism.[10] Results revealed that, when compared to the control group, the mindfulness meditation

---

[4]Egan et al. (2012).
[5]Maricutoiu et al. (2019).
[6]Limberg et al. (2017).
[7]Papadomarkaki and Portinou (2012); Shafran et al. (2016).
[8]Martin (2019).
[9]James and Rimes (2018).
[10]James and Rimes (2018).

group reported a greater reduction in perfectionism and stress at the conclusion of the eight-week study.[11]

In a separate study of community adults, researchers compared a six-week intervention group, which consisted of participants reading a book on mindfulness meditation for perfectionism, to a waiting-list control group.[12] In the book, a variety of meditative exercises were offered, which helped practitioners to accept themselves and anchor themselves to the present moment, rather than pursue rigid, perfectionistic standards.[13] Similar to the previously mentioned study, findings revealed that the intervention group, when compared to the control group, reported a greater reduction in perfectionism and stress, this time over a six-week period of time.[14]

With this research, we can see that mindfulness meditation may help practitioners to shift from perfectionistic tendencies to nonjudgmental, present-moment awareness, decreasing the tendency to establish and pursue unrealistic personal standards. To be sure, when we hold on to rigid, unattainable performance expectations, we may end up criticizing ourselves and struggling to press forward in an imperfect, fallen world. Although mindfulness meditation certainly holds some promise, I would like us to turn to the Christian tradition to make sense of perfectionism, doing so from a biblical worldview.

PERFECTIONISM: A CHRISTIAN UNDERSTANDING

From a Christian perspective, God created humankind in his image (Gen 1:27), to be in relationship with him and others. Yet, because of the fall, brokenness and hardship entered the world (Gen 3:16-19), resulting in our enduring suffering ever since. Fast-forward to the present day, and we repeatedly fall short in keeping God's commandments in daily life. In this fallen state, we are estranged from God and "miss the mark" on a moment-by-moment basis, struggling to carry out God's will each step of the way. In fact, the Bible reveals that we are only reconciled to God through our union with Christ (2 Cor 5:18-21; Col 1:19-23), not by any human effort of our own (Eph 2:8-10; Gal 2:16; Rom 3:28).

However, as Christians, many of us still struggle with legalism, or the notion that we need to somehow earn our salvation by perfectly following God's law.[15] Without a doubt, in attempting to meet extremely high external (emanating from society or the Bible) or internal (arbitrarily constructed on our own) standards, especially

---

[11]James and Rimes (2018).
[12]Wimberley et al. (2016).
[13]Wimberley et al. (2016).
[14]Wimberley et al. (2016).
[15]Anderson et al. (2003).

unattainable ones, we can miss out on the ever-present grace that God offers us on a daily basis. With legalism, we are "seeking to attain, gain, or maintain acceptance with God, or achieve spiritual growth, through keeping a written or unwritten code or standard of performance."[16] Here, we can see that solely relying on our own performance, which often flows from preconceived standards, is antithetical to the Christian notion of grace, or undeserved merit.

With grace, we do not need to earn our favor from God, given we are now friends with God because of our union with Christ. More formally, grace is defined as "undeserved blessing freely bestowed on humans by God—a concept that is at the heart not only of Christian theology but also of all genuinely Christian experience."[17] In the Christian tradition, more specifically, "common grace" refers to the blessings that God offers to all of creation, without favor to any one person, as well as God's providential care in providing for us on a daily basis, whereas "special grace" captures the redemption and sanctification available to those who put their faith in Jesus Christ, transforming our brokenness, meaninglessness, hardship, and suffering as God patiently walks with us along the paths of life.[18]

As we commune with God, walking with him on the arduous trails of life, we can cathartically acknowledge our imperfections, experience much-needed rest (both psychologically and spiritually), and exert a "humble confidence" in knowing that our identity is found in him, not our own unilateral efforts or "good works."[19] By relying on God's grace, not our own perfectionistic tendencies, we are learning to quickly get back on the roads of life when we have drifted in a wayward direction, without ruminating about our mistakes or worrying if our relationship with God has been damaged or ruptured. Rather, each and every time we come up short of God's standards, we can have the confidence that he is welcoming us home with outstretched arms (Lk 15:11-32).

Without God's grace, of course, perfectionism may creep in, especially when we constantly monitor the gap between our pre-established, unrealistic standards and current, imperfect performance. Along the way, we may develop a pattern of self-criticism and self-judgment, attacking ourselves with an internal dialogue that perseverates on mistakes, disorder, and disorganization in this fallen, broken world. Or, we may end up criticizing others, viewing their actions through our personally constructed system of right and wrong, divorced from God's omniscience. In fact, like the Pharisees in Jesus' time, we may end up viewing all of life through our own

---

[16]Anderson et al. (2003, p. 37).
[17]Hughes (2001, p. 529).
[18]Hughes (2001).
[19]Scorgie (2011).

moral lens.[20] Yet, since we are called to love God and others (Mt 22:36-40), human-derived knowledge can get in the way of fulfilling these two foundational commandments, which "all the Law and Prophets hang on" (Mt 22:40), in that our own arbitrary judgments can be antithetical to love.[21]

Perfectionism and the Bible: Pharisaic judgment versus love and God's will. In the New Testament, the Pharisees were religious leaders who created and attempted to enforce a wide variety of rules to govern moral behavior, doing so in a perfectionistic, judgmental manner.[22] Reminiscent of Adam and Eve in the garden, they attempted to be "like God," not "dependent on God," in their knowledge of good and evil.[23] Yet, Jesus responded to the Pharisees by following God's will, not getting caught up in their judgmental moral system.[24] In striving to follow the will of God, Jesus displayed a "freedom and simplicity of all action," emphasizing union and love, not disunion and judgment.[25]

In Jesus' example, then, we have a model for how we should live—instead of relying on our own moral standards for judging our own (and others') behavior, we should, with "freedom and simplicity of all action," focus on following God's will, striving for union and love along the way. In contrast with attempting to be like God in our knowledge of good and evil, in other words, we should be dependent on God, attempting to discern *God's* will from moment to moment.[26] In this process, our eyes are on God, not ourselves. Indeed, the initial misstep of Adam and Eve involved attempting to place themselves, not God, at the center of existence, deciding to pursue their own knowledge of good and evil, consistent with the Pharisees.[27] Yet, in doing so, suffering entered the world, with humankind now overwhelmed by our own rigid, unilaterally derived system of rules and regulations.

Ultimately, when we recognize we are attempting to enforce our own standards (whether applied to ourselves or others), a fitting next step involves simply letting go, surrendering our own imperfect knowledge of good and evil to God and prioritizing his will above our own. Stated differently, we are trading in our Pharisaic thinking for a deeper, more trusting reliance on God's will, recognizing that God (not humankind) is at the center of the proverbial garden. In this two-step process of noticing and shifting, we are relying on an amalgam of God's love and grace as the proverbial bridge, not our own fallen judgments of who we are, how we should

---

[20]Bonhoeffer (1955).
[21]Boyd (2004).
[22]Winter (2005).
[23]Bonhoeffer (1955, 1959).
[24]Bonhoeffer (1955).
[25]Bonhoeffer (1955).
[26]Bonhoeffer (1955).
[27]Bonhoeffer (1955).

perform, or how other people should measure up to our haphazardly created standards. In support of this perspective, recent research has revealed a link between perfectionistic strivings and psychological and spiritual struggles among religious adults, briefly reviewed below, suggesting that perfectionism may carry with it a whole host of challenges in the Christian life.

Perfectionism and psychological and spiritual functioning among religious adults. In a recent study of Latter-day Saints (i.e., Mormons), researchers developed two subscales to assess perfectionism in the context of their relationship with God.[28] The first subscale, "perceived standards from God," tapped into participants' beliefs about God's standards for them (e.g., "God expects the best from me," "God sets very high standards for me"), whereas the second subscale, "perceived discrepancy from God," measured the gap between how participants believed they were performing and whether or not they believed God was satisfied with their performance (e.g., "God is hardly ever satisfied with my performance," "I rarely live up to God's high standards").[29] Results revealed that the "perceived standards from God" subscale was positively linked to religious commitment and positive affect, whereas the "perceived discrepancy from God" subscale was negatively correlated with religious commitment and positive affect and positively associated with guilt, shame, and negative affect.[30]

In a more recent study, researchers explored religious perfectionism among different types of religious adults (e.g., Buddhists, Muslims, Protestant Christians) in China.[31] More specifically, the authors examined two subscales, "zealous religious dedication," which focuses on the level of importance of, and adherence to, religious beliefs and practices in daily life, and "religious self-criticism," which emphasizes dwelling on falling short of religious standards and corresponding feelings of guilt.[32] Results revealed that the "zealous religious dedication" subscale was positively correlated with happiness and life satisfaction, whereas the "religious self-criticism" subscale was positively linked to anxiety.[33] Consistent with the previous study, adherence to a set of religious standards does not seem to be the problem in and of itself. Instead, dwelling on the inevitable gap between our religious standards—emanating from our religious tradition—and imperfect performance seems to contribute more to psychological suffering.

In sum, we can see that having high standards that emanate from God is not unhealthy on its own. However, when we believe that God is dissatisfied and

---

[28]Wang et al. (2018).
[29]Wang et al. (2018).
[30]Wang et al. (2018).
[31]Wang et al. (2020).
[32]Wang et al. (2020).
[33]Wang et al. (2020).

disappointed with us in our struggles to live up to his expectations, we can also have a hard time with committing to our faith, guilt, shame, and negative affect. This type of research, then, prompts a fundamental question—since the Bible calls us to become more like Jesus Christ on a daily basis, which includes displaying the fruit of the Spirit along the way (Gal 5:22-23), how are we to respond to our personal shortcomings, especially when we believe God is disappointed with our imperfections?

Legalism, grace, and mental health among religious adults. In a recent study of Latter-day Saint college students, legalism was negatively associated with experiencing God's grace, as well as positively related to shame and fearing God.[34] On the other hand, experiencing God's grace was negatively linked to depression, anxiety, shame, and fearing God.[35] In addition, "perfectionism disgrepancy" was positively linked to legalism and negatively linked to experiencing God's grace.[36]

From this study we see that legalism is positively correlated with several psychological and spiritual struggles, whereas grace has the opposite relationship. More importantly, "perfectionism disgrepancy," which involves dwelling on the gap between our self-imposed high standards and actual performance, is positively linked to legalism and negatively correlated with grace. To emphasize this finding, experiencing God's grace may help us to let go of the tendency to dwell on our mistakes and shortcomings, given we are aware of God's loving acceptance from moment to moment. Although grace is certainly important in Christian living, especially as an antidote to perfectionism, self-criticism, and self-judgment, how can we best cultivate an awareness of God's loving acceptance in the here-and-now?

Perfectionism and Christian meditation, prayer, and contemplation. In the Christian tradition, grace is a foundational component of mental health, since we live in a fallen, broken world. In other words, God's grace is the proverbial glue that holds us together in our fragile condition, which is undeserved and freely flowing from him.[37] Therefore, rather than pursuing perfection in a legalistic, Pharisaic manner, relying on our own arbitrarly constructed moral system and judgments along the way, we can learn to surrender to God's will in each passing moment, becoming more like Jesus Christ day by day. To do so, Christianity offers a variety of practices, or spiritual disciplines, including meditation, prayer, and contemplation.

With meditation, we can meditate on God's grace, using words and images from Scripture to cultivate an awareness of the undeserved favor he is bestowing on us

---

[34]Judd et al. (2020).
[35]Judd et al. (2020).
[36]Judd et al. (2020).
[37]Knabb (2018).

from moment to moment. As a quick example, like the apostle Paul, we can savor God's promise about the sufficiency of his grace: "My grace is sufficient for you, for my power is made perfect in weakness" (2 Cor 12:9). With this passage, we may ruminate (in a healthy manner) on the short phrase "My grace is sufficient for you" throughout the day, pivoting from perfectionistic tendencies and self-criticism to these words whenever we notice a corresponding feeling of guilt or shame in inevitably coming up short.

In prayer, we may recite the long version of the Jesus Prayer—"Lord Jesus Christ, Son of God, have mercy on me, a sinner"—in order to recognize God's mercy (i.e., loving kindness) throughout the day. Or, we may condense the prayer, slowly reciting, "Lord Jesus, have mercy," so as to end the prayer with an emphasis on Jesus' compassion. As one more example, we may simply call on the name of Jesus, attempting to cultivate a deeper trust in him, not our own unilateral efforts. In doing this, we are learning to shift our focus from ourselves to God, recognizing that we are unable to become more like him without his help. Asking for mercy, therefore, is about asking for Jesus' presence, recognizing that he is the antidote to our fallen, broken condition.

Finally, with contemplation, we can lovingly focus on God, learning to shift from our own unilaterally derived, overly complex, and often inaccurate system of moral standards to the simple awareness that "It is finished" (Jn 19:28-30). To be sure, there is nothing that can disentangle us from God's perfect web of love (Rom 8:31-39), which means we can reach for him in each unfolding moment, basking in a loving awareness that he is with us right now. Along the way, we are learning, rather paradoxically, that the remedy for perfectionism is to simply sit, gazing at Jesus (like Mary), not anxiously striving (reminiscent of Martha) (Lk 10:38-42).

Overall, the four-step process in this workbook, applied to perfectionism, involves (1) noticing our self-criticism (and other perfectionistic tendencies), (2) shifting toward an awareness of God's perfect grace, (3) accepting God's perfect grace, and (4) acting in life based on a deeper communion with, and contentment in, God by making decisions that are consistent with his perfect will, not our own Pharisaic, legalistic ways. To begin this process, I would like you to start to notice your perfectionistic strivings with a daily log.

NOTICING PERFECTIONISM: A DAILY LOG

In this first exercise, you will be attempting to identify the types of perfectionistic tendencies you are engaged in on a daily basis. In particular, notice especially when you are (1) pursuing unrealistic standards, (2) judging or criticizing yourself for struggling to meet such standards, (3) second-guessing your performance in attempting to meet such standards, or (4) distracted by the need to be overly tidy, neat, or organized.[38]

To begin, simply set aside a few minutes, several times per day, to slow down and ask yourself if you are pursuing perfectionism in the here-and-now. If so, write down the type of perfectionism you are engaged in. Next, try to identify the impact that your perfectionistic strivings are having on your thoughts, feelings, behaviors, and relationships, before documenting the impact your perfectionistic, legalistic tendencies are having on your relationship with God. To start the process, I have provided one example. If needed, please use additional paper.

Now that you have had the opportunity to identify some of your perfectionistic tendencies throughout the day, as well as the impact they may have on your psychological and spiritual functioning, begin the first meditative practice in this chapter, drawn from a popular medieval writing, *The Imitation of Christ*.

THE "IMITATION OF CHRIST": RELYING ON GOD'S GRACE IN A FALLEN WORLD

In the 1400s, the medieval writer Thomas à Kempis wrote *The Imitation of Christ*.[39] In this famous work, he provided detailed instructions on the Christian life, especially the inner world. More specifically, in his chapter "On the Value of Divine Grace" he offered a fitting prayer that captures the importance of relying on God's grace from moment to moment. In particular, Thomas prayed the following:

> I plead with you, O Lord, may I find grace in your sight when I have earthly needs, for only your grace is sufficient for me [2 Cor 12:9]. When I am tempted and tormented by many troubles and trials, I will fear no evil as long as your grace remains in me. Your grace is alone my strength, for it brings me counsel and help. It is more powerful than all my enemies and wiser than all the wise ones in the world. Grace is the mistress of truth, the teacher of discipline, the light of the heart, the comfort in anxiety, the reliever of sorrow, the deliverer from fear, the nurse of devotion, and the source of tears of joy. I am just a withered tree without it, a dried-out branch to be cast away. Let your grace, then, always protect and be with me.[40]

Here, we can see just how salient grace is in the Christian life, given it is our source of comfort and relief during our most difficult times. In fact, God's grace is the proverbial glue that holds our fragmented state together,[41] especially when we recognize we are striving, on our own, toward a pseudo-state of perfection. Without God's grace we are merely a "withered tree."

---

[38]Adapted from Egan et al. (2011); Limberg et al. (2017); Slaney et al. (2001).
[39]Thomas (2015).
[40]Thomas (2015, chap. 53, sect. 1, para. 7).
[41]Knabb (2018).

NOTICING PERFECTIONISM

Day of the Week	Time of Day	Type of Perfectionism	Impact on Thoughts, Feelings, Behaviors, and Relationships	Impact on Relationship with God
Monday	11:00am	I'm a worthless parent. I'm not spending enough time with my son today. Although there was a crisis at work today that took up all of my time, I still have no excuse for being such a disappointment as a parent. I shouldn't ever let work get in the way of my relationship with my son.	My self-judgment is leading to a feeling of shame. I don't want to do anything today. I'm overwhelmed with thoughts of worthlessness and feelings of guilt and shame. The last thing I want to do now is spend time with my son. He deserves better.	I want to hide from God. I believe God's judging me right now. God has blessed me with a wonderful son, but I just can't seem to be there for him. I don't feel like reading my Bible or praying today.

Day of the Week	Time of Day	Type of Perfectionism	Impact on Thoughts, Feelings, Behaviors, and Relationships	Impact on Relationship with God

In another part of the chapter, we read Thomas authentically praying through his own struggles in life, viewed through the lens of God's grace:

> I often purpose to do many good things, but because grace is lacking in my weaknesses, I fall back with little resistence and fail. Because of this, I recognize the way of perfection and see clearly what I should do. But pressed down by the weight of my own corruption, I don't rise to the things which are perfect. Your grace is entirely necessary, O Lord, for a good beginning, good progress, and a good completion of life. Without your grace, I can do nothing, but "I can do everything through [you], who gives me strength" [Phil 4:13]. We are powerless, for without your heavenly grace, no gift of nature has any value. Arts, riches, beauty, strength, wit, or eloquence cannot do anything without you, O Lord, and your grace.[42]

In this powerful statement, we can see Thomas's confession of his own inadequacies, as well as the salience of relying exclusively on God's grace to optimally function in life. With these words, Thomas seems to be capturing at least two fundamental components of Christian living: (1) our inability, unilaterally, to both meet our own "earthly needs" and carry out God's will, and (2) our absolute reliance on God's grace, applied to a wide variety of life domains, talents, skills, and so forth, to derive value from life. With the next exercise, therefore, you will have a chance to practice noticing when you are relying on your own standards and efforts, then shifting toward surrendering to God in the present by yielding to his perfect grace.

THE "IMITATION OF CHRIST": AN EXERCISE

In this exercise,[43] set aside ten minutes to spend time with God, practicing shifting from relying on your own perfectionistic standards and efforts to utterly relying on God's grace to press forward with strength and confidence. Find a quiet location, closing your eyes and sitting up straight in a supportive chair. When you are ready, begin the practice below, resting your hands in your lap with your palms up to symbolize your receptivity toward God's perfect grace:

Notice. First, recognize all of the ways that you are striving, on your own, to attain perfection, whether in work life, family life, church life, or any other area of daily living. Notice the standards you have established, which may be unrealistic and divorced from God's perfect grace.

Shift. Second, shift from your perfectionistic tendencies to an awareness of God's active, loving presence. In this very moment, God is offering you undeserved favor, based on no effort of your own. Rather, God is freely giving you merit, extending value to you right now.

---

[42]Thomas (2015, chap. 53, sect. 1, para. 4).
[43]Adapted from Bonhoeffer (1955); Thomas (2015).

Accept. Third, accept God's gift of grace by slowly, softly, and gently repeating the following phrase: "O Lord, may I find grace in your sight when I have earthly needs." Whenever you notice a perfectionistic tendency emerge, simply pivot toward God's grace, acceping the worth he is bestowing upon you right now by reciting the phrase, "O Lord, may I find grace in your sight when I have earthly needs." Over and over again, recite this phrase in response to your perfectionistic strivings.

Act. Fourth, begin to imagine acting in life based on pursuing God's will, built upon union and love, not disunion and judgment. Envision walking with Jesus as you attempt to be more like him, letting go of the tendency to pursue your own standards. In simplicity, let go of any legalistic proclivities, given you have a relationship with God to rely on as you fellowship with him along the roads of life.

After completing the exercise, journal for a few minutes, attempting to answer the following questions:

- What was it like to shift from relying on your own perfectionistic standards to accepting God's grace? What were the benefits? The limitations?

- How well were you able to recite Thomas's prayer, "O Lord, may I find grace in your sight when I have earthly needs,"[44] during the exercise?

- What, if anything, got in your way? Were you able to overcome the obstacles? If so, how? If not, why not?

- How, if at all, can repeating Thomas's prayer help you with perfectionism as you move through the rest of your day?

- How, if at all, can repeating Thomas's prayer help you to accept God's loving presence, minute by minute, and act in a manner that is anchored to fellowshiping with, and finding contentment in, him as you carry out your day?

_____

_____

_____

_____

_____

_____

_____

_____

_____

[44]Thomas (2015).

PURITAN MEDITATION: MEDITATING ON GOD'S GRACE

In the Puritian tradition, *kataphatic* meditation involves "bending of the mind upon some spiritual object."[45] This "spiritual object" can include God's attributes, actions, heaven, and so forth. For this chapter, meditating on God's grace can be an important way to pivot from perfectionistic thoughts and actions to an awareness that God's grace is enough (2 Cor 12:9).

With Puritan meditation, we are typically engaging in several overarching steps, employing cognition as the vehicle through which to give rise to an emotional response and Christlike behavioral action. In fact, this meditative process involves present-moment awareness of God, along with focused, sustained attention on God. Along the way, we are learning to shift from perfectionism to God's grace, over and over again, recognizing that we can let go of our perfectionistic tendencies at any given moment by accepting God's grace as a free gift. In turn, we can get back on the roads of life, walking with God as a friend, trustworthy traveling companion, and perfect source of contentment.

Based on a review of a wide variety of Puritan sources on the topic, below are several steps for Puritan meditation, paying particular attention to God's grace as the "spiritual object," or subject matter:[46]

1. *Select.* Choose a short passage in Scripture to focus all your attention on, selecting a verse that emphasizes God's grace.

2. *Pray.* Say a short prayer to God, asking him to guide you during this meditative practice and offer you his grace.

3. *Shift.* Shift your focus from earthly-mindedness to heavenly-mindedness, letting go of your preoccupation with perfection and shifting toward a single point of focus—a short passage in Scripture that reveals God's grace.

4. *Meditate.* Slowly and gently repeat the passage in Scripture with focused, sustained attention.

5. *Move.* Begin to move from your brain to your heart, focusing on the feeling of being loved by God, which flows from his grace, captured in the short passage in Scripture.

6. *Feel.* Deeply experience the feeling of God's love that flows from his grace.

7. *Commit.* As you conclude the meditation, make a commitment to act on what you have just focused all your attention on by extending God's loving presence and grace to yourself and others throughout the day in a Christlike manner.

---

[45]Hall (2016, chap. 2, sect. 1, para. 1).
[46]Adapted from Ball (2016); Baxter (2015); Beeke and Jones (2012); Hall (2016); Knabb (2018, p. 87); Watson (2012).

8. **Pray.** Say a short prayer to God, thanking him for offering his grace to you and revealing himself to you via Scripture, then asking him to be with you throughout the rest of your day.

In these eight steps, we are able to meditate on God's grace, as well as pray to God, cultivating a deeper communion with him along the way. As we slowly move through the process, we are developing a present-moment loving awareness of God,[47] anchored to his everflowing grace, shifting from our unilateral efforts to achieve perfection to a total reliance on the merit that he bestows on us. Now, try to practice this eight-step process in order to shift from perfectionistic, legalistic tendencies to a more heavenly perspective, wherein God is at the center of reality, before resting in God's love and preparing for Christlike behavioral action through a deeper, more heartfelt experience of him.

PURITAN MEDITATION: AN EXERCISE

In this ten-minute exercise,[48] find a quiet environment, free from distractions, and sit up straight in a supportive chair. Close your eyes, resting your hands in your lap with your palms faced upward to God, symbolizing your willingness to let go of your perfectionistic strivings and rely exclusively on his grace, which he is offering freely to you right now. When you are ready, slowly move through the eight steps below:[49]

1. **Select.** Choose Psalm 103:8 to focus all your attention on, which emphasizes God's compassion, grace, patience, and love: "The LORD is compassionate and gracious, slow to anger, abounding in love."

2. **Pray.** Say a short prayer to God, asking him to guide you during this meditative practice and offer you his free gift of grace.

3. **Shift.** Shift your focus from earthly-mindedness to heavenly-mindedness, letting go of your preoccupation with perfection and moving toward a single point of focus: "The LORD is compassionate and gracious, slow to anger, abounding in love."

4. **Meditate.** Slowly and gently repeat the passage in Scripture with focused, sustained attention: "The LORD is compassionate and gracious, slow to anger, abounding in love."

5. **Move.** Begin to move from your brain to your heart, focusing on the feeling of being loved by God, which flows from his grace.

6. **Feel.** Deeply experience the feeling of God's love that flows from his grace.

---

[47]Knabb and Bates (2020a).
[48]Adapted from Ball (2016); Baxter (2015); Beeke and Jones (2012); Hall (2016); Knabb (2018, p. 87); Watson (2012).
[49]You can also follow along with the audio recording (Track 4), found at ivpress.com/Knabb4.

7. **Commit.** As you conclude the meditation, make a commitment to act on what you have just focused all your attention on by extending God's compassion, grace, patience, and love to yourself and others throughout the day in a Christlike manner.

8. **Pray.** Say a short prayer to God, thanking him for offering his grace to you and revealing himself to you via Scripture, then asking him to be with you throughout the rest of your day.

After completing the exercise, journal for a few minutes, attempting to answer the following questions:

- What was it like to shift from relying on your own perfectionistic standards to accepting God's grace by meditating on a short verse in the Bible? What were the benefits? The limitations?

- How well were you able to recite Psalm 103:8, "The LORD is compassionate and gracious, slow to anger, abounding in love," during the exercise?

- What, if anything, got in your way? Were you able to overcome the obstacles? If so, how? If not, why not?

- How, if at all, can repeating this verse help you with perfectionism as you move through the rest of your day?

- How, if at all, can repeating this verse help you to accept God's loving presence, minute by minute, and act in a manner that is anchored to fellowshiping with, and finding contentment in, him as you carry out your day?

_____

_____

_____

_____

_____

_____

_____

_____

_____

_____

_____

MEDITATING WITH A. W. TOZER: *THE CHRISTIAN BOOK OF MYSTICAL VERSE*

Several decades ago, A. W. Tozer, a prolific Protestant author of the twentieth century, compiled *The Christian Book of Mystical Verse*.[50] With this collection of writings from throughout Christian history, Tozer defined "mystical" as "that personal experience common to the saints of Bible times and well known to multitudes of persons in the post-biblical era" and "mystic" as someone "who has been brought by the gospel into intimate fellowship with the Godhead."[51] Of this type of person, Tozer went on to state the following:

> He differs from the ordinary orthodox Christian only because he experiences his faith down in the depths of his sentient being while the other does not. He exists in a world of spiritual reality. He is quietly, deeply, and sometimes almost ecstatically aware of the Presence of God in his own nature and in the world around him. His religious experience is something elemental, as old as time and the creation. It is immediate acquaintance with God by union with the Eternal Son. It is to know that which passes knowledge.[52]

Here, we can see that "mystical," from Tozer's perspective, consists of a deeper, quieter, simpler, more experiential encounter with God, one that recognizes God's presence from moment to moment in a real relationship, not in an abstract manner. In the context of perfectionism, we can easily get lost in our own performance, unilaterally striving to measure up to our own arbitrarily constructed standards, which are always just out of reach. Yet, in this very instance, God is revealing himself to us, which means we can enter into a simple, quiet, real exchange with the Creator of the universe in the here-and-now. Rather than attempting to be "like God" in pursuing our own knowledge of good and evil, which inevitably leads to a skewed perspective on who we are and God's will for our life, we can exchange our own lens for viewing the world with God's lens, which focalizes his love, forgiveness, mercy, and grace as freely flowing in this very moment.

To practice shifting from your own perfectionistic tendencies to an awareness of God's simple, quiet, gracious presence, slowly meditate on this hymn, included in Tozer's *The Christian Book of Mystical Verse* and written by Oliver Holden, likely in the early 1800s.[53] In this prayer, as you will see, the theme is God's throne of grace (see Heb 4:16), with God's grace present to us right now. As you meditate on this famous hymn, imagine approaching God's throne of grace with a more enduring confidence, since you are exchanging your own standards, which you can never

---

[50]Tozer (1991).
[51]Tozer (1991, introduction, para. 6).
[52]Tozer (1991, introduction, para. 6).
[53]Tozer (1991).

live up to, with the merit your benevolent King freely bestows upon you in this very instance. Ultimately, by shifting from your own standards to a total reliance on God's grace, which is always available from moment to moment, you will be learning to walk with him as a benevolent King and trustworthy traveling companion on the trails of life, steadily heading home with hope and endurance.[54]

MEDITATING WITH A. W. TOZER: AN EXERCISE

In this exercise,[55] set aside ten minutes, finding a comfortable location and sitting in a supportive chair with your eyes closed. When you are ready, slowly move through the following steps, envisioning that you have the ability to approach God's throne of grace in this very moment:

Meditate. First, slowly meditate on Oliver Holden's hymn, paying particular attention to the theme of God's grace, which he is freely offering to you in this very moment, untethered to any effort of your own to earn his favor:

They who seek the throne of grace
Find that throne in every place;
If we live a life of prayer,
God is present everywhere.
In our sickness and our health,
In our want, or in our wealth,
If we look to God in prayer,
God is present everywhere.
When our earthly comforts fail,
When the woes of life prevail,
'Tis the time for earnest prayer;
God is present everywhere.
Then, my soul, in every straight,
To thy father come, and wait;
He will answer every prayer:
God is present everywhere.

Imagine. Second, imagine that you are approaching God's throne of grace. Envision that you are walking up to God, seated on his royal throne. As you slowly move closer to God, you recognize that you are experiencing incredible peace, not fear or anxiety. As you step toward him, you are steadily gaining confidence and boldness, because God is welcoming you to be with him right now. In fact, you now realize you have special favor with your King, who is eagerly summoning you to approach him on his throne in this very instance, given he knows your current

---

[54]Knabb and Bates (2020b).
[55]Adapted from Gallagher (2008); Guthrie (1983); Tozer (1991).

needs. Among them, you have been struggling with a pseudo-need for perfection, falling short over and over again. Because of this, you are in psychological pain and need God to soothe your wounds and accept you in your vulnerable state, not judge, criticize, or shame you.

Let go. Third, as you finally reach God's throne, imagine letting go of your own lofty standards, setting them down at his feet. Envision what it might be like to truly relinquish the grip you have on your own arbitrarily constructed rules for life, with God encouraging you to do so. To be sure, imagine what it might be like for God to actually say, "Let go."

Accept. Fourth, in exchange for your personally developed standards for living, which are unattainable and only lead to shame, imagine that God is freely offering you his favor, which is undeserved, in this very moment. Unquestionably, there is nothing you can do right now to be worthy of this merit. Yet, even so, he is offering you value right now. Your job, thus, is to merely accept his offer. Spend a few minutes simply being with God, as he sits on his throne and offers you his perfect grace. There is nowhere else to be right now, other than in his presence, sitting at his feet as he reigns on his throne. Because you are with him, and because he has freely given you worth and value, you can confidently bask in the reality that you belong to his royal court.

Act. Fifth, once you have received God's free gift of grace, imagine what it might be like to go about the rest of your day, walking out into God's kingdom with boldness in knowing, matter-of-factly, that you get your true worth from God, which is not based on something you have to earn or prove. Instead, in each passing second of the day, God is bestowing upon you infinite value, which is a perfect gift from your King.

After completing the exercise, journal for a few minutes, attempting to answer the following questions:

- What was it like to shift from relying on your own perfectionistic standards to accepting God's grace by meditating on Oliver Holden's hymn? What were the benefits? The limitations?

- How well were you able to meditate on the hymn during the exercise?

- What, if anything, got in your way? Were you able to overcome the obstacles? If so, how? If not, why not?

- How, if at all, can imagining that you are approaching God's throne of grace help you with perfectionism as you move through the rest of your day?

- How, if at all, can imagining that you are approaching God's throne of grace help you to accept God's loving presence, minute by minute, and act in a manner that is anchored to fellowshiping with, and finding contentment in, him as you carry out your day?

_____

_____

_____

_____

_____

_____

_____

_____

_____

_____

_____

TERESA OF ÀVILA'S *THE WAY OF PERFECTION*: AN ALTERNATIVE TO HUMAN-DERIVED STANDARDS

In the 1500s, the Spanish nun Teresa of Àvila wrote *The Way of Perfection*, which offered detailed instructions on spiritual practices in the Christian tradition. As a recurring theme, she advocated for love, detachment, and humility as central to a life of prayer, anchored to the ways in which we show charity toward other people, let go of worldly pursuits, and shed self-preoccupations, all in an effort to follow God's will.[56] Along the way, we are cultivating a more enduring freedom, as we pivot from the personal distractions of status, reputation, esteem, wealth, and physical comfort to a deeper relationship with God.[57] Ultimately, as Christian virtues, love, detachment, and humility are about shifting from ourselves to God, prioritizing him, not our own self-interests and self-preoccupations, at the center of daily living, which can lead to calmness, joy, contentment, and peace.[58] In the context of perfectionism, we are letting go of our own standards, doing so in favor of surrendering to God's plan.

_____

[56]Teresa (2000).
[57]Teresa (2000).
[58]Teresa (2000).

As one type of prayer, Teresa taught the prayer of recollection, which involves focusing all of our attention on God, with an awareness that "He is near" and "never takes His eyes off [us]."[59] Using the image of a palace, she suggested that God is sitting on a throne within our inner world, which represents the human heart.[60] Since he is reigning over our heart, therefore, we should naturally surrender everything to him.[61]

In this prayer of recollection, the "soul collects its faculties together and enters within itself to be with its God," doing so in silence and solitude within the depths of our being.[62] In other words, rather than being easily distracted by sensory experiences in the outer world or thoughts in the inner world, we can converse with God in a simple, calm, straightforward manner, turning inward and imagining that his eyes are on us as he sits on his throne. With God's eyes always on us, we are learning to keep our eyes on him too. In this important exchange, we can "speak with him as with a father, or a brother, or a lord, or as with a spouse; sometimes in one way, at other times in another."[63]

In the context of her prayer of recollection, Teresa emphasized the salience of Jesus' beginning words on prayer: "Our Father" (Mt 6:9). Here, she explained that God is actually *within* our inner world, not far away in some distant heaven, which many of us are accustomed to envisioning. Therefore, with utter simplicity, we are learning to cultivate an awareness of God's presence inside, not somewhere outside, and recognizing that we have an intimate relationship with God as our heavenly Father:

> Do you think it matters little for a soul with a wandering mind to understand this truth and see that there is no need to go to heaven in order to speak to one's Eternal Father or find delight in him? Nor is there any need to shout. However softly we speak, he is near enough to hear us. Neither is there any need for wings to go out to find him. All one need to do is go into solitude and look at him within oneself, and not turn away from so good a Guest but with great humility speak to him as to a father.[64]

Ultimately, the "prayer of recollection" consists of several steps:[65]

1. *Turn.* In solitude, silence, and simplicity, turn inward, recognizing that God is already dwelling within you, not far away in some distant heaven.

2. *Imagine.* Imagine that God is sitting on a throne in a palace within the center of your being, with God's throne symbolizing his dwelling place in your heart.

---

[59]Teresa (2000, pp. 23-24).
[60]Teresa (2000).
[61]Teresa (2000).
[62]Teresa (2000, p. 300).
[63]Teresa (2000, p. 300).
[64]Teresa (2000, p. 299).
[65]Adapted from Teresa (2000).

As he sits on his throne, he is gazing upon you with loving attention. In this very moment, nothing is distracting him from bestowing worth and affection onto you, his faithful subject.

3. ***Surrender.*** Surrender yourself to God, trusting that he is your loving, heavenly Father as he reigns over your inner world. To yield in this way, imagine that your job consists solely of gazing back at him with a simple, loving attention.

4. ***Converse.*** Converse with God as your personal, loving Father, "recollecting" his presence by repeating the words "My Father" as you yield to God and imagine that he is at the center of your inner world, sitting on the throne of your heart.

5. ***Return.*** Whenever you notice you are distracted with something in either the outer (e.g., a sound) or inner (e.g., a thought) world, ever so gently return to your loving gaze with the humble words "My Father," recognizing that God is continuing to watch you with an affection that only a benevolent Father can provide.

Applied to perfectionism, with these steps, we are learning to relinquish the throne that we are currently sitting on to establish and enforce our own standards from moment to moment. As an alternative, we are recognizing that God is already dwelling within our inner world, offering his perfect love as a benevolent King who reigns over our internal kingdom. Because God is a good King, we can surrender our imperfections to him, knowing he is loving us from moment to moment and freely offering us merit, despite our shortcomings. In his reign, there is nothing we can do to earn his favor. Rather, we are simply tasked with basking in his loving presence, acknowledging he is the good King who has our best intentions in mind. To conclude this chapter, practice the prayer of recollection, shifting from sitting on your own inner thrown to recognizing God's benevolent reign within your heart.

TERESA OF ÀVILA'S *THE WAY OF PERFECTION*: AN EXERCISE

In this ten-minute exercise,[66] find a quiet location to rest in silence and solitude with God. Sit in a supportive chair, with your back straight and hands gently resting on your lap. Place your palms up to symbolize your willingness to yield to God's perfect reign within your heart, letting go of your own perfectionistic strivings in favor of God's loving affection. When you are ready, follow along with these steps:

1. ***Turn.*** In solitude, silence, and simplicity, turn inward, recognizing that God is already dwelling within you, not far away in some distant heaven.

2. ***Imagine.*** Imagine that God is sitting on a throne in a palace within the center of your being, with God's throne symbolizing his dwelling place in your heart.

---

[66]Adapted from Teresa (2000).

As he sits on his throne, he is gazing on you with loving attention. In this very moment, nothing is distracting him from bestowing worth and affection onto you, his faithful subject. In other words, he is watching you in loving admiration, not with judgment or criticism.

3. **Surrender.** Surrender yourself to God, trusting that he is your loving, heavenly Father as he reigns over your inner world. To yield in this way, imagine that your job consists solely of gazing back at him with a simple, loving attention. Other than this loving attention, nothing is needed. In fact, you can let go of your efforts to somehow earn his affection with perfectionistic strivings, resting in the notion that God already loves you and simply desires a reciprocating gaze.

4. **Converse.** Converse with God as your loving, personal Father, "recollecting" his presence by repeating the words "My Father" as you yield to God and imagine that he is at the center of your inner world, sitting on the throne of your heart.

5. **Return.** Whenever you notice you are distracted with something in either the outer (e.g., a sound) or inner (e.g., a thought) world, ever so gently return to your loving gaze with the humble words "My Father," recognizing that God is continuing to watch you with an affection that only a benevolent father can provide.

After completing the exercise, try to journal for a few minutes, attempting to answer the following questions:

- What was it like to imagine getting off of your own inner throne and relinquishing your reign to God? What were the benefits? The limitations?

- How well were you able to surrender your own perfectionistic strivings to God during the exercise?

- What, if anything, got in your way? Were you able to overcome the obstacles? If so, how? If not, why not?

- How, if at all, can imagining that God is a benevolent King who dwells in your heart and offers you his loving attention from moment to moment help you with perfectionism as you move through the rest of your day?

- How, if at all, can imagining that God is a benevolent King who dwells in your heart and offers you his loving attention right now help you to accept God's presence, minute by minute, and act in a manner that is anchored to fellowshiping with, and finding contentment in, him as you carry out your day?

REFLECTING ON THE PRACTICE

Throughout the chapter, we have focused on perfectionism. From a psychological perspective, perfectionistic tendencies can quickly impair daily functioning, especially when they become all-consuming, leading to self-criticism and a preoccupation with organization and neatness. Even more, for Christians, perfectionism can get in the way of communing with God, given we are focusing on ourselves, not him. Ever since the fall of humankind, we have struggled with attempting to be "like God," rather than dependent on him.[67] In other words, instead of relying on God's grace from moment to moment, we commonly construct our own personal standards, leading to a wide variety of perfectionistic proclivities in a broken, fragile world. Yet, in this very moment, God is offering us his grace, freely providing his unearned favor, which can take the place of our unilaterally constructed, unattainable standards for daily living. As the antidote to perfectionisim, trusting that God's grace is more than enough is key, letting go of our legalistic strivings in favor of a deeper rest in him.

By shifting from perfectionism to an awareness of God's active, loving presence, we are cultivating a more enduring contentment, found exclusively in him as we steadily walk and talk with him from moment to moment. To develop this friendship with God, based on our union with Christ, we have practiced several meditative exercises, anchored to medieval and Protestant spiritual sources, to (1) notice perfectionism, (2) shift from earthly preoccupations to a heavenly, spiritual reality, (3) accept God's presence and focus on him in each unfolding moment, and (4) act based on a deeper communion with, and contentment in, God. Before concluding this chapter and moving on to the final transdiagnostic process in this workbook—impaired mentalization—reflect on your meditative experiences thus far with a final journaling activity.

---

[67]Bonhoeffer (1955, 1959).

REFLECTING ON THE CHAPTER: A JOURNALING ACTIVITY

To conclude this chapter, spend a few minutes journaling about your experience with relating differently to your sense of self through the use of Christian meditation. Please use additional paper, if necessary. A few questions to consider:

- What was it like for you to notice your perfectionistic tendencies on a daily basis? How well were you able to do so? Were you able to step back and see these perfectionistic patterns in the moment? What can you do to continue to notice your perfectionistic tendencies?

- How well were you able to shift from perfectionism to God? What went well? What do you still need to work on?

- Which exercises, if any, were most helpful in allowing you to get unstuck from your perfectionistic tendencies and shift toward God? How can you build these exercises into daily life?

- How, if at all, did Christian meditation help you to pivot from an earthly perspective to a more transcendent, heavenly reality? What can you do to strengthen this daily practice?

- How did you do with developing the mental skills of attention, present-moment awareness, and acceptance in the context of your relationship with God?

- How, if at all, did your relationship with God change as you spent more time meditating on his Word, the Bible?

- How, if at all, did your ability to commune with God change? How about your ability to find a deeper contentment in him as you made decisions throughout the day?

_____

_____

_____

_____

_____

_____

_____

_____

TARGETING PROBLEMS
with RELATIONSHIPS

Christian Meditation for Impaired Mentalization

To love someone means to see him as God intended him.

FYODOR DOSTOEVSKY

To say that I am made in the image of God is to say that love is the reason
for my existence, for God is love. Love is my true identity. Selflessness
is my true self. Love is my true character. Love is my name.

THOMAS MERTON

A new command I give you: Love one another. As I have
loved you, so you must love one another. By this everyone will
know that you are my disciples, if you love one another.

JOHN 13:34-35

We have the mind of Christ.

1 CORINTHIANS 2:16

In your relationships with one another, have
the same mindset as Christ Jesus.

PHILIPPIANS 2:5

IN THIS EIGHTH AND FINAL CHAPTER, I explore impaired mentalization,[1] including its foundations in secular psychology, link to mental disorders, and relationship with mindfulness meditation. In addition, I discuss impaired mentalization in the context of the Christian tradition, offering a biblical understanding and intervention strategies. As Christians, although we may continue to struggle with fully understanding ourselves from the "outside in" and others (and God) from the "inside out"[2] in a broken world, we can learn to take on the "mind of Christ" (1 Cor 2:16; Phil 2:1-8) and display Christlike loving compassion through a plethora of meditative practices, given that God has called us to love one another (Jn 13:34-35). In fact, by deepening our fellowship with God, we can hold "[God's] mind in mind,"[3] or be mindful of the "mind of Christ," exchanging our own fallen thoughts for God's perfect thoughts so as to act like Jesus as we mercifully walk with others on the arduous roads of life.

As you work through this concluding chapter, you will be able to track the final transdiagnostic process with a log, as well as practice a wide variety of strategies, grounded in several bodies of Christian spiritual writings (e.g., contemporary, Protestant). For ease of use, I explain each exercise along the way, then provide a transcript for you to follow. I also include an audio recording, should you choose to listen to one of the guided exercises. Throughout the chapter, you will have the opportunity to reflect on each practice with journaling exercises in order to gain more insight into the relationship between impaired mentalization, focusing on God, and deepening your contentment in, and communion with, him.

Applied to the transdiagnostic process of impaired mentalization, the four steps in this workbook involve (1) noticing our fallen, imperfect mind (e.g., thoughts, feelings, intentions), as well as the fallen, imperfect mind of others (e.g., thoughts, feelings, intentions); (2) shifting toward the mind of Christ in the present moment; (3) accepting God's mind, trading in our wayward thoughts for his own by being mindful of the mind of Christ; and (4) acting in life with loving compassion, taking on the mind of Christ to display Christlike behavior that is anchored to God's will. To get us started, I would like to introduce mentalization, a popular concept among secular psychologists for understanding uniquely human self-in-relationship processes.

IMPAIRED MENTALIZATION: A SECULAR PSYCHOLOGICAL UNDERSTANDING

In the last few decades, mentalization has emerged in the psychology literature as an important concept for understanding relational, self-and-other functioning in

---

[1]Allen (2008).
[2]Allen et al. (2008).
[3]Allen and Fonagy (2006).

daily life. To mentalize, as humans, means we are able to understand the mental states of ourselves, commonly referred to as "meta-cognition" (i.e., thinking about our own thinking), as well as other people.[4] Stated differently, mentalizing helps us to recognize that we have an inner world, made up of a variety of unique thoughts, feelings, and intentions, as do the diverse people we interact with on a daily basis.

Ultimately, to mentalize means we can identify the connection between external behaviors and internal thoughts and feelings, in both ourselves and others, striving to understand that other people have a separate mind from our own. In this process, we are attempting to accurately "mind read" as we interact with others in daily life. For example, we might walk past an old friend at a local grocery store, quickly recognizing that they have not acknowledged our presence. Rather than interpreting this behavior in a purely negative light, we may mentalize by imagining that they have had a difficult day at work and are rushing home to be with their family. With this human ability to mentalize, most importantly, comes the capacity to make sense of the thoughts and feelings (and corresponding intentions), not just behaviors, of ourselves and others.[5]

To offer a brief summary, mentalizing, applied to the self, may consist of the following overlapping ingredients:[6]

- Displaying compassion toward ourselves

- Striving to make sense of our own intentions

- Viewing our inner world with a bit more distance

- Making sense of our behaviors by attempting to understand our inner world (e.g., thoughts, feelings, beliefs, values, preferences, wishes, desires, concerns)

- Focusing our attention on our "interiors" (e.g., thoughts, feelings), not just "exteriors" (e.g., behaviors, actions, physical displays)

- Thinking about what we might be thinking and "[keeping our own] mind in mind" (i.e., meta-cognition)

- Understanding what we might be feeling

- Seeing ourselves from the outside in

On the other hand, mentalization, in the context of other people, may involve the following overlapping components:[7]

---

[4] Allen (2008).
[5] Aival-Naveh et al. (2019).
[6] Adapted from Aival-Naveh et al. (2019); Allen (2008); Dimitrijevic et al. (2018); Fonagy and Luyten (2009); Gilbert (2010).
[7] Adapted from Aival-Naveh et al. (2019); Allen (2008); Dimitrijevic et al. (2018); Fonagy and Luyten (2009); Gilbert (2010).

- Viewing others as real people, with unique and separate inner experiences, not mere objects to be used or exploited for our own benefit

- Displaying compassion toward others

- Attempting to take the perspective of others

- Striving to make sense of others' intentions

- Making sense of others' behaviors by attempting to understand their inner world (e.g., thoughts, feelings, beliefs, values, preferences, wishes, desires, concerns)

- Focusing on others' "interiors" (e.g., thoughts, feelings), not just "exteriors" (e.g., behaviors, actions, physical displays)

- Thinking about what other people might be thinking and "[keeping others'] mind[s] in mind"

- Empathizing with, and understanding, what other people might be feeling

- Empathizing with others through picking up on nonverbal communication

- Seeing other people from the inside out

- Understanding the "imaginative mental activity" of others

Above all else, the human capacity to observe and make sense of our own inner world from a "balcony view," or an outside-in perspective, as well as imagine what other people may be thinking, feeling, and intending, or an inside-out perspective, means we can look beyond mere behavior in order to better understand our relational world, including crucial self-and-other dynamics. Without this mental ability, a wide variety of struggles can quickly ensue, leading to both short- and long-term psychological challenges in daily life.

Impaired mentalization, psychopathology, and loving compassion. As a transdiagnostic process, mentalization can help us to flexibly observe and understand our own thoughts and feelings, as well as the thoughts and feelings of others,[8] accurately linking these inner states to observable behavior.[9] In other words, we are able to more effectively manage our behaviors when we can clearly recognize this inner-outer connection, given our thoughts and feelings play a vital role in our daily actions.[10] This interior-exterior dynamic, moreover, is vital for our relationships, since healthy interpersonal exchanges involve understanding that others' behaviors are influenced by their own unique thoughts, feelings, and intentions.[11]

---

[8]Malda-Castillo et al. (2019).
[9]Eizirik and Fonagy (2009).
[10]Eizirik and Fonagy (2009).
[11]Eizirik and Fonagy (2009).

As children, we gradually acquire this salient ability to understand our own mental states when we have ongoing, predictable, healthy interactions with caregivers, made up of loving, attentive, and emotionally responsive exchanges, especially when we are distressed and disregulated.[12] Over time, as caregivers understand and mirror our psychological experiences, we develop the ability to understand ourselves, both internally and externally, including our own thoughts and feelings. To be certain, it is as if caregivers hold up a mirror, psychologically speaking, to reflect our experiences, which slowly helps us to understand our own emotional world and better manage our own distressing emotional states. Also in these optimal interactions with caregivers, we slowly learn that our inner world is not always the same as—that is, it does not perfectly match—what is taking place in the outer world,[13] developing a basic understanding that our thoughts and feelings are by no means objective facts, and we do not need to impulsively act on them.[14]

Beyond gaining insight into ourselves, we gradually learn how to understand others in these crucial caregiver-child exchanges, especially the reality that other people may have different, separate mental states that do not fully align with our own.[15] Along the way, we begin to view our mental states from the outside in, as well as others' mental states from the inside out, noticing and tolerating inner-outer and self-other discrepancies in the process.[16] Combined, we can eventually recognize, as a uniquely human skill, that we have a mind, other people have a mind, and these separate minds are made up of idiosyncratic thoughts, feelings, and intentions that may not fully align with outward displays of behavior.

Because of the salience of this capacity, when impaired, we may end up struggling with a variety of individual and interpersonal dynamics, such as managing our emotions, monitoring distortions in our thinking, flexibly shifting perspectives to understand alternative points of view, and understanding the intentions (not just behaviors) of other people.[17] In our struggles, we might develop dichotomous, black-and-white, rigid thinking, believing we know (with certainty) that others have "malevolent" intentions, which prevents us from entertaining a full range of possible motivations (in ourselves and others) with an open, flexible curiosity.[18] With impaired mentalization, moreover, we may go on to struggle with a wide variety of psychiatric symptoms and mental disorders, since the ability to mentalize

---

[12]Bateman and Fonagy (2010).
[13]Eizirik and Fonagy (2009).
[14]Hayes et al. (2012).
[15]Eizirik and Fonagy (2009).
[16]Allen et al. (2008).
[17]Malda-Castillo et al. (2019).
[18]Jain and Fonagy (2020).

is key to better understanding ourselves and others.[19] For instance, in research of late, deficits in mentalizing have been linked to anxiety in close relationships (i.e., attachment anxiety) and neuroticism as a personality feature (e.g., worry, anxiety),[20] as well as symptoms of depression.[21]

More recently, a review of almost two dozen studies revealed that mentalization-based therapies (which focus on helping clients make better sense of their own, as well as the psychotherapist's, mental states) may be helpful for personality disorders (e.g., borderline) and depression.[22] In addition, in a study from only a few years ago, community adults who described themselves as "in love" (i.e., in a romantic relationship) and were "primed" by being shown a picture of their romantic partner and asked to reminisce about a fond memory outperformed a control group in identifying the emotions of strangers in black-and-white photographs.[23] So we can see that mentalizing may be crucial for deepening our relationships, with love possibly bridging this process.

Certainly, "mentalizing enables intimacy, a loving sense of connection with the reality of another person" and "is more than a skill; it is a virtue, a loving act."[24] Put another way, in contrast with mere infatuation, mentalizing with loving affection may help us to "see more clearly and deeply,"[25] letting go of our own self-preoccupations in order to optimally respond to the mental states of others.[26]

In addition to love, compassion may help us to better understand the link between mentalizing and relating to ourselves and others. At least theoretically, compassion—or the ability to be moved by, and responsive to, suffering[27]—for ourselves and others may help us to better mentalize, given we are cultivating a more "compassionate self," slowing down to be kind, nurturing, empathic, and validating toward the plethora of fluctuating thoughts and feelings (and, ultimately, suffering) we experience in the inner world, as well as the suffering of others.[28] More formally, self-compassion involves (1) exercising kindness (not self-criticism) toward ourselves; (2) recognizing that, as humans, we all suffer; and (3) maintaining an awareness of our most difficult thoughts and feelings with distance and flexibility, not dwelling on them and defining ourselves by them,[29] which can also be extended to others.

---

[19]Bateman and Fonagy (2010).
[20]Dimitrijevic et al. (2018).
[21]Fischer-Kern and Tmej (2019).
[22]Malda-Castillo et al. (2019).
[23]Wlodarski and Dunbar (2014).
[24]Allen and Fonagy (2006, p. 23).
[25]Allen et al. (2008, p. 133).
[26]Allen (2013).
[27]Gilbert (2010).
[28]Gilbert (2010).
[29]Neff (2003).

To understand and accept the mental states of ourselves and others with compassion and empathy means we can explore, at a safe distance, the inner workings of the human mind, recognizing that our thoughts and feelings change from moment to moment and influence our behavior, often without our awareness of this vital connection.[30] This more welcoming, kind, and empathic approach to our own mind, as well as the mind of others, means we can let go of the tendency to avoid, disavow, wall off, or flat-out deny that we have an inner world, which sometimes suffers in a fallen world. Instead, we can gently explore, with greater distance, flexibility, and empathy, our thoughts and feelings so that we can be more intentional about our interpersonal exchanges with others, who also struggle from time to time.

In support of this theoretical understanding, in a recent empirical study of community adults, compassion (defined as "the tendency to experience concern and empathy for others") was positively linked to "theory of mind," a component of mentalizing that involves understanding others' perspectives.[31] Here, we can see that improving our ability to mentalize may help to lessen psychopathology, with loving compassion as one potential source of motivation for better understanding the mental states of ourselves and others. To increase this loving and compassionate mentalizing function, the psychology literature has recently advocated for the use of mindfulness meditation, recognizing that the cultivation of compassion can be helpful for slowing down to see ourselves from the outside in and others from the inside out.[32]

Impaired mentalization, mindfulness, and loving compassion. With mindfulness, we are deliberately attending to present-moment inner and outer experiences with acceptance and open curiousity,[33] which means that regular practice may help with self- and other-mentalizing, given we are learning to be mindful of the mental states of ourselves and others.[34] More specifically, because we are developing the ability to notice the inner world with nonjudgment and empathic compassion, we are cultivating a greater capacity to think about our thinking (i.e., meta-cognition) and understand our emotions with greater distance.[35] Stated more succinctly, mentalization is simply "mindfulness of the mind."[36] Ultimately, in changing our relationship to our thoughts and feelings by learning to notice them with less rigidity and more kindness, we are able to recognize that we are

---

[30] Allen (2013).
[31] Allen et al. (2017, p. 600).
[32] Allen et al. (2008).
[33] Feldman et al. (2007).
[34] Allen (2013); Jain and Fonagy (2020).
[35] Aival-Naveh et al. (2019); Allen (2013); Gilbert (2010).
[36] Allen (2013).

more than these impermanent, passing events within the inner world.[37] In turn, we can make relational decisions that are more intentional, rather than being lost in a sea of mindless impulsivity.

In fact, *interpersonal* mindfulness means that we are being especially mindful in social exchanges, including attending (and listening) to the other person, accepting the other person with nonjudgment, and maintaining an awareness of our own, as well as the other person's, emotions.[38] In the context of mentalizing, interpersonal mindfulness can help us to "mind the mind" of the other person.[39] Along the way, we are being fully present, nonreactive, nonjudgmental, and compassionate toward the other person, accepting the reality that they have a unique, separate, real mental world—with different thoughts, feelings, beliefs, values, and intentions than our own—which is active in the here-and-now and contributing to the very conversation before us.[40] Conversely, when we are struggling with impaired mentalization, we are being mindless, not mindful, of the mind of others, merely seeing their behavior, not their thoughts, feelings, and intentions as separate human beings with a will of their own.

Recent research among an online sample of community adults revealed that interpersonal mindfulness was negatively correlated with symptoms of depression, anxiety, and stress and positively correlated with empathy and perspective taking.[41] In a separate study with college students, interpersonal mindfulness was negatively linked to depression and anxiety and positively linked to empathy and perspective taking.[42] Thus, we can see that attempting to be fully present to the other person's mental world can help us walk in their proverbial shoes and take a better look around.

To summarize, mindfulness may help us to cultivate compassion for ourselves and others and better see ourselves from the outside in and others from the inside out.[43] Still, from a Christian perspective, mentalizing is not a solely intrapsychic activity that begins and ends within the individual, but involves God at the center of our mental world, living in us and working through us. In fact, because Christian mental health involves fellowshiping with God from moment to moment and finding a deeper contentment in him,[44] to mentalize, as Christians, means we are regularly taking on the mind of Christ,[45] exchanging our thoughts, feelings, intentions, and behaviors for his own. Next, then, I would like us to explore a Christian

---

[37]Masterpasqua (2016); Wallin (2007).
[38]Pratscher et al. (2019).
[39]Sisti (2014).
[40]Allen (2013); Fonagy and Luyten (2009); Gilbert (2010); Pratscher et al. (2019).
[41]Pratscher et al. (2019).
[42]Pratscher et al. (2018).
[43]Allen (2013); Allen et al. (2008).
[44]Knabb and Bates (2020b).
[45]Zirlott (2017).

understanding of holding the "mind in mind,"[46] or, put another way, "mindfulness of the mind,"[47] which prompts a pressing question, "Whose mind is it anyway?"

IMPAIRED MENTALIZATION: A CHRISTIAN UNDERSTANDING

From a Christian perspective, mentalizing involves a broader triad (God-human-human), not a narrower dyad (human-human), made up of our attempts to understand our own God-given (yet fallen) mind, the God-given (yet also fallen) mind of others, and the (perfect) mind of God. In this triad, we are striving to make sense of our imperfect mind-behavior-intention dynamics and inviting God to sanctify us in our enduring, vulnerable state as the Lord of our mind. For Christians, then, following Jesus Christ and becoming more like him each and every day means *both* thinking *and* acting like him.[48] In doing so, we are intentionally choosing to mentalize with the mind of Christ, meditating on and internalizing Scripture, following God's will, and displaying Christlike loving compassion toward ourselves and others along the way (1 Cor 2:16; Col 3:11-12; Phil 2:1-8; Rom 12:2).[49] In other words, to hold the "mind in mind,"[50] or engage in "mindfulness of the mind,"[51] means we are holding the "[fallen] mind in mind," applied to ourselves and others, recognizing that we need to intentionally shift from our own thoughts to the thoughts of God.[52]

To take on the mind of Christ, more specifically, means we are adopting his "ideas, images, information, and patterns of thinking," pivoting from our own thoughts and behaviors to those modeled by Jesus.[53] This step-by-step process involves (1) noticing our own mind, including the link between our fallen thoughts, feelings, behaviors, and intentions, then (2) shifting toward the mind of Christ, viewing our own fallen thoughts, feelings, behaviors, and intentions and the fallen thoughts, feelings, behaviors, and intentions of others through the lens of Christlike loving compassion. Certainly, this is no easy task, given our imperfect, vulnerable state, which results in impaired mentalization in daily life. However, a variety of meditative practices may help us to be mindful of God's mind throughout the day. Before exploring the ways in which these exercises can help us to be more Christlike in compassionately relating to ourselves and others, though, I would like to further explore a biblical view of mentalizing. With this understanding, the Christian life boils down to trading in our own mind for the mind of Christ, mentalizing with

---

[46]Allen and Fonagy (2006).
[47]Allen (2013).
[48]Stanley (2009).
[49]Mathis (2016); Stanley (2009); Wolpert (2003).
[50]Allen and Fonagy (2006).
[51]Allen (2013).
[52]Goodwin (2015).
[53]Willard (2002).

Christ's mind, not our own, as we attempt to deepen our relationships with both God and others on this side of heaven (Mt 22:36-40).

Impaired mentalization, the Bible, and loving compassion. Because of the fall (Gen 3),[54] as humans, we regularly struggle to understand our own mind, including the link between our thoughts, feelings, behaviors, and intentions, as well as the thoughts, feelings, behaviors, and intentions of others. Because of sin (*hamartano*, Greek), we frequently miss the mark, similar to an archer aiming for, then over-shooting, the intended bullseye.[55] In our estrangement from God, we commonly miss the mark by attempting to define and make sense of ourselves and others outside of our relationship with God,[56] struggling to extend God's loving compassion and mercy to ourselves and others in the process. In these repeated stumbles, we may end up hurting both ourselves and others, psychologically speaking, given the wide variety of misunderstandings that can emanate from our broken existence,[57] especially when we fail to hold God's "mind in mind."[58]

According to the late Trappist monk Thomas Merton,

> God is a consuming Fire. He alone can refine us like gold, and separate us from the slag and dross of our selfish individualities to fuse us into this wholeness of perfect unity that will reflect His own Triune Life forever. As long as we do not permit His love to consume us entirely and to unite us in Himself, the gold that is in us will be hidden by the rock and dirt which keep us separate from one another. As long as we are not purified by the love of God and transformed into Him in the union of pure sanctity, we will remain apart from one another, opposed to one another, and union among us will be a precarious and painful thing, full of labor and sorrow and without lasting cohesion.[59]

From a Christian perspective, the human ability to compassionately hold our "mind in mind"[60] comes from God, whose love serves as our proverbial glue. As Christians, therefore, we should be guided by *God's* loving compassion on a daily basis, given (1) "God is love" (1 Jn 4:7-17); (2) God has already displayed his perfect, loving compassion to us by offering his Son as *the* way to reconcile us to him (Jn 3:16); and (3) loving God and others is the *telos* (i.e., purpose) for this life (Jn 13:34-35). Overlapping with the secular psychology literature, Christlike loving compassion may help us, as Christians, to better understand the bridge between mentalizing and healthy relational functioning.[61]

---

[54]Genesis 3.
[55]Erickson (2013); Strong (2001b).
[56]Bonhoeffer (1955, 1959); Merton (1961).
[57]McMinn (2008).
[58]Allen (2013).
[59]Merton (1961, pp. 70-71).
[60]Allen and Fonagy (2006).
[61]Allen (2013); Allen and Fonagy (2006); Gilbert (2010); Wlodarski and Dunbar (2014).

In the Christian tradition, compassion is defined as "[entering] sympathetically into one's sorrow and pain,"[62] emanating from the New Testament word *eleos*, which frequently conveys God's compassion and mercy for humankind as we suffer in a fallen world.[63] As revealed in Scripture, throughout human history, God has displayed his perfect compassion toward humankind in his loving responsiveness, and we are called, in turn, to show compassion to one another (Ps 103:13; 2 Cor 1:3-4; Eph 4:32; 1 Pet 3:8). In the context of mentalizing, we are tasked with emulating Jesus Christ by taking on his mind (1 Cor 2:16), then showing loving compassion toward others in daily life.

Building on this more general understanding, to take on the mind of Christ means we possess a "renewed mind" that is "divinely influenced," displaying Christlike loving compassion in our relationships with others by following God's will, not our own.[64] Writing to the Romans, the apostle Paul offers followers of Jesus Christ the following:

> Therefore, I urge you, brothers and sisters, in view of God's mercy, to offer your bodies as a living sacrifice, holy and pleasing to God—this is your true and proper worship. Do not conform to the pattern of this world, but be transformed by the renewing of your mind. Then you will be able to test and approve what God's will is—his good, pleasing and perfect will. (Rom 12:1-2)

Paul goes on to encourage Christians to hold the following thoughts in mind:

> Hate what is evil; cling to what is good. Be devoted to one another in love. Honor one another above yourselves. Never be lacking in zeal, but keep your spiritual fervor, serving the Lord. Be joyful in hope, patient in affliction, faithful in prayer. Share with the Lord's people who are in need. Practice hospitality.
>
> Bless those who persecute you; bless and do not curse. Rejoice with those who rejoice; mourn with those who mourn. Live in harmony with one another. Do not be proud, but be willing to associate with people of low position. Do not be conceited.
>
> Do not repay anyone evil for evil. Be careful to do what is right in the eyes of everyone. If it is possible, as far as it depends on you, live at peace with everyone. (Rom 12:9-18)

Within this list, we are given instructions on how to display Christlike loving compassion in the context of both relationships and life events, taking on the mind of Christ by "renewing our minds" to conform to Jesus' mind. In Romans 12, thus, to have God's "mind in mind"[65] means the following:

---

[62]Stewart (1998, p. 324).
[63]Strong (2001b).
[64]Keener (2016).
[65]Allen and Fonagy (2006).

- We are to have an accurate view of ourselves and others, believing we are equal to (not better than) other people.

- We are to love, honor, share with, maintain peace with, bless, and devote ourselves to others, even when we believe we are being "persecuted," by doing what is "good" and "right."

- We are to maintain joy, hope, patience, and faith in the midst of life's challenges.

Certainly, God, who offers his loving compassion to us in each unfolding moment, plays a central role along the way, sanctifying us so that we can better understand and relate to ourselves and others in our pursuit of a more "lasting cohesion."[66] Therefore, in this fallen world, God can help us to relate differently to ourselves and others, modeled by Jesus Christ, by (1) noticing our own (and others') fallen mental states, (2) shifting toward the mind of Christ, and (3) displaying Christlike loving compassion toward ourselves and others.

But how, exactly, do we begin this process of maintaining an awareness of our imperfect mind from the outside in, as well as others' imperfect mind from the inside out,[67] trading in our fallen mind for the mind of Christ and displaying Christlike loving compassion along the way? We can begin by gaining further insight into three separate "minds," two of which are fallen and one of which is not: (1) our own thoughts, feelings, and intentions, as well as the link between these mental processes and our behavior; (2) others' thoughts, feelings, and intentions, as well as the link between others' mental processes and their behavior; and (3) the mind of Christ.

To get us started, we can ask several overarching, interwoven questions in the present moment so as to cultivate the ability to mentalize with the mind of Christ and display Christlike loving compassion:

Self

- What am I thinking and feeling right now? What am I intending to do right now? What am I actually doing?

- How can I mentalize with the mind of Christ right now, thinking Jesus' thoughts, not my own?

- How can I display Christlike loving compassion toward myself right now?

Others

- What is this person thinking and feeling right now? What are they intending to do right now? What are they actually doing?

---

[66]Merton (1961).
[67]Allen et al. (2008).

- How can I mentalize with the mind of Christ right thoughts about this person, not my own?

- How can I display Christlike loving compassion toward this pers͜

God

- What is Jesus thinking and feeling right now? What is Jesus doing right now?[68]

- How can I mentalize with the mind of Christ right now, thinking Jesus' thoughts?

- How can I display Christlike loving compassion right now?

When we have a hard time understanding our own mind, the mind of others, and the mind of God, we can easily lose our way in life, struggling to prioritize the mind of Christ and deepen our relationship with both God and others. In fact, in the last several years, researchers in the psychology literature have attempted to better understand the theoretical role that mentalizing (including impaired mentalization) plays in the human ability to pursue and maintain a relationship with God.

Imaired mentalization, the psychology of religion, and God. In the psychology literature, some authors have recently argued that relating to God requires mentalizing, given that many religious adults believe God is intentional, with separate mental states than us.[69] From this perspective, we need to be able to mentalize to relate to God, beyond reading about God's attributes and actions in the Bible, since we are relying on our imagination to enter into and maintain a relationship that is perceived to be real.[70] In other words, to imagine what God has believed about us in the past, what he believes about us in the present, and what he will believe about us in the future requires us to mentalize, as does being able to reflect on our own beliefs about God.[71] Mentalizing, too, is required when we attempt to understand others' relationship with God, which is separate from our own, whether making sense of a spouse's, child's, neighbor's, or coworker's experience of God. In each of these dyads (or triads), we are recognizing that we have a God-given mind, others have God-given minds, and God has a mind of his own.

Impaired mentalization and sanctification. Beyond merely believing that God has perfect mental states that are in contrast with our own (and others') fallen mental states, the Christian concept of sanctification may help us to better understand this mental exchange process, wherein we hold God's "mind in mind"[72] throughout the day. In other words, beyond the first step of simply attempting to understand God's mental state, which is different from our own, we can actually

---

[68]Unlike fallen humans, though, Jesus' intentions and actions are one and the same.
[69]Allen (2013); Schaap-Jonker and Corveleyn (2014).
[70]Allen (2013).
[71]Schaap-Jonker and Corveleyn (2014).
[72]Allen and Fonagy (2006).

to take on the mind of Christ, becoming more like him—which includes thinking like he thinks[73]—from moment to moment. Certainly, for Christians, God desires for us to become more like him each passing day, on our way to being with him, face to face, in heaven.[74]

With sanctification, God is leading us through a process of transformation, wherein we are renewed in the image of God to be more Christlike in our thoughts and actions and live out God's will in daily life.[75] The process of sanctification, of course, involves communing with God based on our union with Christ, doing so by faith, not overly relying on our own works.[76] Yet, the process is also collaborative, in that we make efforts to emulate Jesus, who reveals himself to us in Scripture (1 Cor 11:1; Eph 5:1; Phil 2:5-11).[77] As a quick example, purposefully displaying kindness and compassion through loving, forgiving, and serving others, just like Jesus did, is foundational to Christlikeness (Eph 4:32; 5:2; Phil 2:5-11).[78]

Interestingly, in the psychology literature, sanctification is defined as "a psychological process through which aspects of life are perceived by people as having [divine] character and significance" and has been empirically explored in recent years as a psychospiritual, not just theological, concept.[79] For example, sancitification has been applied to family life, including the relationship between both husbands and wives and parents and children, with religious individuals "[perceiving] an object as being a manifestation of [their] images, beliefs, or experience of God."[80] In religious family life, undoubtedly, relationships are perceived to be a triad, not dyad—with God active and present in marital (i.e., spouse-spouse) and family-child interactions.[81] To date, research among community adults has revealed that sancitification as a "manifestation of God" is positively correlated with prayer and church attendance among both spouses and parents[82] and positively correlated with collaborative problem solving and affection among spouses.[83]

In sum, in this line of psychological research on *theistic* sanctification, mentalizing appears to be taking place, given the "divine character and significance"[84] of key interpersonal exchanges in family life often emanate from an attempt to take on the mind of Christ, exchanging our own fallen thoughts and actions for

---

[73]Willard (2002).
[74]Knabb and Bates (2020b).
[75]Hoekema (1987).
[76]Hoekema (1987).
[77]Hoekema (1987).
[78]Hoekema (1987).
[79]Mahoney et al. (2003, p. 221); Pargament and Mahoney (2005, p. 183).
[80]Mahoney et al. (2003, p. 221).
[81]Mahoney et al. (2003).
[82]Mahoney et al. (2003).
[83]Kusner et al. (2014).
[84]Pargament and Mahoney (2005 p. 183).

Christlike relational functioning. In other words, when we are attempting to be Christlike in our human relationships, we are striving to recognize God's presence, role, actions, teachings, and will,[85] which requires holding God's "mind in mind."[86] But how, exactly, can we utilize classic spiritual practices in the Christian tradition to better mentalize in our God-human and God-human-human relational exchanges in daily living?

Impaired mentalization and Christian meditation, prayer, and contemplation. When we pray, we are mentalizing, in that we are creating imaginative mental space to reciprocally converse with God,[87] striving to make sense of our own, as well as others' (and God's), mental processes. Through Christian meditation, prayer, and contemplation, we are attempting to take on the mind of Christ, thinking and acting like Jesus as we walk with him in this life.[88] More specifically, with meditation, we can ponder God's attributes and actions so as to better understand the mind of God, doing so with the intention of knowing God on a more intimate level. For prayer, moreover, we are conversing with God in a reciprocal manner, sharing our own mind with him, as well as asking for him to reveal his mind to us. In doing so, we are petitioning God to help us exchange our fallen mind for his perfect mind, trading in our imperfect, wayward thoughts and actions for Jesus' compassionate, humble thoughts and actions. Finally, with contemplation, we are learning to gaze upon God with a loving attentiveness, faithfully entering into a "cloud of unknowing" to commune with him and placing our own distracting thoughts beneath a "cloud of forgetting."[89] Along the way, we are striving to trade our fallen mind for God's perfect mind, gently returning to our loving gaze when we notice we have become distracted.

Ultimately, in each of these practices—meditation, prayer, and contemplation—we are developing Christlikeness, (1) noticing when our ability to mentalize is impaired, (2) shifting toward the mind of Christ, (3) accepting Jesus' thoughts and actions, and (4) acting like Jesus in life based on a more enduring contentment in, and fellowship with, him. Over and over again, through these salient psychospiritual exercises, we are learning to recognize our fallen mind, then take on Jesus' mind, which is different from our own. To do so, we need to be able to mentalize in the first place (i.e., as a starting point), recognizing that we have a (fallen) mind, other people have a (fallen) mind, and God has a perfect mind, which we want to rely on.

---

[85]Mahoney et al. (2003).
[86]Allen and Fonagy (2006).
[87]Schaap-Jonker and Corveleyn (2014).
[88]Taylor (2002); Wolpert (2003).
[89]Bangley (2006).

To start this process, therefore, try keeping track of your ability to recognize that you have a (imperfect) mind, other people have a (imperfect) mind, and God has a (perfect) mind, linking your thought-feeling-intention-behavior dynamics in daily relationships and offering loving compassion toward yourself and others whenever you notice you have struggled to recognize this reality in key interpersonal exchanges. Fill out the mentalization log below.

Now that you have had the opportunity to recognize your own fallen, imperfect mind, the fallen, imperfect mind of others, and God's perfect mind, I would like you to begin the first meditative practice in this chapter, drawn from contemporary Christian spirituality.

CENTERING PRAYER: "CONSENTING TO GOD'S PRESENCE AND ACTION WITHIN"

Centering prayer is a contemporary repackaging of the contemplative instructions within the *Cloud of Unknowing*.[90] As a type of contemplative prayer, the practice of centering prayer is about cultivating "objectless awareness" of God, not focused attention, which can help us to surrender our inner world to him and cultivate an attitude of consent to his divine presence, given he is always moving within the center of our being.[91] In the Christian life, unfortunately, we can quickly construct an entire self in our own mind that is outside of God's will,[92] which is revealed in centering prayer when we practice letting go of our mind's attempt to operate outside of God's loving action. Therefore, over time, we are developing the ability to relinquish the grip we have on this unilaterally constructed self, then resting in God's divine presence by returning to him over and over again.[93]

Early on in life, we begin to develop this false self, in response to a variety of traumatic experiences, organized around the ubiquitious human needs of safety (e.g., comfort, protection), esteem (e.g., value, reputation, worth, status), and control (e.g., power).[94] Gradually, we end up overly relying on this human-created false self, instead of God, who is our real source of safety, esteem, and control. In essence, centering prayer is about letting go of this identity, modeled after Jesus' self-emptying (*kenosis,* Greek) in Philippians (Phil 2:5-8), by taking on the "same mindset of Christ Jesus." In other words, centering prayer is really just "*kenosis* in meditation form,"[95] given we are shifting from an earthly to heavenly perspective through the arduous path of self-renunciation as we pivot from being preoccupied with our own mind to the mind of Christ.

---

[90]Keating (2006).
[91]Bourgeault (2004, 2016).
[92]Keating (2006); Merton (1961).
[93]Bourgeault (2016).
[94]Keating (2006).
[95]Bourgeault (2016).

MENTALIZATION: A DAY LOG

Day of the Week	Time of Day	Relational Exchange	My Own Fallen Mind (Thoughts, Feelings, Intentions, Behaviors)	Other Person's Fallen Mind (Thoughts, Feelings, Intentions, Behaviors)	God's Perfect Mind (Mind of Christ)
Monday	1:00pm	I got into an argument with my boss at work. She told me I wasn't performing well on a specific task. I attempted to defend myself, which seemed to only make things worse.	I thought to myself, "I really must be useless as an employee, especially since I have worked so hard to improve, to no avail." I ended up feeling shame, sort of like I did growing up in my family. Although I've intended to improve, I have come up short once again. After this exchange, I hid in my office for the rest of the day.	My boss probably has it out to get me. She's probably thinking that I'm useless, too. She's clearly angry toward me and may be bringing up my performance to get me fired.	To take on the mind of Christ, I need to think and act like Jesus, not based on my own fallen mind. Jesus sees my boss as being created in his image and loves her as his creation. Jesus also teaches his followers to love and pray for our enemies, according to Matthew 5:43–48, and serve others, as per Luke 22:26–27. To have loving compassion for my boss, maybe I can recognize that she, too, struggles. She might have had a bad day and unintentionally took it out on me. She may have added stress right now due to a deadline. Even though I received less-than-optimal feedback, I will do my best to forgive her, serve my company, and have compassion for her throughout the rest of the week.

Day of the Week	Time of Day	Relational Exchange	My Own Fallen Mind (Thoughts, Feelings, Intentions, Behaviors)	Other Person's Fallen Mind (Thoughts, Feelings, Intentions, Behaviors)	God's Perfect Mind (Mind of Christ)

Rather than functioning as a concentrative form of practice, though, centering prayer is more of a receptive activity, in that we are engaging in the process of yielding to God's "presence and action within," over and over again in the here-and-now, not attempting to concentrate on God's attributes, actions, and so forth.[96] Consistent with the *Cloud of Unknowing*, thus, we are placing everything other than God beneath a "cloud of forgetting," even a false notion of who we have created ourselves to be within our mind.[97] To do so, we are mentalizing, noticing the inner workings of our own mind (e.g., thoughts, feelings, memories), then gently pivoting to God's divine mind. Second by second, we are repeating this self-emptying process, lovingly returning to God by consenting to his divine activity at the center of our inner world.

During formal practice, which takes place in solitude and silence, the instructions are as follows:[98]

1. Choose a sacred word as the symbol of your intention to consent to God's presence and action within.

2. Sitting comfortably and with eyes closed, settle briefly and silently introduce the sacred word as the symbol of your consent to God's presence and action within.

3. When engaged with your thoughts, return ever so gently to the sacred word.

4. At the end of the prayer period, remain in silence with eyes closed for a couple of minutes.

We begin the practice by selecting a "sacred word," which captures our willingness to surrender to God in the present. In doing so, we are learning to better mentalize, recognizing that we have an overactive mind, filled with distracting (and often unhelpful) thoughts, then shifting toward our "sacred word" to reflect our willingness to yield to God's loving activity within our inner being. With this repeated pivot, we are recognizing, then letting go of, our own mental habits in an effort to take on the mind of Christ.[99] Over time, we are learning a particular process—sitting in silence with God as we watch our fallen, imperfect mind with him and prioritize his mind above our own. In this process, we are recognizing his loving, compassionate presence, which is all we need as he sanctifies us from the inside out, and cultivating awareness and acceptance, two mental skills that are vital for decreasing impaired mentalization.

Next, try practicing centering prayer during a formal period of time. Given that the heart of this type of prayer involves noticing and letting go (i.e.,

---

[96]Bangley (2006); Bourgeault (2004).
[97]Bangley (2006); Bourgeault (2016).
[98]Keating (2006, pp. 177-78).
[99]Frenette (2012).

minding our own mind), then taking on the mind of Christ (i.e., minding God's mind), regular practice can help us to mentalize in a way that deepens our relationship with him. Of course, patience is also necessary, especially when we realize just how active our imperfect, vulnerable mind is in distracting us from God's active, loving presence. As a result, try to extend Jesus' loving compassion to yourself as you get to know your mind, God's mind, and the gap between the two.

CENTERING PRAYER: AN EXERCISE

For this ten-minute exercise, find a quiet location, free from distractions, and sit up straight in a supportive chair. Rest your hands comfortably in your lap, closing your eyes as you begin the practice. When you are ready, start by slowly following along with the below directions:[100]

1. Choose the prayer word *Christ*, which captures your willingness to pivot from your own mind to the mind of Christ, surrendering to Jesus' presence within the depths of your being.

2. Settle into a comfortable position, then gently begin reciting the prayer word, *Christ*, saying it as a way to take on the mind of Christ within.

3. Whenever you recognize that you are distracted by your own mind (e.g., a thought or feeling), slowly and gently shift toward your prayer word, *Christ*, taking on Jesus' mind in place of your own.

4. When the practice concludes, sit in silence for a few minutes, resting in God's presence as you receive his loving compassion.

After completing the exercise, journal for a few minutes, attempting to answer the following questions:

- What was it like to shift from your own mind to the mind of Christ by slowly and gently repeating the prayer word, *Christ*, then returning to the word when you noticed you were lost in your own fallen, imperfect mind? What were the benefits? The limitations?

- How well were you able to take on the mind of Christ during the exercise?

- What, if anything, got in your way? Were you able to overcome the obstacles? If so, how? If not, why not?

- How, if at all, can taking on the mind of Christ help you with impaired mentalization as you move through the rest of your day?

---

[100]Slightly adapted from Keating (2006, pp. 177-78).

● How, if at all, can taking on the mind of Christ help you to accept God's loving compassion, minute by minute, and act in a manner that is anchored to fellowshiping with, and finding contentment in, him as you carry out your day?

_____

_____

_____

_____

_____

_____

_____

_____

_____

_____

_____

THE WELCOMING PRAYER: RECOGNIZING GOD'S PRESENCE THROUGHOUT THE DAY

As a way to extend centering prayer to the rest of your day—letting go of your need for safety, esteem, and control on an ongoing basis—the welcoming prayer is a practice for surrendering, over and over again, to the mind of Christ.[101] With the welcoming prayer, we are learning to mentalize, in that we are recognizing the activity of our mind, then inviting Jesus Christ to be with us in the inner world. Over time, the practice can help us develop the habit of noticing and shifting as we go about our day, swapping our fallen, imperfect mind for Jesus' mind.

The original version of the exercise involves three important steps:[102]

1. Feel and sink into what you are experiencing this moment in your body.

2. "Welcome" what you are experiencing this moment in your body as an opportunity to consent to the divine indwelling.

3. Let go by saying, "I let go of my desire for security, affection, and control and embrace this moment as it is."

---

[101]Bourgeault (2004).
[102]Contemplative Outreach (n.d.).

Notice, here, that the essence of the practice involves acknowledging and accepting our psychological experiences in the present moment, then inviting God into such experiences, before relinquishing our grip on—or detaching from—our unilateral pursuit of safety, esteem, and power. Throughout the day, this practice can help us to notice our own (fallen) mind, invite God into our (fallen) mind, and pivot toward an awareness of God's (perfect) mind, rather than relying on our own efforts to make sense of daily life and provide for our moment-by-moment needs. What follows, therefore, is a modified version of the welcoming prayer for you to practice, given how crucial it is to notice and shift in each passing moment.

THE WELCOMING PRAYER: AN EXERCISE

To extend centering prayer to daily life, try practicing the welcoming prayer for ten minutes in the morning, with an understanding that the formal exercise will help you to apply the process to the plethora of interactions you have throughout the course of your day. To practice formally, set aside ten minutes, finding a quiet location, sitting in a supportive chair, and closing your eyes. Place your hands in your lap, with your palms facing upward to capture your willingness to let go of your grip on a false sense of self, replacing this pseudo-self with the mind of Christ.

As a modified formal exercise, taking into consideration the mentalization-based approaches in this chapter, the directions for the welcoming prayer[103] are below:[104]

1. *Notice.* Observe your thoughts, feelings, and intentions right now, without attempting to do anything with your mind. Rather, just accept your mind with an open curiousity, watching what is unfolding in the present moment. Here, simply mentalize, paying attention to the inner workings of your own mind.

2. *Invite.* With your own "mind in mind," invite Jesus into the experience, surrendering to him by asking him to be with you as you take on his mind in the here-and-now.

3. *Let go.* Now, with Jesus' "mind in mind," relinquish the grip you have on your own fallen, imperfect mind, taking on the mind of Christ by letting go of your need to think, feel, or act in a certain way. Instead, you are consenting to Jesus living through you, displaying Christlike loving compassion toward yourself and others in the process. With this last step, maintain an awareness of God's "presence and action within" throughout your day, being mindful of Jesus' mind within you.

---

[103]Adapted from Allen (2013); Bourgeault (2004).
[104]You can also follow along with the audio recording (Track 5), found at ivpress.com/Knabb5.

After completing the exercise, journal for a few minutes, attempting to answer the following questions:

- What was it like to notice, invite, and let go during the formal practice? What were the benefits? The limitations?

- How well were you able to notice, invite, and let go during the exercise?

- What, if anything, got in your way? Were you able to overcome the obstacles? If so, how? If not, why not?

- How, if at all, can noticing, inviting, and letting go help you with impaired mentalization as you move through the rest of your day?

- How, if at all, can noticing, inviting, and letting go help you to accept God's loving compassion, minute by minute, and act in a manner that is anchored to fellowshiping with, and finding contentment in, him as you carry out your day?

_____

_____

_____

_____

_____

_____

_____

_____

_____

_____

_____

_____

_____

_____

THE "GAME OF MINUTES": HOLDING GOD'S "MIND IN MIND" THROUGHOUT THE DAY

Dating back to the early twentieth century, Frank Laubach,[105] an evangelical missionary and mystical author, penned a variety of letters that captured his "game of

---

[105]Laubach (2007).

minutes," which involves finding novel ways throughout the day to place God's presence at the forefront of the mind. Eventually published as *Letters by a Modern Mystic*, Laubach's book further elaborated on this approach, which emanates from the Protestant tradition:

> For the past few days I have been experimenting in a more complete surrender than ever before. I am taking, by deliberate act of will, enough time from each hour to give God much thought. Yesterday and today I have made a new adventure, which is not easy to express. I am feeling God in each movement, by an act of will—willing that He shall direct these fingers that now strike this typewriter—willing that He shall pour through my steps as I walk—willing that He shall direct my words as I speak, and my very jaws as I eat![106]

To surrender to God in the here-and-now, according to Laubach, involves attempting to "be like Jesus" and "respond to God as a violin responds to the bow of the master."[107] With this game of minutes, then, our task is to remember God throughout the day, carrying out a variety of deliberate activities in the process (e.g., singing to God, talking to God, reading Scripture).[108]

Applied to mentalizing, as Christians, we are striving to be mindful of Jesus' mind over the course of the day, practicing God's presence through daily tasks, both large and small. To get into this daily rhythm, we can ask three important questions:[109]

1. What am I thinking, feeling, doing, and intending as I carry out this activity right now?

2. What is Jesus thinking, feeling, and doing right now?[110]

3. How can I carry out this activity with Jesus' mind (not my own) in mind?

Here, we can see that these salient questions help us to "invite [God] to share everything [we] do or say or think,"[111] effectively mentalizing by shifting from what the Protestant pastor and theologian Gregory Boyd calls the "flesh-mind-set" to "single-mindedness."[112] Along the way, we are pivoting from seeing our mind in isolation (e.g., *I* am going to this place or that place, *I* am thinking this thought or that thought) to viewing God as the Lord of our mind (e.g., *We* are going to this place or that place, *We* are thinking this thought or that thought). Over time, we are better at noticing the inner chatter of our imperfect mind, then recognizing that Jesus is the Lord over both our inner and outer world, turning from an *I* to *we* in

---

[106]Laubach (2007).
[107]Laubach (2007).
[108]Laubach (2007).
[109]Adapted from Allen (2013); Laubach (2007).
[110]Jesus' behaviors and intentions are one and the same.
[111]Laubach (2007).
[112]Boyd (2010).

the process.[113] Next, I would like you to practice this game of minutes throughout the day, recording your experiences as you interact with others and carry out your tasks on the roads of life.

THE GAME OF MINUTES: AN EXERCISE

For this next exercise, try to select a specific day to practice the game of minutes, recording your hourly efforts to shift from *I* to *we* as you interact with others, fulfill your obligations, and carry out activities that keep your attention on God, holding God's "mind in mind" along the way.[114]

GAME OF MINUTES

Time	Activity	My Mind (*I*) (Thoughts, Feelings, Behaviors, Intentions)	Jesus' Mind (*We*) (Thoughts, Feelings, Behaviors)
2:30pm	Mowing the lawn at home on a Sunday afternoon	I hate mowing the lawn. Why should I have to do it on a Sunday afternoon? I should get to relax. I've worked a long week. I'm so frustrated right now. Why can't someone else mow the lawn, not me? I'm not even doing a good job. I want to spend time with my friends and family instead. I miss them.	"Whatever you do, work at it with all your heart, as working for [me], not human masters, since you know that you will receive an inheritance from [me] as a reward. It is [me] you are serving" (Col 3:23–24).

---

[113]Boyd (2010).
[114]Adapted from Allen (2013); Boyd (2010); Laubach (2007).

Time	Activity	My Mind (*I*) (Thoughts, Feelings, Behaviors, Intentions)	Jesus' Mind (*We*) (Thoughts, Feelings, Behaviors)

Time	Activity	My Mind (*I*) (Thoughts, Feelings, Behaviors, Intentions)	Jesus' Mind (*We*) (Thoughts, Feelings, Behaviors)

In the example I give in the table, notice that our own mind may be inconsistent with Jesus' mind, which is revealed in Scripture. In fact, as a starting point, learning what Jesus thinks about something can come directly from the Bible, since Scripture is God's Word. Therefore, as you begin to hold God's "mind in mind,"[115] try to internalize verses in the Bible, given that "all Scripture is God-breathed and useful for teaching, rebuking, correcting and training in righteousness, so that the servant of God may be thoroughly equipped for every good work" (2 Tim 3:16-17).

After completing the exercise, journal for a few minutes, attempting to answer the following questions:

- What was it like to practice the game of minutes throughout your day? What were the benefits? The limitations?

- How well were you able to shift from *I* to *we* during the exercise?

- What, if anything, got in your way? Were you able to overcome the obstacles? If so, how? If not, why not?

- How, if at all, can shifting from *I* to *we* help you with impaired mentalization as you move through the rest of your day?

---

[115]Allen (2013).

● How, if at all, can shifting from *I* to *we* help you to accept God's loving compassion, minute by minute, and act in a manner that is anchored to fellowshiping with, and finding contentment in, him as you carry out your day?

_____

_____

_____

_____

_____

_____

_____

_____

_____

_____

_____

REFLECTING ON THE PRACTICE

In this final chapter, it seems fitting that we have explored the reality that we have a mind, which we are only sometimes aware of, and is fallen and different from God's mind. As a result, to take on the mind of Christ, we need to practice God's presence, recognizing our own inner world, then shifting to an awareness that God is the Lord of our thoughts, feelings, behaviors, and intentions. In other words, Jesus Christ is the Lord of *all*.[116] In our interactions with both ourselves and others, thus, we are recognizing this triadic, not dyadic, dynamic at play, "consenting to God's presence and action within" from moment to moment.[117] In doing so, we are learning to (1) notice our (fallen) mind, along with the (fallen) mind of others; (2) shift toward an awareness of God's (perfect) mind; (3) accept God's presence in the here-and-now; and (4) act in life based on God's will, not our own, which involves Christlike loving compassion in our interactions with others, with God at the center of our existence.

---

[116] Johnson (1997).
[117] Keating (2006).

This chapter, of course, is consistent with the previous four intervention chapters, which start with a contemporary, secular psychological understanding of "mind-brain-body-behavior" patterns,[118] then help you to shift toward a more heavenly, transcendent, spiritual perspective, wherein God is the author of contentment. In the meditative process, you are learning to steadily walk home with God,[119] surrendering to his providential care as the antidote to your temporary suffering and recognizing that the psychological pain in this world is time-limited and need not get in the way of Christlike behavioral action.

With the exercises threaded throughout this workbook, my hope is that you have been able to get into the daily rhythm of walking with God. Although mindfulness-based practices are ubiquitous in contemporary Western society, as Christians, we have our own meditative tradition to draw from, one that takes our *telos* (i.e., purpose)—communing with God as we walk home with him[120]—into consideration. Although by no means exhaustive in fully capturing life's problems and solutions, this workbook can serve as a catalyst, emboldening you to go deeper in psychotherapy and professional counseling with the process of fellowshiping with God at the center, not on the periphery, of the change process. Before concluding the workbook, though, I would like you to set aside a few minutes to reflect on your overall experience, taking into consideration this eighth and final chapter, as well as the other four intervention chapters you have interacted with along the way. Then, we will end with Ignatius of Loyola's famous prayer, which fittingly captures what we have been striving for all along in this four-step meditative process.

REFLECTING ON THE CHAPTER AND WORKBOOK: A JOURNALING ACTIVITY

To conclude both this chapter and workbook, spend a few minutes journaling about your experience with relating differently to your thoughts, feelings, behaviors, sense of self, and relationships through the use of Christian meditation. Please use additional paper, if necessary. A few questions to consider:

- What was it like for you to notice these transdiagnostic processes on a daily basis? How well were you able to do so? Were you able to step back and see these patterns in the moment? What can you do to continue to notice these "mind-brain-body-behavior"[121] tendencies?

- How well were you able to shift from these patterns to God? What went well? What do you still need to work on?

---

[118]Greeson et al. (2014).
[119]Knabb and Bates (2020b).
[120]Knabb and Bates (2020b).
[121]Greeson et al. (2014).

- Which exercises, if any, were most helpful in allowing you to get unstuck from these tendencies and shift toward God? How can you build these exercises into daily life?

- How, if at all, did Christian meditation help you to pivot from an earthly perspective to a more transcendent, heavenly reality? What can you do to strengthen this daily practice?

- How did you do with developing the mental skills of attention, present-moment awareness, and acceptance in the context of your relationship with God?

- How, if at all, did your relationship with God change as you spent more time meditating on his word, the Bible?

- How, if at all, did your ability to commune with God change? How about your ability to find a deeper contentment in him as you made decisions throughout the day?

_____

_____

_____

_____

_____

_____

_____

_____

_____

A FINAL PRAYER

To end this workbook, I leave you with a final prayer, attributed to Ignatius of Loyola in the 1500s, which appropriately captures what we are aiming for in the Christian life, whether walking through seasons of celebration or suffering:

> Take, Lord, and receive all my liberty, my memory, my understanding, and my entire will, all I have and call my own. You have given all to me. To you, Lord, I return it. Everything is yours; do with it what you will. Give me only your love and your grace, that is enough for me.[122]

May you continue to steadily walk with God through suffering as you slowly and courageously head toward your final destination, in lockstep with him.

---

[122]Greeson et al. (2014).

REFERENCES

Aival-Naveh, E., Rothschild-Yakar, L., & Kurman, J. (2019). Keeping culture in mind: A systematic review and initial conceptualization of mentalizing from a cross-cultural perspective. *Clinical Psychology: Science and Practice, 26*(4), 1-25.

Allen, J. (2008). Mentalizing as a conceptual bridge from psychodynamic to cognitive-behavioral therapies. *European Psychotherapy, 8*, 103-21.

Allen, J. (2013). *Mentalizing in the development and treatment of attachment trauma.* Routledge.

Allen, J. (2013). *Restoring mentalizing in attachment relationships: Treating trauma with plain old therapy.* American Psychiatric Publishing.

Allen, J., & Fonagy, P. (Eds.). (2006). *Handbook of mentalisation-based treatment.* John Wiley & Sons.

Allen, J., Fonagy, P., & Bateman, A. (2008). *Mentalizing in clinical practice.* American Psychiatric Publishing.

Allen, T., Rueter, A., Abram, S., Brown, J., & Deyoung, C. (2017). Personality and neural correlates of mentalizing ability. *European Journal of Personality, 31*, 599-613.

American Dictionary and Cyclopedia. (1900). *Accept.* Dictionary and Cyclopedia Co.

American Psychiatric Association. (2013). *Diagnostic and statistical manual of mental disorders* (5th ed.). Author.

Anderson, N., Miller, R., & Travis, P. (2003). *When trying harder isn't enough: Breaking the bondage of legalism.* Harvest House Publishers.

Anderson, T., Clark, W., & Naugle, D. (2017). *An introduction to Christian worldview: Pursuing God's perspective in a pluralistic world.* InterVarsity Press.

Antoine, P., Andreotti, E., Congard, A., Dauvier, B., Illy, J., & Poinsot, R. (2018). A mindfulness-based intervention: Differential effects on affective and processual evolution. *Applied Psychology: Health and Well-Being, 10*, 368-90.

Atwood, G., & Stolorow, R. (1993). *Faces in a cloud: Intersubjectivity in personality theory.* Rowman & Littlefield.

Augustine. (2011). *On Christian doctrine* [ebook edition]. Aeterna Press. Amazon.com

Austin, M., & Geivett, R. (Eds.). (2012). *Being good: Christian virtues for everyday life.* Eerdmans.

Ball, J. (2016). *A treatise of divine meditation.* Puritan Publications.

Ballester, M. (1983). Prayer. In G. Wakefield (Ed.), *The Westminster dictionary of Christian spirituality* (pp. 307-314). Westminster Press.

Bangley, B. (Ed.). (2006). *The cloud of unknowing: Contemporary English edition.* Paraclete Press.

Barclay, W. (1974). *New Testament words.* Westminster John Knox Press.

Barclay, W. (2001). *The Gospel of Matthew: Volume I.* Westminster John Knox Press.

Barlow, D., Farchione, T., Fairholme, C., Ellard, K., Boisseau, C., Allen, L., & Ehrenreich-May, J. (2011). *Unified protocol for transdiagnostic treatment of emotional disorders: Therapist guide*. Oxford University Press.

Barry, W. (1991). *Finding God in all things: A companion to the spiritual exercises of St. Ignatius*. Ave Maria Press.

Bateman, A., & Fonagy, P. (2010). Mentalization based treatment for borderline personality disorder. *World Psychiatry, 9*, 11-15.

Baxter, R. (2015). *The saints' everlasting rest*. GLH Publishing.

Baxter, R. (2017). *Walking with God*. Gideon House Books.

Bebane, S., Flowe, H., & Maltby, J. (2015). Re-refining the measurement of distress intolerance. *Personality and Individual Differences, 85*, 159-64.

Beeke, J., & Jones, M. (2012). *A Puritan theology: Doctrine for life* [ebook edition]. Reformation Heritage Books. Amazon.com

Benner, D. (1989). Toward a psychology of spirituality: Implications for personality and psychotherapy. *Journal of Psychology and Christianity, 8*, 19-30.

Benner, D. (2010). *Opening to God: Lectio divina and life as prayer*. InterVarsity Press.

Bernard, of Clairvaux. (2016). *Commentary on the Song of Songs* (M. Henry, Trans.). Jazzybee Verlag.

Bernstein, A., Marshall, E., & Zvolensky, M. (2011). Multi-method evaluation of distress tolerance measures and construct(s): Concurrent relations to mood and anxiety psychopathology and quality of life. *Journal of Experimental Psychopathology, 2*, 386-99.

Bieling, P., Israeli, A., & Antony, M. (2004). Is perfectionism good, bad, or both? Examining models of the perfectionism construct. *Personality and Individual Differences, 36*, 1373-85.

Bill, J. (2016). *Holy silence: The gift of Quaker spirituality* (2nd ed.). Eerdmans.

Bishop, S., Lau, M., Shapiro, S., Carlson, L., Anderson, N., Carmody, J., Segal, Z., Abbey, S., Speca, M., Velting, D., & Devins, G. (2004). Mindfulness: A proposed operational definition. *Clinical Psychology: Science and Practice, 11*, 230-41.

Boersma, H. (2018). *Seeing God: The beautiful vision in Christian tradition*. Eerdmans.

Bonhoeffer, D. (1955). *Ethics*. Touchstone.

Bonhoeffer, D. (1959). *Creation and fall*. Touchstone.

Borgman, B. (2009). *Feelings and faith: Cultivating godly emotions in the Christian life*. Crossway Books.

Botella, C., Molinari, G., Fernandez-Alvarez, J., Guillen, V., Garcia-Palacios, A., Banos, R., & Tomas, J. (2018). Development and validation of the openness to the future scale: A prospective protective factor. *Health and Quality of Life Outcomes, 16*, 1-16.

Bourgeault, C. (2004). *Centering prayer and inner awakening*. Cowley Publications.

Bourgeault, C. (2016). *The heart of centering prayer: Nondual Christianity in theory and practice*. Shambhala Publications.

Boyd, G. (2004). *Repenting of religion: Turning from judgment to the love of God*. Baker Books.

Boyd, G. (2010). *Present perfect: Finding God in the now*. Zondervan.

Brakke, D. (2006). *Demons and the making of the monk: Spiritual combat in early Christianity*. Harvard University Press.

Brinton, H. (2018). *Guide to Quaker practice*. Pendle Hill Publications.

Bruce, F. (1984). *The epistles to the Colossians, to Philemon, and to the Ephesians*. Eerdmans.

Brueggemann, W. (1984). *The message of the Psalms: A theological commentary*. Augsburg Publishing House.

Bullock, H. (2015). *Psalms—volume I: Psalms 1-72*. Baker Books.

Burg, J., & Michalak, J. (2011). The healthy quality of mindful breathing: Associations with rumination and depression. *Cognitive Therapy Research, 35*, 179-85.

Burroughs, J. (2010). *Heavenly-mindedness recommended: In a discourse on Colossians 3:2*. Gale ECCO.

Burroughs, J. (2014). *A treatise on earthly-mindedness*. GLH Publishing.

Burroughs, J. (2018). *The rare jewel of Christian contentment: Abridged and in modern English* (R. Summers, Trans.). Author.

Burton-Christie, D. (1993). *The word in the desert: Scripture and the quest for holiness in early Christian monasticism*. Oxford University Press.

Butler, E. (1926). *Western mysticism: Augustine, Gregory, and Bernard on contemplation and the contemplative life*. E. P. Dutton.

Byfield, N. (2013). *The promises of God*. Puritan Publications.

Calamy, E. (1680). *The art of divine meditation*. London.

Calhoun, A. (2005). *Spiritual disciplines handbook: Practices that transform us*. InterVarsity Press.

Carpenter, J., Sanford, J., & Hofmann, S. (2019). The effect of a brief mindfulness training on distress tolerance and stress reactivity. *Behavior Therapy, 50*, 630-45.

Cassian, J. (1997). *The conferences* (B. Ramsey, Trans.). Paulist Press.

Chandler, D. (2014). *Christian spiritual formation: An integrated approach to personal and relational wholeness*. InterVarsity Press.

Chappelle, W. (2000). A series of progressive legal and ethical decision-making steps for using Christian spiritual interventions in psychotherapy. *Journal of Psychology and Theology, 28*, 43-53.

Chryssavgis, J. (2008). *In the heart of the desert, revised: The spirituality of the desert mothers and fathers*. Word Wisdom.

Chumley, N. (2014). *Be still and know: God's presence in silence*. Augsburg Fortress.

Clarke, T., Barnes, P., Black, L., Stussman, B., & Nahin, R. (2018). *Use of yoga, meditation, and chiropractors among U.S. adults aged 18 and over. NCHS Data Brief, no. 325*. National Center for Health Statistics.

Classic Christian ebooks. (2019). *An introduction to the spiritual disciplines of the Christian life: 25 classic works on spiritual formation and spiritual growth in the life of the believer* [ebook edition]. Christian Classics Treasury. Amazon.com

Claude, d. l. C. (1983). *Trustful surrender to divine providence: The secret to peace and happiness* [ebook edition]. TAN Books. Amazon.com

Colombiere, C. (1983). *Trustful surrender to divine providence: The secret of peace and happiness*. TAN Books.

Coniaris, A. (1998). *Philokalia: The Bible of Orthodox spirituality*. Light & Life Publishing Company.

Coniaris, A. (2004). *Confronting and controlling thoughts according to the fathers of the Philokalia*. Light & Life Publishing Company.

Contemplative Outreach. (n.d.). *Welcoming prayer*. www.contemplativeoutreach.org/welcoming-prayer

Cooper, D., Yap, K., & Batalha, L. (2018). Mindfulness-based interventions and their effects on emotional clarity: A systematic review and meta-analysis. *Journal of Affective Disorders, 235*, 265-76.

Cosby, B. (2012). *Suffering and sovereignty: John Flavel and the Puritans on afflictive providence*. Reformation Heritage Books.

Cramer, H., Hall, H., Leach, M., Frawley, J., Zhang, Y., Leung, B., Adams, J., & Lauche, R. (2016). Prevalence, patterns, and predictors of meditation use among US adults: A nationally representative survey. *Scientific Reports, 6,* 1-9.

Crane, R. (2009). *Mindfulness-based cognitive therapy.* Routledge.

Craske, M. (2012). Transdiagnostic treatment for anxiety and depression. *Depression and Anxiety, 29,* 749-53.

Dandelion, P. (2008). *The Quakers: A very short introduction.* Oxford University Press.

Davis, J. (2012). *Meditation and communion with God: Contemplating scripture in an age of distraction.* InterVarsity Press.

Demarest, B. (2011). Apophatic and kataphatic ways. In G. Scorgie (Ed.), *Dictionary of Christian spirituality.* Zondervan.

Desrosiers, A., Vine, V., Klernanski, D., & Hoeksema, S. (2013). Mindfulness and emotion regulation in depression and anxiety: Common and distinct mechanisms of action. *Depression & Anxiety, 30,* 654-61.

Dimitrijevic, A., Hanak, N., Dimitrijevic, A., & Marjanovic, Z. (2018). The mentalization scale (MentS): A self-report measure for the assessment of mentalizing capacity. *Journal of Personality Assessment, 100,* 268-80.

Dorjee, D. (2016). Defining contemplative science: The metacognitive self-regulatory capacity of the mind, context of meditation practice and modes of existential awareness. *Frontiers in Psychology, 7,* 1-15.

Dudley, R., Kuyken, W., & Padesky, C. (2011). Disorder specific and trans-diagnostic case conceptualisation. *Clinical Psychology Review, 31,* 213-24.

Dugas, M., & Robichaud, M. (2007). *Cognitive-behavioral treatment for generalized anxiety disorder: From science to practice.* Routledge.

Dunn, J. (1996). *The epistles to the Colossians and to Philemon: A commentary on the Greek text.* Eerdmans.

Dyer, J. (1999). The Psalms in monastic prayer. In N. Van Deusen (Ed.), *The place of the Psalms in the intellectual culture of the middle ages* (p. 59). State University of New York Press.

Earle, M. (2011). *Celtic Christian spirituality: Essential writings—annotated & explained.* SkyLight Paths Publishing.

Earle, M., & Maddox, S. (2004). *Holy companions: Spiritual practices from the Celtic saints.* Morehouse Publishing.

Eck, B. (2002). An exploration of the therapeutic use of spiritual disciplines in clinical practice. *Journal of Psychology and Christianity, 21,* 266-80.

Egan, K. (2005). Contemplation. In P. Sheldrake (Ed.), *The new Westminster dictionary of Christian spirituality* (pp. 211-13). Westminster John Knox Press.

Egan, S., Wade, T., & Shafran, R. (2011). Perfectionism as a transdiagnostic process: A clinical review. *Clinical Psychology Review, 31,* 203-12.

Egan, S., Wade, T., & Shafran, R. (2012). The transdiagnostic process of perfectionism. *Spanish Journal of Clinical Psychology, 17,* 279-94.

Ehring, T., & Watkins, E. (2008). Repetitive negative thinking as a transdiagnostic process. *International Journal of Cognitive Therapy, 1,* 192-205.

Ehring, T., Zetsche, U., Weidacker, K., Wahl, K., Schonfeld, S., & Ehlers, A. (2011). The Perseverative Thinking Questionnaire (PTQ): Validation of a content-independent measure of repetitive negative thinking. *Journal of Behavior Therapy and Experimental Psychiatry, 42,* 225-32.

Eifring, H. (2016). Types of meditation. In H. Eifring (Ed.), *Asian traditions of meditation* (pp. 27-47). University of Hawai'i Press.

Eisendrath, S. (Ed.). (2016). *Mindfulness-based cognitive therapy: Innovative applications.* Springer International Publishing.

Eizirik, M., & Fonagy, P. (2009). Mentalization-based treatment for patients with borderline personality disorder: An overview. *Brazilian Journal of Psychiatry, 31,* 72-75.

Elliott, M. (2006). *Faithful feelings: Rethinking emotion in the New Testament.* Kregel Publications.

Endean, P. (1990). The Ignatian prayer of the senses. *The Heythrop Journal, 31,* 391-418.

Erickson, M. (2013). *Christian theology* (3rd ed.). Baker Academic.

Evagrius. (2009). *Talking back: A monastic handbook for combating demons.* Liturgical Press.

Fall, J., & Tenney, M. (2011). *Zondervan illustrated Bible dictionary.* Zondervan.

Fanous, S., & Gillespie, V. (Eds.). (2011). *The Cambridge companion to Medieval English mysticism.* Cambridge University Press.

Farag, L. (2012). *Balance of the heart: Desert spirituality for twenty-first-century Christians.* Cascade Books.

Farb, N. (2014). From retreat center to clinic to boardroom? Perils and promises of the modern mindfulness movement. *Religions, 5,* 1062-1086.

Feldman, G., Hayes, A., Kumar, S., Greeson, J., & Laurenceau, J. (2007). Mindfulness and emotion regulation: The development and initial validation of the Cognitive and Affective Mindfulness Scale-Revisited (CAMS-R). *Journal of Psychopathology and Behavioral Assessment, 29,* 177-90.

Fénelon, F. (2010). *The inner life* [ebook edition]. Amazon.com

Ferguson, J., Willemsen, E., & Castaneto, M. (2010). Centering prayer as a healing response to everyday stress: A psychological and spiritual process. *Pastoral Psychology, 59,* 305-29.

Finley, J. (2004). *Christian meditation: Experiencing the presence of God.* HarperCollins.

Fischer-Kern, M., & Tmej, A. (2019). Mentalization and depression: Theoretical concepts, treatment approaches and empirical studies—an overview. *Journal of Psychosomatic Medicine and Psychotherapy, 65,* 162-77.

Flavel, J. (1754). *The whole works of the Reverend Mr. John Flavel.* John Orr.

Flett, G., Nepon, T., Hewitt, P., & Rose, A. (2020). Why perfectionism is antithetical to mindfulness: A conceptual and empirical analysis and consideration of treatment implications. *International Journal of Mental Health and Addiction.* Advance online publication.

Fonagy, P., & Luyten, P. (2009). A developmental, mentalization-based approach to the understanding and treatment of borderline personality disorder. *Development and Psychopathology, 21,* 1355-81.

Foster, R. (1998). *Streams of living water: Essential practices from the six great traditions of Christian faith.* HarperCollins.

Foster, R. (2018). *Celebration of discipline: The path to spiritual growth.* HarperCollins.

France, R. (1985). *The Gospel according to Matthew: An introduction and commentary.* Eerdmans.

Francis, d. S. (2011). *Treatise on the love of God—contemporary English edition.* Paraclete Press.

Francis, d. S. (2015). *Introduction to the devout life.* Catholic Way Publishing.

Frenette, D. (2012). *The path of centering prayer: Deepening your experience of God.* Sounds True.

Gallagher, T. (2006). *The examen prayer: Ignatian wisdom for our lives today.* Crossroad.

Gallagher, T. (2008). *Meditation and contemplation: An Ignatian guide to praying with Scripture.* Crossroad.

Gamez, W., Chmielewski, M., Kotov, R., Ruggero, C., & Watson, D. (2011). Development of a measure of experiential avoidance: The Multidimensional Experiential Avoidance Questionnaire. *Psychological Assessment, 23*, 692-713.

Germer, C. (2009). *The mindful path to self-compassion: Freeing yourself from destructive thoughts and emotions.* Guilford.

Germer, C., & Neff, K. (2019). *Teaching the mindful self-compassion program: A guide for professionals.* Guilford.

Gilbert, P. (2010). *Compassion focused therapy.* Routledge.

Gillet, L. (1985). *On the invocation of the name of Jesus.* Templegate Publishers.

Gillingham, S. (2012). *Psalms through the centuries: Volume one.* John Wiley & Sons.

Gnilka, P., & Broda, M. (2019). Multidimensional perfectionism, depression, and anxiety: Tests of a social support mediation model. *Personality and Individual Differences, 139*, 295-300.

Goggin, J., & Strobel, K. (Ed.). (2013). *Reading the Christian spiritual classics: A guide for evangelicals.* InterVarsity Press.

Gohm, C., & Clore, G. (2000). Individual differences in emotional experience: Mapping available scales to processes. *Personality and Social Psychology Bulletin, 26*, 679-97.

Goodwin, T. (2015). *The vanity of thoughts.* Chapel Library.

Goyal, M., Singh, S., Sibinga, E., Gould, N., Rowland-Seymour, A., Sharma, R., Berger, Z., Sleicher, D., Maron, D., Shihab, H., Ranasinghe, P., Linn, S., Saha, S., Bass, E., & Haythornthwaite, J. (2014). Meditation programs for psychological stress and well-being: A systematic review and meta-analysis. *Journal of the American Medical Association, 174*, 357-68.

Gratz, K., & Roemer, L. (2004). Multidimensional assessment of emotion regulation and dysregulation: Development, factor structure, and initial validation of the difficulties in emotion regulation scale. *Journal of Psychopathology and Behavioral Assessment, 26*, 41-54.

Greeson, J., Garland, E., & Black, D. (2014). Mindfulness: A transtherapeutic approach for transdiagnostic mental processes. In A. Ie, C. Ngnoumen, & E. Langer (Eds.), *The Wiley Blackwell handbook of mindfulness* (pp. 533-62). John Wiley & Sons.

Gu, J., Strauss, C., Bond, R., & Cavanagh, K. (2015). How do mindfulness-based cognitive therapy and mindfulness-based stress reduction improve mental health and wellbeing? A systematic review and meta-analysis of mediation studies. *Clinical Psychology Review, 37*, 1-12.

Guigo II. (2012). *The ladder of monks* (P. Nau, Trans.) [ebook edition]. Sr. Pascale Dominique Nau. Amazon.com

Gunaratana, B. (2017). *Loving-kindness in plain English: The practice of metta.* Wisdom Publications.

Guthrie, D. (1983). *The epistle to the Hebrews: An introduction and commentary.* Eerdmans.

Guyon, J. (2010). *A short and easy method of prayer.* Trinity Press.

Guyon, J. (2011). *Works of Madame Jeanne Guyon* [ebook edition]. www.classicchristian ebooks.com

Hall, J. (2016). *The art of divine meditation* [ebook edition]. Titus Books. Amazon.com

Hansen, G. (2012). *Kneeling with giants: Learning to pray with history's best teachers.* InterVarsity Press.

Hareli, S., & Hess, U. (2012). The social signal value of emotions. *Cognition and Emotion, 26*, 385-89.

Harmless, W. (2004). *Desert Christians: An introduction to the literature of early monasticism.* Oxford University Press.

Harmless, W. (2008). *Mystics.* Oxford University Press.

Harris, R. (2009). *ACT made simple: An easy-to-read primer on Acceptance and Commitment Therapy.* New Harbinger Publications.

Harris, R. (2011). *The confidence gap: A guide to overcoming fear and self-doubt.* Trumpeter.

Harvey, A., Watkins, E., Mansell, W., & Shafran, R. (2004). *Cognitive behavioural processes across psychological disorders: A transdiagnostic approach to research and treatment.* Oxford University Press.

Hayes, S., Strosahl, K., & Wilson, K. (2012). *Acceptance and commitment therapy: The process and practice of mindful change* (2nd ed.). Guilford.

Henriques, G. (2019). Toward a metaphysical empirical psychology. In T. Teo (Ed.), *Palgrave studies in the theory and history of psychology* (pp. 209-38). Springer Nature.

Henry, M. (2005). *Matthew Henry's commentary on the whole Bible: Complete and unabridged in one volume.* Hendrickson Publishers.

Henry, M. (2011). *Daily communion with God.* Digital Puritan Press.

Hilton, W. (1991). *The scale of perfection* (J. Clark & R. Dorward, Trans.). Paulist Press.

Hoare, E. (2016). *Using the Bible in spiritual direction.* Morehouse Publishing.

Hoekema, A. (1987). The reformed perspective. In M. Dieter, A. Hoekema, S. Horton, J. Mc-Quilkin, & J. Walvoord (Eds.), *Five views on sanctification* (pp. 59-90). Zondervan.

Hofmann, S., Grossman, P., & Hinton, D. (2011). Loving-kindness and compassion meditation: Potential for psychological interventions. *Clinical Psychology Review, 31,* 1126-32.

Holman Illustrated Bible Dictionary. (1998). *Contentment.* Holman Bible Publishers.

Howells, E. (2005). Apophatic spirituality. In P. Sheldrake (Ed.), *The new Westminster dictionary of Christian spirituality* (pp. 117-19). Westminster John Knox Press.

Hughes, P. (2001). Grace. In W. Elwell (Ed.), *Evangelical dictionary of theology* (pp. 519-22). Baker Academic.

Ignatian Spirituality. (n.d.). *The daily examen.* www.ignatianspirituality.com/ignatian-prayer/the-examen

Ivens, M. (1998). *Understanding the Spiritual Exercises: Text and commentary—a handbook for retreat directors.* Cromwell Press.

Jain, F., & Fonagy, P. (2020). Mentalizing imagery therapy: Theory and case series of imagery and mindfulness techniques to understand self and others. *Mindfulness, 11,* 153-65.

James, K., & Rimes, K. (2018). Mindfulness-based cognitive therapy versus pure cognitive behavioural self-help for perfectionism: A pilot randomized study. *Mindfulness, 9,* 801-14.

Jaoudi, M. (2010). *Medieval and renaissance spirituality: Discovering the treasures of the great masters.* Paulist Press.

Jean-Pierre, d. C. (2008). *The joy of full surrender* [ebook edition]. Paraclete Press. Amazon.com

Johnson, C. (2010). *The globalization of hesychasm and the Jesus Prayer: Contesting contemplation.* Continuum.

Johnson, E. (1997). Christ, the Lord of psychology. *Journal of Psychology and Theology, 25,* 11-27.

Johnson, E. (2007). *Foundations of soul care: A Christian psychology proposal.* InterVarsity Press.

Johnson, E. (Ed.). (2010). *Christianity and psychology: Five views* (2nd ed.). InterVarsity Press.

Johnson, E., Worthington, E., Hook, J., & Aten, J. (2013). Evidence-based practice in light of the Christian tradition(s): Reflections and future directions. In E. Worthington, E. Johnson, J. Hook, & J. Aten (Eds.), *Evidence-based practices for Christian counseling and psychotherapy* (pp. 325-46). InterVarsity Press.

Johnston, W. (Ed.). (2014). *The cloud of unknowing.* Image.

Jollie, T. (2015). *A treatise on heavenly mindedness.* Puritan Publications.

Judd, D., Dyer, W., & Top, J. (2020). Grace, legalism, and mental health: Examining direct and mediating relationships. *Psychology of Religion and Spirituality, 12,* 26-35.

Kabat-Zinn, J. (1994). *Wherever you go, there you are: Mindfulness meditation in everyday life.* Hyperion.

Kabat-Zinn, J. (2013). *Full catastrophe living: Using the wisdom of your body and mind to face stress, pain, and illness.* Bantam Books.

Kachan, D., Olano, H., Tannenbaum, S., Annane, D., Mehta, A., Arheart, K., Fleming, L., Yang, X., McClure, L., & Lee, D. (2017). *Prevalence of mindfulness practices in the US workforce: National health interview survey.* www.cdc.gov/pcd/issues/2017/16_0034.htm

Keating, T. (2006). *Open mind, open heart: 20th anniversary edition.* Bloomsbury.

Keating, T. (2019). *Open mind, open heart.* Continuum.

Keener, C. (2016). *The mind of the spirit: Paul's approach to transformed thinking.* Baker Academic.

Keller, D. (2011). *Desert banquet: A year of wisdom from the desert mothers and fathers.* Liturgical Press.

Keller, T. (2016a). *Jesus the King: Understanding the life and death of the Son of God.* Penguin Books.

Keller, T. (2016b). *Shaped by the gospel: Doing balanced, Gospel-centered ministry in your city.* Zondervan.

Kessler, R., Petukhova, M., Sampson, N., Zaslavsky, A., & Wittchen, H. (2012). Twelve-month and lifetime prevalence morbid risk of anxiety and mood disorders in the United States. *International Journal of Methods in Psychiatric Research, 21,* 169-84.

Khoury, B., Lecomte, T., Fortin, G., Masse, M., Therien, P., Bouchard, V., Chapleau, M., Paquin, K., & Hofmann, S. (2013). Mindfulness-based therapy: A comprehensive meta-analysis. *Clinical Psychology Review, 33,* 763-71.

Kloepfer, J. (2003). Disposition. In K. Beasley-Topliffe (Ed.), *The upper room dictionary of Christian spiritual formation* (p. 86). Upper Room Books.

Knabb, J. (2016). *Faith-based ACT for Christian clients: An integrative treatment approach.* Routledge.

Knabb, J. (2018). *The compassion-based workbook for Christian clients: Finding freedom from shame and negative self-judgments.* Routledge.

Knabb, J., & Bates, M. (2020a). "Holy desire" within the "Cloud of Unknowing": The psychological contributions of medieval apophatic contemplation to Christian mental health in the 21st century. *Journal of Psychology and Christianity, 39,* 24-39.

Knabb, J., & Bates, M. (2020b). Walking home with God: Toward an indigenous Christian psychology. In T. Sisemore & J. Knabb (Eds.), *The psychology of world religions and spiritualities: An indigenous perspective* (pp. 85-116). Templeton Press.

Knabb, J., & Frederick, T. (2017). *Contemplative prayer for Christians with chronic worry: An eight-week program.* Routledge.

Knabb, J., & Grigorian-Routon, A. (2014). The role of experiential avoidance in the relationship between faith maturity, religious coping, and psychological adjustment among Christian university students. *Mental Health, Religion & Culture, 17,* 458-69.

Knabb, J., & Vazquez, V. (2018). A randomized controlled trial of a two-week Internet-based contemplative prayer program for Christians with daily stress. *Spirituality in Clinical Practice, 5,* 37-53.

Knabb, J., & Wang, K. (2019). The Communion with God Scale: Shifting from an etic to emic perspective to assess fellowshipping with the triune God. *Psychology of Religion and Spirituality.* Advance online publication.

Knabb, J., Frederick, T., & Cumming, G. (2017). Surrendering to God's providence: A three-part study on providence-focused therapy for recurrent worry (PFT-RW). *Psychology of Religion and Spirituality, 9,* 180-96.

Knabb, J., Johnson, E., Bates, T., & Sisemore, T. (2019). *Christian psychotherapy in context: Theoretical and empirical explorations in faith-based mental health*. Routledge.

Knabb, J., Pate, R., Sullivan, S., Salley, E., Miller, A., & Boyer, W. (2020). "Walking with God": Developing and pilot testing a manualized four-week program combining Christian meditation and light-to-moderate physical activity for daily stress. *Mental Health, Religion & Culture, 23*, 756-776.

Knabb, J., Pelletier, J., & Grigorian-Routon, A. (2014). Towards a psychological understanding of servanthood: An empirical investigation of the relationship between orthodox beliefs, experiential avoidance, and self-sacrificial behaviors among Christians at a religiously-affiliated university. *Journal of Psychology & Theology, 42*, 269-83.

Knabb, J., Vazquez, V., Garzon, F., Ford, K., Wang, K., Conner, K., Warren, S., & Weston, D. (2020). Christian meditation for repetitive negative thinking: A multi-site randomized trial examining the effects of a four-week preventative program. *Spirituality in Clinical Practice, 7*, 34-50.

Knabb, J., Vazquez, V., & Pate, R. (2019). 'Set your minds on things above': Shifting from trauma-based ruminations to ruminating on God. *Mental Health, Religion & Culture, 22*, 384-99.

Knabb, J., Vazquez, V., & Wang, K. (2020). The Christian Contentment Scale: An emic measure for assessing inner satisfaction within the Christian tradition. *Journal of Psychology and Theology*. Advance online publication.

Knabb, J., Vazquez, V., Wang, K., & Bates, T. (2018). "Unknowing" in the 21st century: Humble detachment for Christians with repetitive negative thinking. *Spirituality in Clinical Practice, 5*, 170-87.

Koessler, J. (1999). *God our father*. Moody Press.

Koessler, J. (2003). *True discipleship: The art of following Jesus*. Moody Publishers.

Kok, B., Waugh, C., & Fredrickson, B. (2013). Meditation and health: The search for mechanisms of action. *Social and Personality Psychology Compass, 7*, 27-39.

Koltko-Rivera, M. (2004). The psychology of worldviews. *Review of General Psychology, 8*, 3-58.

Konstantinovsky, J. (2016). Evagrius Ponticus and Maximus the Confessor: The building of the self in praxis and contemplation. In J. Kalvesmaki & R. Young (Ed.), *Evagrius and his legacy*. University of Notre Dame Press.

Kristeller, J., & Johnson, T. (2005). Cultivating loving kindness: A two-stage model of the effects of meditation on empathy, compassion, and altruism. *Zygon, 40*, 391-407.

Krystal, H. (1988). *Integration and self-healing: Affect, trauma, alexithymia*. Routledge.

Kusner, K., Mahoney, A., Pargament, K., & DeMaris, A. (2014). Sanctification of marriage and spiritual intimacy predicting observed marital interactions across the transition to parenthood. *Journal of Family Psychology, 28*, 604-14.

Kuyper, A. (1931). *Lectures on Calvinism: Six lectures delivered at Princeton University*. Eerdmans.

Kuyper, A. (2015). *Common grace: God's gifts for a fallen world*. Lexham Press.

Kyabgon, T. (2014). *The essence of Buddhism: An introduction to its philosophy and practice*. Shambhala.

Laird, M. (2006). *Into the silent land: A guide to the Christian practice of contemplation*. Oxford University Press.

Larsen, T. (2007). Defining and locating evangelicalism. In T. Larsen & D. Treier (Eds.), *The Cambridge companion to evangelical theology* (pp. 1-14). Cambridge University Press.

Laubach, F. (2007). *Letters by a modern mystic* [ebook edition]. Purposeful Design Publications. Amazon.com

Lawrence, B. (2015). *The practice of the presence of God.* (S. Sciurba, Trans.). ICS Publications.

Lehrhaupt, L., & Meibert, P. (2017). *Mindfulness-based stress reduction: The MBSR program for enhancing health and vitality.* New World Library.

Lewis, C. (2001). *The screwtape letters.* HarperCollins.

Leyro, T., Zvolensky, M., & Bernstein, A. (2010). Distress tolerance and psychopathological symptoms and disorders: A review of the empirical literature among adults. *Psychological Bulletin, 136,* 576-600.

Lilienfeld, S., Smith, S., & Watts, A. (2017). Diagnosis: Conceptual issues and controversies. In W. Craighead, D. Miklowitz, & L. Craighead (Eds.), *Psychopathology: History, diagnosis, and empirical foundations* (pp. 1-38). John Wiley & Sons.

Limburg, K., Watson, H., Hagger, M., & Egan, S. (2017). The relationship between perfectionism and psychopathology: A meta-analysis. *Journal of Clinical Psychology, 73,* 1301-26.

Lippelt, D., Hommel, B., & Colzato, L. (2014). Focused attention, open monitoring and loving kindness meditation: Effects on attention, conflict monitoring, and creativity—a review. *Frontiers in Psychology, 5,* 1-5.

Lischetzke, T., & Eid, M. (2017). The functionality of emotional clarity: A process-oriented approach to understanding the relation between emotional clarity and well-being. In M. Robinson & M. Eid (Eds.), *The happy mind: Cognitive contributions to well-being* (pp. 371-88). Springer.

Loyola Press. (n.d.). *Suscipe.* www.loyolapress.com/catholic-resources/prayer/traditional-catholic-prayers/saints-prayers/suscipe-prayer-saint-ignatius-of-loyola

Lutz, A., Slagter, H., Dunne, J., & Davidson, R. (2008). Attention regulation and monitoring in meditation. *Trends in Cognitive Science, 12,* 163-69.

Macatee, R., Albanese, B., Allan, N., Schmidt, N., & Cougle, J. (2016). Distress intolerance as a moderator of the relationship between daily stressors and affective symptoms: Tests of incremental and prospective relationships. *Journal of Affective Disorders, 206,* 125-32.

Mahoney, A., Pargament, K., Murray-Swank, A., & Murray-Swank, N. (2003). Religion and the sanctification of family relationships. *Review of Religious Research, 44,* 220-36.

Main, J. (2001). *Christian meditation: The Gethsemani talks.* Medio Media Publishing.

Main, J. (2006). *Word into silence: A manual for Christian meditation.* World Community for Christian Meditation.

Malda-Castillo, J., Browne, C., & Perez-Algorta, G. (2019). Mentalization-based treatment and its evidence-base: A systematic literature review. *Psychology and Psychotherapy: Theory, Research and Practice, 92,* 465-98.

Manney, J. (2011). *The prayer that changes everything: Discovering the power of St. Loyola's examen.* Loyola Press.

Mansell, W., Harvey, A., Watkins, E., & Shafran, R. (2009). Conceptual foundations of the transdiagnostic approach to CBT. *Journal of Cognitive Psychotherapy: An International Quarterly, 23,* 6-19.

Maricutoiu, L., Magurean, S., & Tulbure, B. (2019). Perfectionism in a transdiagnostic context: An investigation of the criterion validity of the almost perfect scale-revised. *European Journal of Psychological Assessment.* Advance online publication.

Mars, T., & Abbey, H. (2010). Mindfulness meditation practice as a healthcare intervention: A systematic review. *International Journal of Osteopathic Medicine, 13,* 56-66.

Martin, S. (2019). *The CBT workbook for perfectionism: Evidence-based skills to help you let go of self-criticism, build self-esteem & find balance*. New Harbinger Publications.

Masterpasqua, F. (2016). Mindfulness mentalizing humanism: A transtheoretical convergence. *Journal of Psychotherapy Integration, 26*, 5-10.

Masters, K., & Spielmans, G. (2007). Prayer and health: Review, meta-analysis, and research agenda. *Journal of Behavioral Medicine, 30*, 329-38.

Mathis, D. (2016). *Habits of grace: Enjoying Jesus through the spiritual disciplines*. Crossway.

Matter, E. (2012). Lectio divina. In A. Hollywood & P. Beckman (Eds.), *The Cambridge companion to Christian mysticism* (pp. 147-56). Cambridge University Press.

McCown, D., Reibel, D., & Micozzi, M. (2010). *Teaching mindfulness: A practical guide for clinicians and educators*. Springer.

McGinn, B. (2006). *The essential writings of Christian mysticism*. Random House.

McGrath, A. (2011). *Christian theology: An introduction* (5th ed.). John Wiley & Sons.

McHugh, R., & Otto, M. (2012). Refining the measurement of distress intolerance. *Behavioral Therapy, 43*, 641-51.

McMinn, M. (2008). *Sin and grace in Christian counseling: An integrative paradigm*. InterVarsity Press.

McMinn, M., & McRay, B. (1997). Spiritual disciplines and the practice of integration: Possibilities for Christian psychologists. *Journal of Psychology and Theology, 25*, 102-10.

McPherson, C. (2002). *Keeping silence: Christian practices for entering stillness*. Morehouse Publishing.

Meiklejohn, J., Philips, C., Freedman, M., Griffin, M., Biegel, G., Roach, A., Frank, J., Burke, C., Pinger, L., Soloway, G., Isberg, R., Sibinga, E., Grossman, L., & Saltzman, A. (2012). Integrating mindfulness training into K-12 education: Fostering the resilience of teachers and students. *Mindfulness, 3*, 291-307.

Merriam Webster's Desk Dictionary. (1995). *Accept*. Merriam-Webster, Incorporated.

Merton, T. (1960). *Spiritual direction and meditation*. Liturgical Press.

Merton, T. (1961). *New seeds of contemplation*. New Directions Books.

Merton, T. (1969). *Contemplative prayer*. Image Books.

Merton, T. (1998). *The seven storey mountain: An autobiography of faith*. Harcourt.

Miles, M. (1983). Detachment. In G. Wakefield (Ed.), *The Westminster dictionary of Christian spirituality* (p. 111). Westminster Press.

Morgan, D. (2010). *Essential Buddhism: A comprehensive guide to belief and practice*. Praeger.

Murray, A. (1888). *Abide in Christ: Thoughts on the blessed life of fellowship with the Son of God*. James Nisbet.

Neff, K. (2003). The development and validation of a scale to measure self-compassion. *Self and Identity, 2*, 223-50.

Neff, K., & Germer, C. (2018). *The mindful self-compassion program: A proven way to accept yourself, build inner strength, and thrive*. Guilford.

Nhat Hanh, T. (1976). *The miracle of mindfulness: An introduction to the practice of meditation*. Beacon Press.

Nikodimos. (Ed.). (1782). *Philokalia*. R. P. Pryne.

Nila, K., Holt, D., Ditzen, B., & Aguilar-Raab, C. (2016). Mindfulness-based stress reduction (MBSR) enhances distress tolerance and resilience through changes in mindfulness. *Mental Health & Prevention, 4*, 36-41.

Oatley, K., & Johnson-Laird, P. (1996). The communicative theory of emotions: Empirical tests, mental models, and implications for social interaction. In L. Martin & A. Tesser (Eds.), *Striving and feeling: Interactions among goals, affect, and self-regulation* (pp. 363-93). Lawrence Erlbaum Associates.

O'Grady, K., & Slife, B. (2017). A prominent worldview of psychological research. In B. Slife, K. O'Grady, & R. Kosits (Eds.), *The hidden worldviews of psychology's theory, research, and practice*. Routledge.

Ottenbreit, N., & Dobson, K. (2004). Avoidance and depression: The construct of the cognitive-behavioral avoidance scale. *Behaviour Research and Therapy, 42*, 293-313.

Owen, J. (2007). *Communion with the triune God.* Crossway.

Owen, J. (2016). *Spiritual mindedness.* GLH Publishing.

Packer, J. (1990). *A quest for godliness: The Puritan vision of the Christian life.* Crossway.

Paintner, C. (2011). *Lectio divina—the sacred art: Transforming words and images into heart-centered prayer.* SkyLight Paths Publishing.

Paintner, C. (2012). *Desert fathers and mothers: Early Christian wisdom sayings—annotated & explained.* SkyLight Paths Publishing.

Papadomarkaki, E., & Portinou, S. (2012). Clinical perfectionism and cognitive behavioral therapy. *Psychiatriki, 23*, 61-71.

Pargament, K., & Mahoney, A. (2005). Sacred matters: Sanctification as a vital topic for the psychology of religion. *The International Journal for the Psychology of Religion, 15*, 179-98.

Park, J., & Naragon-Gainey, K. (2019). Daily experiences of emotional clarity and their association with internalizing symptoms in naturalistic settings. *Emotion, 19*, 764-75.

Perez-De-Albeniz, A., & Holmes, J. (2000). Meditation: Concepts, effects and uses in therapy. *International Journal of Psychotherapy, 5*, 49-58.

Peterson, D. (1992). *Engaging with God: A biblical theology of worship.* InterVarsity Press.

Pew Forum. (2015). *America's changing religious landscape.* The Pew Forum on Religion & Public Life.

Pew Research Center. (2018). *Meditation is common across many religious groups in the U.S.* www.pewresearch.org/fact-tank/2018/01/02/meditation-is-common-across-many-religious -groups-in-the-u-s

Pink, A. (2012). *An exposition of Hebrews.* Start Publishing.

Poloma, M., & Pendleton, B. (1991). The effects of prayer and prayer experiences on measures of general well-being. *Journal of Psychology and Theology, 19*, 71-83.

Pratscher, S., Rose, A., Markovitz, L., & Bettencourt, A. (2018). Interpersonal mindfulness: Investigating mindfulness in interpersonal interactions, co-rumination, and friendship quality. *Mindfulness, 9*, 1206-15.

Pratscher, S., Wood, P., King, L., & Bettencourt, B. (2019). Interpersonal mindfulness: Scale development and initial construct validation. *Mindfulness, 10*, 1044-61.

Price, R. (1816). On heavenly-mindedness. In W. Morgan (Ed.), *The works of Richard Price* (pp. 185- 204). A. Strahan.

Raffone, A., & Srinivasan, N. (2010). The exploration of meditation in the neuroscience of attention and consciousness. *Cognitive Processing, 11*, 1-7.

Ranew, N. (1995). *Solitude improved by divine meditation.* Soli Deo Gloria.

Reformed Church in America. (n.d.). *Belgic confession, article 13: The doctrine of God's providence.* www.rca.org/resources/belgic-confession-article-13-doctrine-gods-providence

Richter, M. (2014). Is anxiety best conceived as a unitary condition? The benefits of lumping compared with splitting. *The Canadian Journal of Psychiatry, 59*, 291-93.

Roberts, R. (2007). *Spiritual emotions: A psychology of Christian virtues.* Eerdmans.

Robichaud, M., & Dugas, M. (2005). Negative problem orientation (part I): Psychometric properties of a new measure. *Behaviour Research and Therapy, 43*, 391-401.

Robins, C., Schmidt, H., & Linehan, M. (2004). Dialectical behavior therapy: Synthesizing radical acceptance with skillful means. In S. Hayes, V. Follette, & M. Linehan (Eds.), *Mindfulness and acceptance: Expanding the cognitive-behavioral tradition* (pp. 30-44). Guilford.

Rowe, J. (1672). *Heavenly-mindedness and earthly-mindedness: In two parts.* Francis Tyton.

Rubin, J. (2003). Close encounters of a new kind: Toward an integration of psychoanalysis and Buddhism. In S. Segall (Ed.), *Encountering Buddhism: Western psychology and Buddhist teachings* (pp. 31-60). State University of New York Press.

Ruffing, J. (2005). The affirmative way. In P. Sheldrake (Ed.), *The new Westminster dictionary of Christian spirituality* (pp. 91-92). Westminster John Knox Press.

Ruffing, J. (2005). Kataphatic spirituality. In P. Sheldrake (Ed.), *The new Westminster dictionary of Christian spirituality* (pp. 393-94). Westminster John Knox Press.

Ruge-Jones, P. (2008). *Cross in tensions: Luther's theology of the cross as theologico-social critique.* Pickwick Publications.

Sahdra, B., Shaver, P., & Brown, K. (2010). A scale to measure nonattachment: A Buddhist complement to Western research on attachment and adaptive functioning. *Journal of Personality Assessment, 92*, 116-27.

Saint-Jure, J., & Colombiere, C. (1983). *Trustful surrender to divine providence: The secret to peace and happiness.* TAN Books.

Salzberg, S. (1995). *Loving-kindness: The revolutionary art of happiness.* Shambhala.

Sauer, S., Walach, H., Schmidt, S., Hinterberger, T., Lynch, S., Bussing, A., & Kohls, N. (2013). Assessment of mindfulness: Review on state of the art. *Mindfulness, 4*, 3-17.

Saxton, D. (2015). *God's battle plan for the mind: The Puritan practice of biblical meditation.* Reformation Heritage Books.

Schaap-Jonker, H., & Corveleyn, J. (2014). Mentalizing and religion: A promising combination for psychology of religion, illustrated by the case of prayer. *Archive for the Psychology of Religion, 36*, 303-22.

Schwanda, T. (2012). *Soul recreation: The contemplative-mystical piety of Puritanism.* Pickwick Publications.

Scorgie, G. (Ed.). (2011). *Dictionary of Christian spirituality.* Zondervan.

Segal, Z., Teasdale, J., & Williams, J. (2004). Mindfulness-based cognitive therapy: Theoretical rationale and empirical status. In S. Hayes, V. Follette, & M. Linehan (Eds.), *Mindfulness and acceptance: Expanding the cognitive-behavioral tradition* (pp. 45-65). Guilford.

Segal, Z., Williams, J., & Teasdale, J. (2012). *Mindfulness-based cognitive therapy for depression* (2nd ed.). Guilford.

Sexton, K., & Dugas, M. (2009). Defining distinct negative beliefs about uncertainty: Validating the factor structure of the Intolerance of Uncertainty Scale. *Psychological Assessment, 21*, 176-86.

Shafran, R., Coughtrey, A., & Kothari, R. (2016). New frontiers in the treatment of perfectionism. *International Journal of Cognitive Therapy, 9*, 156-70.

Shankman, R. (2015). *The art and skill of Buddhist meditation: Mindfulness, concentration, and insight.* New Harbinger Publications.

Siegel, R. (2010). *The mindfulness solution: Everyday practice for everyday problems.* Guildford.

Singh, N., Lancioni, G., Wahler, R., Winton, A., & Singh, J. (2008). Mindfulness approaches in cognitive behavior therapy. *Behavioural and Cognitive Psychotherapy, 36,* 659-66.

Sisemore, T., & Knabb, J. (Eds.). (2020). *The psychology of world religions and spiritualities: An indigenous perspective.* Templeton Press.

Sisti, M. (2014). Compassion in contextual psychotherapies. In J. Stewart (Ed.), *Mindfulness, acceptance, and the psychodynamic evolution: Bringing values into treatment planning and enhancing psychodynamic work with Buddhist psychology* (pp. 91-110). New Harbinger Publications.

Slaney, R., Rice, K., Mobley, M., Trippi, J., & Ashby, J. (2001). The revised Almost Perfect Scale. *Measurement and Evaluation in Counseling and Development, 34,* 130-45.

Slife, B., & Reber, J. (2012). Conceptualizing religious practices in psychological research: Problems and prospects. *Pastoral Psychology, 61,* 735-46.

Slife, B., & Whoolery, M. (2006). Biased against the worldview of many religious people? *Journal of Psychology and Theology, 34,* 217-31.

Slife, B., Martin, G., & Sasser, S. (2017). A prominent worldview of professional psychology. In B. Slife, K. O'Grady, & R. Kosits (Eds.), *The hidden worldviews of psychology's theory, research, and practice.* Routledge.

Snodgrass, K. (1996). *The NIV application commentary: Ephesians.* Zondervan.

Society of Jesus. (n.d.). *The spiritual exercises.* https://jesuits.org/spirituality?PAGE=DTN-20130520125429

Spurgeon, C. (2013). *The complete works of C. H. Spurgeon: Volume 50, Sermons 2864-2915.* Delmarva Publications.

Stanley, C. (2009). *Practicing basic spiritual disciplines: Focus on the foundational principles of Christian living.* Thomas Nelson.

Steere, D. (Ed.). (1984). *Quaker spirituality: Selected writings.* Paulist Press.

Steel, Z., Marnane, C., Iranpour, C., Chey, T., Jackson, J., Patel, V., & Silove, D. (2014). The global prevalence of common mental disorders: A systematic review and meta-analysis 1980-2013. *International Journal of Epidemiology, 2014,* 476-93.

Stewart, D. (1998). Compassion. In C. Brand, C. Draper, & A. England (Eds.), *Holman illustrated Bible dictionary* (p. 324). Holman Reference.

Stolorow, R., Brandchaft, B., & Atwood, G. (1995). *Psychoanalytic treatment: An intersubjective approach.* Routledge.

Stout, H., Minkema, K., & Neele, A. (Eds.). (2017). *The Jonathan Edwards encyclopedia.* Eerdmans.

Strong, J. (2001a). *The new Strong's expanded dictionary of the words in the Hebrew Bible.* Thomas Nelson.

Strong, J. (2001b). *The new Strong's expanded dictionary of the words in the Greek New Testament.* Thomas Nelson.

Strong, W. (2015). *The saint's communion with God.* Puritan Publications.

Sulmasy, D. (2002). A biopsychosocial-spiritual model for the care of patients at the end of life. *The Gerontologist, 42,* 24-33.

Talbot, J. (2002). *Come to the quiet: The principles of Christian meditation.* Putnam.

Talbot, J. (2013). *The Jesus Prayer: A cry for mercy, a path of renewal.* InterVarsity Press.

Taylor, B. (2002). *Becoming Christ: Transformation through contemplation.* Cowley Publications.

Taylor, S., & Clark, D. (2009). Transdiagnostic cognitive-behavioral treatments for mood and anxiety disorders: Introduction to the special issue. *Journal of Cognitive Psychotherapy: An International Quarterly, 23,* 3-5.

Teresa, of Á. (2000). *The way of perfection: A study edition* (K. Kavanaugh, Trans.). ICS Publications.

Thaddeus, E. (2012). *Our thoughts determine our lives: The life and teachings of elder Thaddeus of Vitovnica.* St. Herman of Alaska Brotherhood.

Thomas, a. K. (1983). *The imitation of Christ.* Crown Publishing Group.

Thomas, a. K. (2015). *The imitation of Christ: Classic devotions in today's language.* Worthy Inspired.

Thompson, R., Boden, M., & Gotlib, I. (2017). Emotional variability and clarity in depression and social anxiety. *Cognition and Emotion, 31,* 98-108.

Thondup, T. (2008). *The healing power of loving-kindness: A guided Buddhist meditation.* Shambhala.

Tozer, A. (1991). *The Christian book of mystical verse: A collection of poems, hymns, and prayers for devotional reading.* Moody Publishers.

Treier, D. (2007). Scripture and hermeneutics. In T. Larsen & D. Treier (Eds.), *The Cambridge companion to evangelical theology* (pp. 35-50). Cambridge University Press.

Ursinus, Z. (1852). *The commentary of Dr. Zacharius Ursinus on the Heidelberg catechism* (2nd ed.) (G. Williard, Trans.). Scott & Bascom.

Valerio, A. (2016). Owning mindfulness: A bibliometric analysis of mindfulness literature trends within and outside of Buddhist contexts. *Contemporary Buddhism: An Interdisciplinary Journal, 17,* 157-83.

Valle, R. (2019). Toward a psychology of silence. *The Humanistic Psychologist.* Advance online publication.

Van Dam, N., van Vugt, M., Vago, D., Schmalzl, L., Saron, C., Olendzki, A., Meissner, T., Lazar, S., Kerr, C., Gorchov, J., Fox, K., Field, B., Britton, W., Brefczynski-Lewis, J., & Meyer, D. (2018). Mind the hype: A critical evaluation and prescriptive agenda for research on mindfulness and mediation. *Perspectives on Psychological Science, 13,* 36-61.

Vine, V., & Aldao, A. (2014). Impaired emotional clarity and psychopathology: A transdiagnostic deficit with symptom-specific pathways through emotion regulation. *Journal of Social and Clinical Psychology, 33,* 319-42.

Wahl, K., Ehring, T., Kley, H., Lieb, R., Meyer, A., Kordon, A., Heinzel, C., Mazanec, M., & Schonfeld, S. (2019). Is repetitive negative thinking a transdiagnostic process? A comparison of key processes of RNT in depression, generalized anxiety disorder, objsessive-compulsive disorder, and community controls. *Journal of Behavior Therapy and Experimental Psychiatry, 64,* 45-53.

Wallin, D. (2007). *Attachment in psychotherapy.* Guilford.

Walsh, R., & Shapiro, S. (2006). The meeting of meditative disciplines and Western psychology: A mutually enriching dialogue. *American Psychologist, 61,* 227-39.

Wang, K., Allen, G., Stokes, H., & Suh, H. (2018). Perceived perfectionism from God scale: Development and initial evidence. *Journal of Religion and Health, 57,* 2207-23.

Wang, K., Xie, Z., Parsley, A., & Johnson, A. (2020). Religious perfectionism scale among believers of multiple faiths in China: Development and psychometric analysis. *Journal of Religion and Health, 59,* 318-33.

Ward, J. (1983). Contemplation. In G. Wakefield (Ed.), *The Westminster dictionary of Christian spirituality* (pp. 95-96). Westminster Press.

Ware, K. (1986). *The power of the name: The Jesus Prayer in Orthodox spiritualty.* SLG Press.

Ware, K. (2000). *The inner kingdom.* St. Vladimir's Seminary Press.

Ware, K. (2005). St. Nikodimos and the Philokalia. In D. Conomos & G. Speake (Eds.), *Mount Athos the sacred bridge: The spirituality of the holy mountain* (pp. 69-122). Peter Lang.

Ware, K. (2013). Foreword. In I. Brianchaninov (Ed.), *On the prayer of Jesus* (pp. vii-xxxiii). New Seeds.

Ware, K. (2014). *The Jesus Prayer*. Catholic Truth Society.

Watson, D., & Stasik, S. (2014). Examining the comorbidity between depression and the anxiety disorders from the perspective of the quadripartite model. In C. Steven Richards & M. O'Hara (Eds.), *The Oxford handbook of depression and comorbidity* (pp. 46-65). Oxford University Press.

Watson, T. (2012). *A treatise concerning meditation* [ebook edition]. Waxkeep Publishing. Amazon.com.

Watson, T. (2017). *The art of divine contentment* (J. Roth, Trans.). Jason Roth.

Westminster Shorter Catechism. (n.d.). *The Westminster shorter catechism*. www.westminster confession.org/confessional-standards/the-westminster-shorter-catechism.php

Whitney, D. (2014). *Spiritual disciplines for the Christian life*. NavPress.

Wieczner, J. (2016, March 12). Meditation has become a billion-dollar business. *Fortune*, 1-2.

Wilhoit, J., & Howard, E. (2012). *Discovering lectio divina: Bringing Scripture into ordinary life*. InterVarsity Press.

Wilken, R. (2003). *The spirit of early Christian thought*. Yale University Press.

Willard, D. (1998). Spiritual disciplines, spiritual formation, and the restoration of the soul. *Journal of Psychology and Theology, 26*, 101-9.

Willard, D. (1999). *The spirit of the disciplines: Understanding how God changes lives*. HarperCollins.

Willard, D. (2002). *Renovation of the heart: Putting on the character of Christ*. NavPress.

Wimberley, T., Mintz, L., & Suh, H. (2016). Perfectionism and mindfulness: Effectiveness of a bibliotherapy intervention. *Mindfulness, 7*, 433-44.

Windeatt, B. (Ed.). (2015). *Julian of Norwich: Revelations of divine love*. Oxford University Press.

Winter, R. (2005). *The pursuit of excellence and the perils of perfectionism*. InterVarsity Press.

Witherington, B. (2011). *Paul's letter to the Philippians: A socio-rhetorical commentary*. Eerdmans.

Wlodarski, R., & Dunbar, R. (2014). The effects of romantic love on mentalizing abilities. *Review of General Psychology, 18*, 313-21.

Wolpert, D. (2003). *Creating a life with God: The call of ancient prayer practices*. Upper Room Books.

Wolters, A. (2005). *Creation regained: Biblical basics for a reformational worldview* (2nd ed.). Eerdmans.

Wong-McDonald, A., & Gorsuch, R. (2000). Surrender to God: An additional coping style? *Journal of Psychology and Theology, 28*, 149-61.

Wortley, J. (2012). *The book of the elders: Sayings of the desert fathers—the systematic collection*. Cistercian.

Wright, N. (1992). *The New Testament and the people of God*. Fortress Press.

Yuille, S. (2013). *Looking unto Jesus: The Christ-centered piety of seventeenth-century Baptists*. Pickwick Publications.

Zeng, X., Chlu, C., Wang, R., Oei, T., & Leung, F. (2015). The effect of loving-kindness meditation on positive emotions: A meta-analytic review. *Frontiers in Psychology, 6*, 1-14.

Zirlott, C. (2017). Discipline. In K. Beasley-Topliffe (Ed.), *The upper room dictionary of Christian spiritual formation*. Upper Room Books.

Zvolensky, M., Vujanovic, A., Bernstein, A., & Leyro, T. (2010). Distress tolerance: Theory, measurement, and relations to psychopathology. *Current Directions in Psychological Science, 19*, 406-10.

GENERAL INDEX

SCRIPTURE INDEX

An Association for Christian Psychologists,
Therapists, Counselors and Academicians

CAPS is a vibrant Christian organization with a rich tradition. Founded in 1956 by a small group of Christian mental health professionals, chaplains and pastors, CAPS has grown to more than 2,100 members in the U.S., Canada and more than 25 other countries.

CAPS encourages in-depth consideration of therapeutic, research, theoretical and theological issues. The association is a forum for creative new ideas. In fact, their publications and conferences are the birthplace for many of the formative concepts in our field today.

CAPS members represent a variety of denominations, professional groups and theoretical orientations; yet all are united in their commitment to Christ and to professional excellence.

CAPS is a non-profit, member-supported organization. It is led by a fully functioning board of directors, and the membership has a voice in the direction of CAPS.

CAPS is more than a professional association. It is a fellowship, and in addition to national and international activities, the organization strongly encourages regional, local and area activities which provide networking and fellowship opportunities as well as professional enrichment.

To learn more about CAPS, visit www.caps.net.

The joint publishing venture between IVP Academic and CAPS aims to promote the understanding of the relationship between Christianity and the behavioral sciences at both the clinical/counseling and the theoretical/research levels. These books will be of particular value for students and practitioners, teachers and researchers.

For more information about CAPS Books, visit InterVarsity Press's website at www.ivpress.com/christian-association-for-psychological-studies-books-set.